THE GREAT
PURSUIT

THE GREAT PURSUIT

HERBERT MOLLOY MASON, JR.

SMITHMARK

This edition published in 1995 by SMITHMARK Publishers Inc.,
16 East 32nd Street, New York, NY 10016

SMITHMARK books are available for bulk purchase for sales
promotion and premium use. For details write or call the
manager of special sales, SMITHMARK Publishers Inc.,
16 East 32nd Street, New York, NY 10016; (212) 532-6600.

This edition published by arrangement with John Hawkins
& Associates, Inc., New York and with Konecky & Konecky
Associates, Inc.

ISBN: 0-8317-5707-8

Printed In the United States of America

10 9 8 7 6 5 4 3 2 1

TO

Rigmor and Berit

"Poor Mexico. So far from God and so near the United States."

—PORFIRIO DÍAZ

Contents

CONTENTS

THE GREAT PURSUIT

1

Villa Lights the Fuse

A few minutes past midnight on March 9, 1916, First Lieutenant John P. Lucas stepped off the train at the dreary little station in Columbus, New Mexico. It had been a long ride from El Paso, seventy-five miles to the east, and even at that late hour the "Drunkard's Special," as the train was known locally, was crowded with drummers headed westward and with troopers getting off at Columbus, home to the 13th Cavalry Regiment at Camp Furlong.

The twenty-six-year-old lieutenant was returning from a week's leave in El Paso, which he had spent playing polo with other cavalry officers stationed at Fort Bliss. Exhausted from the noisy, rattling train ride, he decided to go directly to his quarters, a small adobe house about a hundred yards southwest of the station. Lucas, who commanded the machine-gun troop, had been in Columbus for seventeen months; he knew every square inch of the little garrison town, whose inhabitants barely numbered three hundred men, women and children. To Lucas, who had recently spent three years enjoying the "vivid colors and exotic atmosphere" of the Philippines, the sprawling Southwestern hamlet only three miles from the Mexican border "presented a picture horrible to the eye." Columbus was a random collection of adobe and frame houses, two hotels, a bank, a post office and several stores. The town was bisected east and west by the railroad tracks that ran parallel to the main street, and north and south by a dirt road running from the Mexican border, through Columbus and on to Deming, thirty-two miles to the north. The barracks, stables and tents of Camp Furlong occupied the southeast quadrant of the town. The railroad tracks separated the camp from the business section, while west of the Deming road there were scattered residences. The country here was flat and desolate, the monotonous terrain relieved only by growths of cactus and tumbleweed, and by the three peaks of the Tres Hermanas mountains a few miles northwest of town.

Despite Lucas' familiarity with the terrain, he picked his way carefully from the station to his quarters. There was no electricity in Columbus, and kerosene for the lamps was in short supply. The moon hung low over the horizon, nearly gone, but the skies were clear, affording the lieutenant enough visibility to get across the rutted wagon road and the deep drainage ditch that barred the way to his house. When Lucas reached his quarters he found the interior dark and his roommate, First Lieutenant Clarence C. Benson, gone to one of the border outposts where his troop was stationed, like many others, as a precaution against incursions by Mexican bandits. The Mexican Revolution, then in its sixth year, had spawned lawless gangs preying on unguarded settlements near the border. The 13th Cavalry was deployed in order to keep the Mexicans on their own side of the line.

Lucas got a lamp going, then cautiously poked around the floor and under the beds to make sure he would not be sharing the room that night with rattlesnakes. Out of habit he checked his .45 Colt revolver. It was unloaded. Lucas guessed that Benson had taken the ammunition with him to the border. Although he ordinarily would not have bothered, "a pure hunch" made him find the keys to the trunk room, where he laboriously shoved boxes and trunks around until he found his own footlocker. He took out a box of shells, reloaded the pistol, replaced the heavy weapon in its holster and hung it on a peg in the wall. Then he pulled off his boots, shucked his pants and shirt and got into bed.

Several hundred yards to the northeast, across the tracks, slept the regiment's commanding officer, Colonel Herbert J. Slocum, a crusty, well-to-do Ohioan only a few weeks away from his sixty-first birthday. Slocum slept soundly, convinced that he had done everything possible in the face of a confused situation along the border; the previous few days had been filled with conflicting reports and disturbing rumors concerning the movements of General Francisco "Pancho" Villa and his ragged band of marauders. On March 5 Slocum had received a letter from Headquarters, Southern Department, at Fort Sam Houston in San Antonio, Texas. The letter, marked "Confidential" and signed by Major General Frederick Funston, stated that "reliable" information had been received to the effect that Villa was planning to cross the border with the intention of giving himself up to American authorities, while "unreliable" information warned that Villa intended to raid American towns along the border. Only two days later, on Tuesday afternoon, March 7, Slocum had listened to a tale related by two Mexicans who said they had barely managed to escape with their lives after blundering into a band of Villistas camped just fifteen miles below the border. Both men, forty-year-old Juan Favela and old Antonio Muñoz, worked for the Palomas Land and Cattle Company, which controlled thousands of acres of ranch land in northern Chihuahua.

Favela had told Slocum that he, Muñoz and an American cowboy named William K. Corbett were driving part of the herd toward Boyd's Ranch, along the Casas Grandes River, when a large group of armed men swept down on them on horseback. Corbett threw up his hands and awaited capture, but Favela and Muñoz spurred their horses and rode for their lives; they did not wait to see what happened to Corbett.

Slocum did not know whether to believe the report fully or not; within the past week he had received "reliable" reports that Villa and his men were at Palomas, eight miles south of Columbus; far down the Casas Grandes River, forty-five miles southwest of Columbus, and at the Rancho Nogales, nearly sixty-five miles southwest of Columbus. The answer to the vexing question *Where is Villa?* could easily have been found by sending an experienced scout or a small patrol across the border, but President Woodrow Wilson's policy toward strife-torn Mexico proscribed that course of action, whatever the urgency. However, there was nothing to keep Slocum from sending a Mexican across the border into his own country, and this he proceeded to do.

By promising Antonio Muñoz twenty dollars, Slocum had persuaded the old man to return to the scene of his recent encounter in an attempt to discover Villa's intentions. On the morning of March 8, Muñoz was driven to Gibson's Ranch, fourteen miles west of Columbus, where a detachment of the 13th was already stationed under the command of Major Elmer Lindsley, who recalled:

"Muñoz arrived early that morning with a letter from Slocum asking me to furnish Muñoz with a rifle and a pair of glasses. He returned to our side of the border just at sundown, and I took him in the Ford car to Slocum, who had no working knowledge of the Spanish language. He reported that he had gone to Boca Grande and found the place deserted. Villa's gang had left about 3 A.M. that day, March 8, as the ashes in the campfire were still warm.

"From a high point near the Vado de Fusiles he had seen through his field glasses two or three mounted men on the road down the river towards Guzmán, and had deemed it best to return to the Gibson Ranch and report to me."

Muñoz went on to say that he believed approximately one hundred and twenty of Villa's men had first continued north toward Palomas but had then turned south and east, away from the border and away from Columbus. "Antonio is too scared to be lying," said Lindsley. Colonel Slocum paid the "spy" and dismissed him. The two officers decided that this report was as reliable as any they were apt to get, and it had the blessing of being current. Lindsley returned to his border outpost, leaving Slocum alone with the ultimate responsibility of command.

Slocum's concern lay beyond the town of Columbus; his area of responsibility covered sixty-five miles of vacant border, from Noria in the east, stretching westward to the insignificant hamlet of Hermanas. To patrol this desolate stretch of ground, Slocum had at his disposal twenty-one officers and five hundred and thirty-two troopers, of whom seventy-nine were considered noncombatants, or about one man for every six hundred feet of border. Although Slocum's arrogance toward subordinates did not endear him to his command, he was no amateur soldier: he had spent forty years in the U.S. Army, including active service in the Indian wars and the Spanish-American War.

Since the U.S. Army had no intelligence service capable of either gathering information or of evaluating rumors, Slocum could only guess at Villa's intentions. Upon receipt of Funston's letter of March 5, Slocum and Major Lindsley drove down to the barbed-wire fence separating the United States and Mexico, and at the border gate admitting passage to the little town of Palomas, Slocum and Lindsley sought to question the Mexican regular troops there. But the Mexican commander was not only uncommunicative, he was hostile; when the American officers approached the gate they found the Mexican troops behind barricades, ready to fire, as though they expected an attack from the north.

On March 6, then, Slocum deployed his command, hoping to meet whatever contingency might arise. He beefed up Lindsley's outpost for a total of 7 officers and 151 riflemen. He sent one rifle troop—2 officers and 65 men—to the border gate. This left Columbus protected by the bulk of his command, 7 officers and 341 men, including Headquarters and Machine-Gun Troops and the noncombatants. Slocum ordered patrols sent out day and night. These patrols, he cautioned, must be mounted at irregular intervals so that neither bandits nor regular Mexican troops could establish a pattern of movement.

Slocum considered the report given by Antonio Muñoz, and decided to leave his command deployed as it was, convinced that further shifting of his slender force would result only in tiring of men and horses.

As Slocum headed for his house that night of March 8, he was depressed by the darkness of streets and even of the houses. Sentries had complained that they could not see "twenty feet in front of us," and previous requisitions for oil and street lamps to remedy the situation had been routinely disapproved. Columbus would remain dark.

When Muñoz and Favela had managed to escape from the pursuing Villistas on the morning of March 7, they did not realize just how lucky they were. But Corbett, the American cowboy, quickly regretted his thoughtless act of surrender.

The Mexicans ushered him into the center of their camp and forced him to dismount. He soon discovered that he was not the only captive there. He recognized his foreman, Arthur McKinney, and one of the outfit's cooks, James O'Neil. McKinney told Corbett that he had witnessed the chase of Muñoz and Favela, led by a Villista "colonel" named Hernández, and that his own capture had taken place only a short time before when he mistook the bandits for regular Mexican troops.

Now, totally cut off from aid and unarmed in the middle of

what seemed to be at least five hundred hostile-looking guerrillas, they could only await the mercy of Pancho Villa.

Some distance away sat yet another Villa captive, Edwin R. "Buck" Spencer, a Negro who had been captured two days earlier near Ojitas. Spencer had first seen McKinney and Corbett made prisoner, then watched Corbett surrender shortly afterward. Spencer saw a young Villista, obviously delighted at Corbett's capture, ride off to Villa's headquarters. He returned a few minutes later with an order for execution. Villa rode over to watch the killings in person.

It was the first time Spencer had ever seen the legendary outlaw general. Astride a horse Villa, thick-necked and heavy-shouldered, seemed immense, his massive chest and big belly hanging over the saddle pommel. His full face, the color of deep copper, loomed menacingly even under the oversized hat, and a heavy reddish mustache draped his thick and sensuous lips. Unkempt black curly hair poked from beneath the high-crowned, sweat-stained sombrero. Villa dismounted, and some of the impressive bulk vanished. Villa's casklike torso was set on short, bowed legs that resembled barrel staves. He walked with a pigeon-toed shamble, as unfamiliar with the rocky terrain as a sailor too long at sea, his long arms swinging like a simian's. Villa's true home was on a horse, where man and beast were splendidly welded together into a centaur figure.

Villa growled a command and Corbett and McKinney were hauled to their feet, roughly stripped of clothing and shoved toward the nearest tree. Their hands were tied behind their backs and ropes draped over their heads and tightened around their necks. They were jerked into the air and slowly strangled.

James O'Neil was then shoved forward and forced to lie spread-eagle on the desert floor; he knew then that he would escape hanging but could not imagine what the Mexicans had in mind. He quickly found out. A dozen horsemen galloped for his prostrate body, intending to trample him to death. O'Neil somehow managed to twist away from the first two horses that swept over him, and Spencer watched in horrified admiration as O'Neil scrambled to his feet as the third horse bore down. O'Neil grabbed the stirrup and swung himself upward. He managed to get his hands around the rider's throat and was choking the Mexican to death when he was shot down from behind.

Buck Spencer wondered when his turn would come.

But when the Villistas broke camp before sunrise the next morning, his captors only motioned him to get in the saddle and ride on as before. The band rode north, toward the border, then turned east. Spencer was afraid he would have to follow the bandits into the interior of Mexico, but later that evening they changed direction and started northward again. A new terror rose inside Spencer when the riders began a ragged chant that began, "*Mata los gringos!*"—"Death to the gringos!"

Spencer prayed that his black skin would disqualify him as a gringo.

Shortly before one o'clock at night on Thursday, March 9, a section foreman for the El Paso & Southwestern Railroad named S. H. McCulloch noticed a bright orange glow a short distance down the tracks leading through the center of Columbus. He ran forward to investigate and found a grass fire crackling alongside the rails. He beat at the flames with a toe sack and stomped at the edges where the fire had eaten. The flames disappeared, leaving only tendrils of smoke rising in the clear, black air. Then McCulloch walked back along the silent tracks to his house and went to sleep. A little more than an hour later the moon slid below the horizon, and only a few pale yellow squares gave evidence that there was still life in Columbus.

It was about then that the first group of Villistas crossed over into the United States. The penetration was made three miles west of the border gate at Palomas, where Slocum had deployed 65 men and 2 officers, and eleven miles east of where Major Lindsley's two troops, 151 men and 7 officers, manned an outpost. Villa's men simply cut the border-fence wire between the two cavalry detachments and silently began making their way for Columbus, barely three miles away. About a mile from the slumbering town, Villa divided his five hundred raiders into two columns. One column set out for Camp Furlong, east of the main road, while the other moved forward to strike at Columbus from the west.

Lieutenant Lucas was the first to see them come. He was pulled out of his sleep by the sounds of horses moving past his house. It was just before four-thirty and pitch-black outside, but Lucas

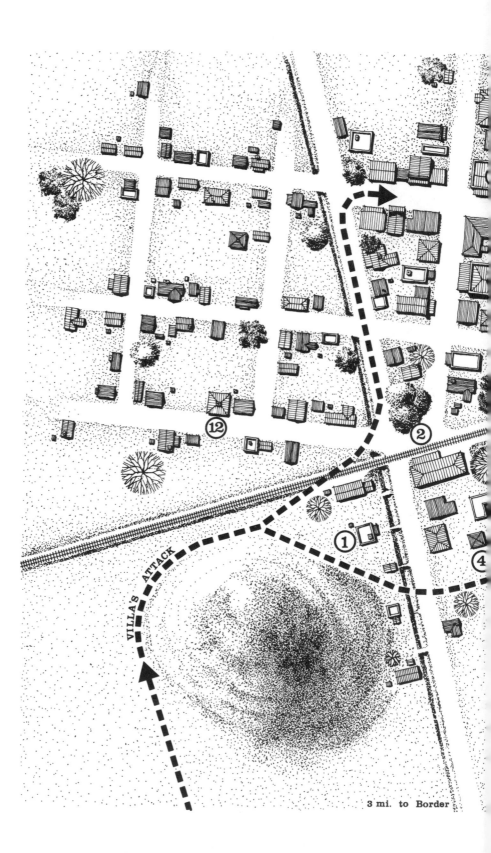

VILLA'S ATTACK

⑫

②

①

④

3 mi. to Border

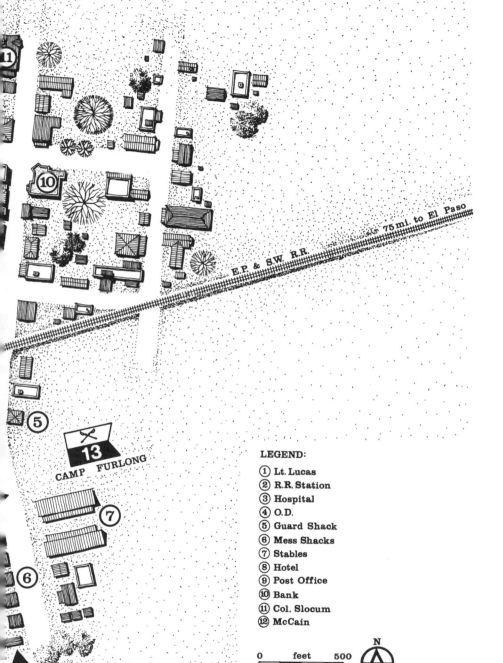

LEGEND:
1. Lt. Lucas
2. R.R. Station
3. Hospital
4. O.D.
5. Guard Shack
6. Mess Shacks
7. Stables
8. Hotel
9. Post Office
10. Bank
11. Col. Slocum
12. McCain

E.P. & S.W. R.R.

75 mi. to El Paso

CAMP FURLONG

13

0   feet   500

N

THE DARK HOURS
COLUMBUS, N.M   9 MARCH 1916

could make out the shadowy forms of mounted men wearing traditional Mexican sombreros. Lucas' window faced north, and he watched the Mexicans heading east for the road and the camp just on the other side. There were a great many horsemen, and Lucas believed that his house was surrounded. Alone in the dark room and wearing only his underwear, Lucas pulled his .45 pistol from the holster hanging on the wall and stationed himself in the center of the room, "determined to get a few of them before they got me."

At that moment Private Fred Griffin, K Troop, who was on guard near the headquarters building at Camp Furlong, only a few hundred feet to the right of Lucas' house, wheeled at the sound of thudding footsteps coming on the double. Griffin shouted a challenge and was answered by a rifle shot. The slug hit him in the belly but he managed to return the fire, killing three Mexicans before he slumped, dying, to the ground.

At this first burst of gunfire, the Mexicans surrounding Lucas' house galloped off. Lucas quickly drew on his pants and put on a shirt, but in the darkness could not find his boots. Barefoot and with the pistol in his hand, he rushed out of the door and ran hard for the road and the barrack housing the men of his machine-gun troop.

The firing brought the officer of the day, thirty-nine-year-old Lieutenant James P. Castleman, out of his shack at a dead run, pistol in hand. He rounded a corner and collided with one of the dismounted raiders. Castleman fired first, saw the man drop, and kept going. He encountered some of his men of F Troop, led by Sergeant Michael Fody, and was relieved to see that they were ready for combat if not fully uniformed. Assuming command, Castleman led the troop across the railroad tracks toward the main part of town.

Sergeant Fody recalled that after advancing two hundred yards, the men of F Troop "encountered heavy fire, so close that the flash almost scorched our faces. Instantly every man in the troop dropped to the ground and opened fire. On account of the darkness it was impossible to distinguish anyone, and for a moment I was under the impression that we were being fired on by some of our own regiment who had preceded us to the scene. When I heard Mexican voices opposite us you can imagine my relief."

Castleman guessed that the bandits would make an effort to

loot the town's only bank, at the eastern end of Main Street. When the fire slackened, Castleman stood upright and shouted "Forward!" His men jumped up and started running for the central part of town, where the firing seemed to be heaviest. Private Jesse P. Taylor was hit in the leg and went down. Fody told him to stay where he was, that he would be picked up later.

Castleman's advance toward the bank was stopped first by a barbed-wire fence obscure in the darkness. A private named Revielle tripped, discharging a round from his heavy Springfield rifle only inches before his nose, which streamed blood from the concussion. The flash attracted the Mexicans' attention, and Castleman's men were forced to go to ground under a lash of bullets. Private Thomas Butler was hit, but he disregarded the wound and kept working the bolt of his rifle. He was hit again during another brief dash toward the bank, and the men flopped back to earth.

"We made four stands in 500 yards," said Fody, "and Butler would not give up and went on with us until he had been hit five distinct times, the last wound proving fatal."

Castleman was finally able to get his men to Main Street before the Mexicans could reach the bank. He deployed his riflemen near the entrance, where they lay prone, shooting at the tiny blossoms of fire at the other end of the street.

While Castleman had been fighting his way toward town, Lucas continued his barefooted dash for the men of Machine-Gun Troop, which had been organized by transferring men from other outfits in the regiment. "It requires no unusual deductive powers," Lucas once commented, "to determine which ones I got. I loved them all, and the worse they were the more I loved them. They caused me considerable worry and they were hard to handle, but they were fighting men, all of them." This last would be quickly proved.

Lucas reached the barracks area and found the men of Machine-Gun Troop struggling into uniform, loosening slings on rifles, shouting questions, cursing the darkness—and in general acting like men roused from sleep by unexpected attack. Lucas grabbed the acting first sergeant and ordered him to muster the troops and follow him to the guard shack, two hundred yards away. Because machine guns could be sold across the border to Mexican revolutionaries for as much as $600 apiece, they were always kept locked and Lucas had one of the keys. Lucas did not wait for his command to form, but ran for the shack where the guns and ammunition were stored, followed by Horseshoer Frank T. Kindvall, twenty-six, and a corporal named Michael Barmazel.

The area swarmed with Mexicans. One of them rose from the ground and fired at Lucas, but missed. "He was so close," Lucas recalled, "that I easily killed him with a pistol and I was never noted for excellence in pistol practice."

When they reached the guard shack Lucas discovered a bloody figure sprawled at the entrance. It was Private John C. Yarborough of K Troop, a sentry who had dueled with the raiders only minutes earlier. He was still alive, but his right arm was shot through. Lucas and the others helped him to his feet and ordered him to make his way back to the Army hospital. Instead, Yarborough picked up his Springfield with his good hand and leaned into the darkness, moving toward town where the firing seemed to be concentrated.

Lucas unlocked the door and stumbled inside to get one of the machine guns, a French-designed Benét-Mercié adopted by the U. S. Army in 1910. The "Ben-A," as the troops called it, weighed only twenty-seven pounds, but had a high muzzle velocity and could spit out seven hundred rounds per minute; and there were only twenty-five parts to care for in the entire assembly. But here praise for the gun ran out; loading was a painstaking procedure even in full daylight. The thirty-round clip had to be flipped over so that the flat side faced upward, then inserted with almost surgical precision into a frustratingly narrow feed slot on the right side of the receiver before cocking and firing. Lucas' men had also complained that the sear and extractor had to be worked over with emery paper to achieve tolerances needed for foolproof full automatic fire. The light weight of the gun, which was such a blessing on training marches, proved a handicap in action; the gun would not stay on target because of heavy recoil.

Lucas, Barmazel and Kindvall grabbed one of the guns and several bags of clips and dashed for the railroad tracks. They set up the gun near one of the crossings, pointing the muzzle toward town. Barmazel lay prone with Lucas beside him. Lucas excitedly slid home the first clip and Barmazel squeezed the trigger. The gun barked a few times, then jammed. Cursing, Lucas and Barmazel abandoned the useless weapon and ran back to the guard shack for another. Kindvall left them and went off to search for his own buddies of K Troop. He was killed shortly afterward.

Lucas and the corporal returned to the crossing with a second Benét-Mercié and this time their gun did not jam; as fast as Barmazel emptied one clip, Lucas loaded another. Barmazel aimed low, spraying bullets toward the flashes from the Mexican rifles along the western end of town. The rest of the men of Machine-Gun Troop ran up, bringing with them the remaining two guns and the reserve ammunition, followed by about thirty riflemen under the command of Lieutenant Horace Stringfellow, Jr. Lucas deployed Stringfellow's riflemen to protect his left flank and stationed the other machine gunners along the railroad tracks to enfilade Main Street. To Lucas, it seemed that his handful of men were the only ones staving off at least a thousand of the enemy. The first Ben-A was put back in action, and within the next ninety minutes Lucas and his men poured twenty thousand rounds of machine-gun fire into the streets of Columbus.

Not without reason did Lucas feel alone; many of the regimental officers lived with their families in quarters scattered throughout the town and were cut off by bands of attacking Mexicans.

Captain Rudolph E. Smyser, his wife and two children lived on the western end of town and were awakened at the first outbreak of firing. Smyser got them all out of a rear window as the Mexicans battered down the front door. The four of them huddled inside the outhouse, listening to the raiders ransacking their quarters. Fearing discovery, Smyser moved his family from the outhouse and hid them in a mesquite patch not far away. They were all lacerated by cactus thorns, but no one cried out. They lay there until dawn, afraid to move.

On the southwestern edge of town lived Lieutenant William A. McCain with his wife and little girl. McCain's orderly stayed in the house as well. When the shooting started, all four Americans escaped from the house and ran in the darkness until they reached the scanty protection of a clump of brush. They were joined a few minutes later by the regimental adjutant, Captain George Williams, who walked into their hiding place by accident. They could hear firing all over town; the officers ached to join their troops but dared not leave the woman and the child unprotected.

When the first wave of attackers ran up against the hot fire directed at them by Lucas' machine guns and Castleman's riflemen, many of them fell back in groups and alone.

One of the Mexicans stumbled into the bush where the Americans were hiding, but before he could bring his rifle to bear, McCain's orderly swung a shotgun and pulled the trigger. The sudden blast knocked down the enemy but did not kill him. Williams and McCain grabbed the Mexican, and dragging him farther into the bush, stifled his cries. Both officers were armed with .45 automatics, but they were afraid to fire. While the wounded Mexican kicked and tried to scream, the Americans frantically sought to put an end to his resistance. One of the officers pulled out a pocketknife and began sawing at the man's throat, but the blade was dull and would not cut through. McCain's wife pulled the child closer to her and turned away in horror as the gruesome struggle went on. The deadly pantomime finally ended with a rain of blows delivered with the butt of a heavy pistol.

Not far away Mrs. John G. Nivergelt and her small daughter lay beside the body of Sergeant Nivergelt, fifty, a member of the regimental band. Nivergelt had been killed trying to get his family from their quarters to the camp.

When the shooting began, the wife of Captain Thomas F. Ryan was alone in her house on the Deming road that ran past headquarters. She dashed for the safety of the bulletproof adobe garage. A Mexican grabbed her arm as she came out of the house and asked her where she was going. "Nowhere," she replied. The Mexican shrugged and let her go. She walked on to the garage and stretched out on the earthen floor, listening to the sounds of combat.

The Villistas penetrated as far as the Commercial Hotel, about halfway up Main Street. They poured into the hotel, one group bounding up the stairs to the second floor, where the nine guests had been sleeping. "Uncle" Steven Burchfield, a longtime border resident, opened his door and in fluent Spanish told the invaders he would give them all the money he had. He pulled a handful of bills and coins from his pocket and scattered them across the floor. While the bandits fought over the loot Burchfield closed the door, crawled out of the window and made his way to safety down the fire escape.

Another guest, Walton R. Walker, was jerked away from his wife and shot to death on the stairs. Two other civilians, Dr. H. M. Hart, a veterinarian, and Charles De Witt Miller, an engineer, were hustled into the street, robbed and shot down.

The proprietor, William T. Ritchie, had gathered his wife and three daughters on the second floor and was standing in front of the terrified females when one of the Mexicans ordered him into the street. Ritchie's family pleaded with him to stay, but he followed the Mexican and was killed in the lobby. Other bandits began pulling at the rings of the distraught Ritchie women, dislocating Mrs. Ritchie's finger when they tore off her wedding band.

Across the street was the Lemmon & Romney grocery store. Gallons of kerosene were sluiced over the wooden building and set ablaze. Flames roared up and fanned across Main Street, setting fire to the hotel. The Mexicans who had been upstairs ransacking dresser drawers and firing rifle shots through closet doors fled the hotel to escape the flames. Juan Favela, who had so recently escaped Villista vengeance, left his house at the rear of the hotel, and with a young customs official named Jolly Garner, rushed up the back stairs of the hotel to see if there were any guests still alive. They discovered Mrs. Ritchie and her daughters and helped them down the stairs to safety.*

The Mexicans opened fire on any home that showed a light. The druggist, C. C. Miller, was killed, and so was a grocer named James Dean. One volley killed Mrs. Milton James and wounded her husband, a railroad worker. Harry Davis, who had arrived in Columbus only the day before, was killed, as was a man named W. A. Dividson.

Roughly half of the Villa raiding force struck at Camp Furlong from the southeast, directing their attack at the complex of barracks, tents, stables and mess shacks. The primary target was the stables, and the raiders managed to spook away a great many horses, but American rifle fire drove the attackers to seek shelter beside the adobe walls of the mess shacks before the stables could be set on fire.

The cooks were already wide awake and hard at work inside the mess shacks when the fighting started. Brewing on top of the wood-fueled iron ranges were steaming cauldrons of black coffee.

* Jolly Garner, younger brother of John Nance Garner, later married Myrtle Ritchie, one of the girls he had helped save from the fire.

Mexicans crouching outside the cookhouses were slaughtered by close-range blasts from large-bore shotguns kept handy by the cooks, who used them to bag fresh game. The raiders ran frantically from the mess area to escape those awful scatterguns, but the fires set in town now lighted the entire area, making the Mexicans visible in flickering relief. Lucas turned one of the machine guns toward the adobe kitchens and opened fire, not afraid of hitting the cooks safe behind the thick walls. The bullets ricocheted off the hard desert floor, killing and maiming Mexicans everywhere.

A group of frantic Mexicans beat down the door of one of the shacks, seeking shelter inside. The kitchen crew was waiting for them. The cook flung a huge kettle of scalding coffee on the intruders and the cook's helper laid into them with the ax he used to chop firewood. A cavalry major later walked through the area and counted several pieces of human skull as large as his hand; bone, he recalled, "with the long hair of the Yaqui Indian still attached."

Heavy fire from Machine-Gun Troop was taking its toll of raiders, beating them back from the center of town, but in turn, Lucas' own men were being killed and wounded. Corporal Barmazel was hit in the jaw and spewed blood all over his gun, but with a handkerchief bound over the wound he kept firing. Sergeant Mark Dobbs, twenty-four, was shot through the liver early in the fighting, but he refused to leave his Ben-A and continued to pour bursts at the Mexicans until he collapsed and died. Three others of Lucas' troop were wounded, but not put out of action.

One of the firing pins split, and two of the gunners ran back with the gun to the hospital building a hundred yards from the tracks. There, they believed, they would be able to use a flashlight in safety and replace the pin. But when they tried to get inside the building they found the door barricaded by shirkers, who shouted for them to go away "because they might draw fire."

The Mexicans had suffered heavy casualties and were slowly withdrawing from the business section of town, moving westward toward the residential section where the officers lived. With a gun and a handful of men, Lucas crossed the tracks and moved down Main Street, "intending to clear the town and do what I could to protect the families of officers from the greasers." He came upon a wounded Villista, apparently awaiting capture, but as Lucas approached, the bandit pulled a gun and fired. The bullet thudded into a wall only inches from the officer's head. Lucas shot the Mexican with the .45 he held in his hand and continued down the eerily lighted street.

The Mexicans withdrew from town and began retreating toward the border, heading in the direction from which they had come. Officers who, along with their families, had been trapped inside their homes, dashed for various parts of the town and the camp. Major Frank Tompkins, forty-eight, left his house and ran to the town's only high ground, Cootes Hill, a small promontory south of the tracks, immediately behind Lucas' quarters. He found Colonel Slocum, who had arrived only minutes before, standing on top of the hill observing the efforts of a handful of riflemen firing prone at the retreating Mexicans. Dawn was breaking and the targets were clearly visible.

Tompkins saw that the Mexicans were in full flight and asked Slocum for permission to "mount up a troop and take the offensive." Slocum assented, and Tompkins rushed down the hill to organize the hot pursuit. He ran into Captain Smyser, who had finally emerged from the mesquite after his ignominious flight with his family to the outhouse. Eager for revenge, the captain asked Tompkins to mount H Troop for the chase. Twenty minutes later, enough horses had been rounded up for thirty-two of Smyser's men and they started riding after the Mexicans.

A half mile out of camp they came across the McCain party and the Mexican they had bludgeoned to death. Tompkins dismounted one of Smyser's men to allow Captain Williams to join in the chase. While the trooper was getting off his horse Tompkins noticed movement in the brush about a hundred yards away. One of the men rode over to investigate and found Mrs. J. J. Moore feebly signaling for help; she had been shot in the leg and had lost a great deal of blood. She said that the Villistas had burst into her home on their way out of Columbus, killing her husband and setting fire to the house. A bandit twisted a ring from her finger, and when she fled, shot her. Mrs. Moore, who ran a small store in Columbus, had sold the same Mexican a pair of pants only the day before.

. . .

Tompkins was joined by Lieutenant Castleman with twenty-seven men of F Troop, giving him a total of fifty-six with which to pursue four hundred or more Villistas. The raiders crossed the international line with Tompkins at their heels. The Mexicans left a rear guard atop a ridge, but Tompkins put in a mounted pistol charge that drove the Mexicans from the hill. Tompkins' men jumped from their saddles and opened fire with Springfields, killing thirty-two of the enemy.

When Tompkins ordered cease-fire, the full realization that he had violated Mexican territory sank in. He watched the Mexicans gallop for a ridge a mile farther away, where they dismounted, waiting to see what the Americans would do. Tompkins reached for his message pad and wrote out a brief appreciation of the situation for Slocum, requesting permission to continue the chase. Forty-five minutes later the messenger returned on a lathered horse with Slocum's noncommittal reply. "Use your own judgment," it said.

Tompkins put in three more charges that morning, driving the Mexicans fifteen miles deep inside their own country, before ammunition and water shortages made it imperative that he get his troopers back across the border. Tompkins and Captain Williams were grazed by Mexican bullets, and one trooper had his horse killed underneath him, but there were no other casualties. With the Mexicans raising dust far to the south, Tompkins ordered his troopers to start back for Columbus.

The Americans passed bodies and equipment scattered everywhere. Nearly a hundred dead Villistas were counted, along with dozens of dead and wounded horses; pistol shots ended the suffering. They picked up two of Villa's machine guns abandoned in flight, as well as loot the raiders had taken from the town. The exhausted detachment reached Camp Furlong a few minutes before one o'clock that afternoon, and found disposal parties hard at work. The corpses of sixty-seven Mexican raiders had been dragged to the outskirts of town, doused with kerosene and set ablaze, adding to the stench of smoldering wood from the gutted area along Main Street.

.   .   .

Back in his quarters, Lieutenant Lucas sat on his bunk. He was red-eyed and grimy, and with a pocketknife and a pair of tweezers he began the painful removal of tiny barbs from sandburs imbedded in the raw, bleeding soles of his feet. It wasn't until after the shooting had stopped that Lucas realized that he had fought barefoot throughout the entire action.

𝟡𝟚

The Cauldron

News of the attack upon Columbus was sent out even while the fighting was in progress. Mrs. G. E. Parks, the night telephone operator, was at her switchboard when the gunfire erupted. Bullets shattered the windows of her tiny office, and flying splinters of glass raked her face and arms. Despite her bleeding from the superficial cuts, Susie Parks did not panic; she blew out the kerosene lamps, and cranking furiously, managed to raise her counterpart in Deming. For two hours Susie Parks sat in the darkness, describing the attack as she imagined it from the frightening sounds of combat raging just outside her window.

Full news of the assault reached the Associated Press even before all the details were known in Washington, D.C. The enterprising AP bureau chief in El Paso, George Seese, thirty-three, had been tipped off by one of his Mexican sources in town that Villa was planning a raid on Columbus. Although Seese received many such tips concerning intentions of various Mexican revolutionaries, some sixth sense compelled him to take a train for Columbus on the night of March 3. He talked to Colonel Slocum and anybody else who would answer his questions, then called for AP telegrapher Edwin Van Camp to leave his post in El Paso and come to Columbus. Van Camp arrived on the night of March 8, only hours before the raid.

Both men survived the attack by taking cover inside the Columbus Hotel, and when the fighting in the streets had stopped they dashed for the railroad station, where they forced the door to the telegraph office. Van Camp sat at the key clicking out thousands of words dictated by Seesc in what was one of the major journalistic scoops of the decade.

Quick reaction on the part of the junior officers and noncoms, coupled with the uncommon bravery of several troopers, had prevented a massacre. Seventeen Americans were killed during the fighting, including nine civilians. Four troopers and two officers were wounded, as well as one civilian, Mrs. Moore. Only eight of Villa's raiders were taken prisoner, and all of these were badly hit. Among them was a twelve-year-old boy named Jesús Bayez, whose father had taken him from school in Chihuahua City to join up.

There was no doubt that the killings were the work of Pancho Villa. A search of the dead turned up a pair of large wallets on the body of a Villa aide. They were stuffed with papers, and among them was a lengthy letter from Villa to the revolutionary leader, Emiliano Zapata, then fighting in the southern part of Mexico. Translations were wired to the State Department in Washington and to General Funston in San Antonio. From the letter it was clear that Villa had planned to violate United States territory as early as January 8 of that year. He urged Zapata to come north with his army "to join in a concerted attack upon the United States." Villa set a six-month deadline for the concentration of forces in Chihuahua, informing Zapata that he had "sent couriers to all states to incite the populace against the Americans," whom Villa termed "common enemies of the Mexicans." It was Villa's habit to send numerous copies of any field correspondence by separate couriers, to make sure that one of them would get through. It was assumed that Zapata had received a copy of the letter, but among the prisoners taken at Columbus, none were Zapata's men.

Further proof that Villa had led the raid was given by an American woman, Mrs. Maud Hawkes Wright, who had been held captive by Villa's irregulars for ten days prior to the battle, not knowing from one day to the next whether she would live or die. She rode into Columbus shortly after the raiders had been driven out. Gaunt and disheveled, near exhaustion, she had to be helped from the saddle by an officer of the 13th. Buck Spencer's brief captivity in no way matched the ordeal of Maud Wright.

Maud and E. J. Wright were among many Americans who had chosen to live in Mexico. They worked a small ranch near Colonia Hernández, about one hundred and twenty miles south of the border, and had stayed on through the nearly six years of bloody revolution. Until the morning of March 1, 1916, they had seen no reason to leave. On that day Maud Wright was alone at the ranch house with her infant daughter. Twelve armed horsemen rode through the gate and dismounted. Maud Wright, accustomed to such sudden visits, came out to greet the Mexicans and to offer the hospitality of the house. This was refused, and Colonel Nicólás Hernández informed her that she was a prisoner of the Division of the North. A little later E. J. Wright and another American, by the name of Hayden, rode up and were also made captive. The Wrights were forced at gunpoint to leave their child to the care of a Mexican woman, then were ordered to mount. The Mexicans and their three prisoners rode all that afternoon and most of the night until they reached the small settlement of Cave Valle, where camp-fires glowed and hundreds of men and horses moved restlessly.

At daybreak Wright and Hayden were taken before Villa, and when the Americans returned, Wright told his wife that Villa would say neither why they had been taken prisoner, nor what would become of them. Wright and Hayden were then taken away. Maud Wright never saw them again; later she learned that both men had been executed.

The Mexicans fed themselves before breaking camp, but offered nothing to Maud Wright. Colonel Hernández told her to get ready to ride, adding that "Villa intends for you to die a horrible death. You will ride day and night until we reach Columbus—if you live that long." The raiding party set a killing pace, but Maud Wright had lived a lifetime in the open and hardship was no stranger. After three punishing days in the saddle, subsisting on scraps of food left her by the Mexicans, she still managed to keep up the pace, knowing that if she collapsed she would probably be shot and left for the buzzards that wheel in the skies over Chihuahua.

During the nightmare days and nights of hard riding that followed, Maud Wright went from one Villista officer to another, begging to be allowed to go back to her child. She was largely ignored. Villa granted her a short interview at his campfire, but only scowled and said that she should talk to Hernández. The colonel told her that Villa admired her "gameness and courage" and that he would probably set her free after they had accomplished their purpose in Columbus. Maud Wright asked what that purpose was.

"To burn and loot the town and kill every American there," Hernández replied.

Maud Wright grimly hung on until the raiding force reached the outskirts of town. She dismounted and was placed under guard. She heard the whispered shouts of command and saw Villa trot up to the head of one of the attack columns. She watched the dark shapes of hundreds of horsemen plunge forward, then she was alone with her guard. She listened as heavy firing burst out in the town, watched the darkened sky light up when the buildings on Main Street were set ablaze. Then she was swept up with the retreating invaders and brought back across the border. The raiders paused briefly at the little mud settlement of Palomas across the fence line.

Villa ambled over to Maud Wright and asked her if she would like to return to the United States.

"If you would do me that favor," she replied in Spanish. Villa told her to take her horse and leave.

Mrs. Wright later returned to the ranch at Colonia Hernández and found her daughter unharmed.

President Thomas Woodrow Wilson received word of the "outrage of Columbus" by a telephone call to the White House placed by Secretary of State Robert Lansing late in the morning of March 9. The news of the raid was a terrible blow. After three frustrating years of complicated—and often inept—political maneuvering trying to shape Mexico into the desired Wilsonian mold, and after one rueful decision that sent U.S. Marines storming ashore in Mexico with bloody results, Wilson realized that Columbus meant the end of the long and fretful period of "watchful waiting." Wilson hung up the receiver, then summoned his private secretary and personal friend, Joseph P. Tumulty, and told him to call a Cabinet meeting early the following morning. But Wilson's decision was already made: the U. S. Army would be ordered to invade Mexico in force, and God only knew where it would end.

Shortly before Wilson assumed the Presidency on March 4, 1913, he had commented to his wife, "It would be an irony of fate if my administration had to deal chiefly with foreign affairs."

Wilson, who had hoped to devote his energies to sweeping social reforms at home, instead faced thorny diplomatic problems with Mexico, a burden inherited from his predecessor, William Howard Taft.

The first half of Taft's term had coincided with the decline of power held by the Mexican dictator, Porfirio Díaz, who had occupied the President's chair in Mexico City for more than thirty years. Díaz was almost eighty years old, but he appeared robust, clear of eye, and held his large frame militarily erect. Outside of Mexico, Díaz was held in awe. Theodore Roosevelt called him "the greatest statesman now living." In Russia, Leo Tolstoy proclaimed him "a prodigy of nature." Díaz, the friend of foreign investors and of Mexican big businessmen, drew an accolade from Andrew Carnegie, who said that the dictator "should be held up to the hero-worship of mankind."

Lavish praise from capitalist quarters was not surprising; Díaz made Mexico a safe place in which to turn high profits from the country's great wealth in silver, copper, oil and cattle. Under laws passed by Díaz, only 4 percent of the country's natural resources rested in the hands of the population. The people, largely Indian and 85 percent of them illiterate, had been stripped of lands traditionally theirs. Díaz had managed to create a feudal society in which the relationship between peons and large landowners was similar to that between serfs and *grands seigneurs* in medieval Europe—with one important exception. The Mexican peon shared nothing with his master, nor did the master feel obliged to protect those who toiled to bring in the crops during every daylight hour. The peon was generally much worse off than the average Negro slave in the ante-bellum South. It was the peon who paid the price for financial stability in Mexico, a stability which American and British business interests in particular hoped to perpetuate.

Anita Brenner, an American who grew up in Mexico during and after the Díaz years, recalled:

"Justice was carried out according to an unwritten, unbreakable law which required that a case be settled in rigid observance of who the attorney was, who the client. Cases involving a foreigner against a Mexican were decided according to the principle that the foreigner must be right, unless word came from Don Porfirio, exceptionally, to discover otherwise. In the remotest places judges understood the fine points of these usages, and could interpret skillfully the precept taught by the U. S. State Department that Americans were guests and must be spared the judicial annoyances unavoidable to Mexicans; that every American working and living in Mexico, from plant manager to gang foreman and oil driller, and every company that had American money in it— even if it were only one red cent, said the Embassy—had the same kind of right of extraterritorial immunity."

Díaz ruthlessly crushed any opposition to the regime or attempts by workers to better their lot. On June 1, 1906, more than five thousand Mexican miners employed by the American-owned Consolidated Copper Company walked off the job, asking for more than the $1.50 they earned for an eleven-hour day. Two thousand American miners working for Consolidated earned twice that amount and worked fewer hours; nevertheless, representatives of the Mexican strikers approached the Americans and asked them to join the strike. The Americans greeted the Mexicans with gunfire, and a general riot broke out. Mine officials called for help from the governor of Sonora, and state troops and federal *rurales* were rushed in. Twenty-three Mexican miners were killed, a like number were wounded and martial law was declared. Fifty of the strike leaders were put in chains and sent to the dungeons at Veracruz.

An even worse incident occurred several months later. On January 7, 1907, textile workers in a factory at Río Blanco went on strike and began wrecking mill property in a frenzy of emotion. Don Porfirio sent troops to ring the great mill, and they dispassionately poured rifle and machine-gun fire into the courtyard packed with humanity. More than two hundred men, women and children were indiscriminately shot down. Strikers fleeing from the rain of bullets were caught, then killed by firing squads that had much experience in this work.

Although Díaz could still point with pride to the fact that there was a surplus in gold worth 62.5 million pesos—and each peso was worth 47 cents—in the national treasury, he could feel the foundations of his power beginning to crack beneath his feet. In 1909 President Díaz wrote to President Taft proposing a public meeting between the two heads of state. Díaz believed that if he were given a symbolic *abrazo*, an embrace, by the newly elected American President his stock would soar at home and his prestige would be further strengthened abroad. Taft agreed to meet with

Díaz, in El Paso, where his special train would in any case be stopping during its long cross-country parabola scheduled for the fall.

The Presidential Special arrived in El Paso shortly before noon on October 16, 1909. Taft went to the El Paso Chamber of Commerce building, found an unused office and lay down on a leather couch and went to sleep. He was awakened in time to meet Díaz in the center of the International Bridge, which connects El Paso with Juárez, and the two men —one resplendent in a tailored uniform with epaulets, the other corpulent and wearing a tentlike frock coat that billowed in the warm breeze—shook hands. There was a noisy parade through the streets of El Paso, then the two men retired to the Chamber of Commerce building and got down to business.

Díaz asked Taft for "full friendship and support" for his regime. Taft countered with a request for renewal of U. S. naval leases on bases at Magdalena Bay in Lower California. Acutely concerned over antiforeign feelings at home, Díaz refused. In turn, Taft gave Díaz only rhetoric and no firm assurances.

While the Presidential Special was still en route to El Paso, Taft had confided to his wife in a letter: "I am glad to aid him for the reason that we have two billions of American capital in Mexico that will be greatly endangered if Díaz were to die and his government go to pieces. I can only hope and pray that his demise does not come until I am out of office . . ."

Taft's prayers were not answered, but the real headache would be all Woodrow Wilson's.

In the fall of 1910, Mexico exploded. Small, disorganized bands of men staged uprisings in towns and villages all over the country. Said Miss Brenner: "Some wanted a full meal, some a new pair of pants; some wanted only a gun to blow to pieces a hated master." These scattered risings, crushed as soon as they began, were fires of insurrection that Díaz frantically tried to stamp out even as he was being inaugurated for his eighth term as President. The flames of rebellion were fanned into full-scale revolution by an unlikely figure, thirty-five-year-old Francisco Ignacio Madero, a lawyer, a vegetarian, an ascetic, a splendid horseman who stood only five feet three inches tall. Madero was wealthy; he shared in the profits from more than a million acres of land. There was money from cattle, cotton, lumber, smelting, rubber, distilleries and banking. Madero was not of the people, but his heart bled for them. Nor did he forget that once during his childhood an ouija board had predicted that someday he would become President.

As head of the Anti-Reelectionist party Madero had campaigned against Díaz, and in June 1910 he was put in the state penitentiary at San Luis Potosí for inciting rebellion. Out on bail, Madero disguised himself as a railway brakeman and escaped to Texas. In San Antonio, Madero and a handful of followers plotted the overthrow of Díaz. In February the next year Madero was back in Mexico gathering armed men, and on April 19, 1911, Madero and fifteen hundred men moved on the federal garrison at Juárez.

The federal commander, General Juan Navarro, had less than a thousand men under arms in the town, and their backs were against the Rio Grande. Navarro prepared his outnumbered force to meet an immediate attack, but Madero loathed bloodshed and dallied on the outskirts of town hoping that Navarro would surrender and that any day now Díaz might remove himself from the National Palace voluntarily. Madero's commanders grew tired of waiting and began the assault on Juárez without orders. On the other side of the river, citizens of El Paso scrambled for vantage points on top of freight cars and inside office buildings to watch the battle. An American newspaper man named Timothy Turner who attached himself to the Madero forces described the investment of Juárez that began on the night of May 8:

"With Garibaldi* I moved into the outskirts of town. We went along for a block or two until there was the rattle of a machine gun, very close, and the men ahead of us fell back, one of them wounded in the arm. Garibaldi's men broke into a house, got onto the roof and began preparations for Latin American warfare.

"It was three o'clock and I decided that it was no place for me. I worked my way back and got out into the hills again and met Raul Madero, Francisco's younger brother, who had charge of the big homemade gun set on a hillock commanding a good view of the town. We saw the river road swarming with *insurrectos* moving into Juárez. They moved in no formation whatsoever, just an irregular stream of them, silhouettes of men and rifles. They

* Giuseppe "Peppino" Garibaldi, then thirty-two, was the adventuresome nephew of the great nineteenth-century Italian patriot-general of the same name.

would fight awhile, then come back to rest, sleep and eat to return refreshed to the front.

"The European soldiers [among us] raved against this, tried to turn them back, to make everybody fight at the same time. But that was not the way of these chaps from Chihuahua; they knew their business well. The *insurrectos* were always fresh and in high spirits, while the little brown federals, with no sleep and with little food and water, with their officers behind them with pistols ready to kill quitters, soon lost their morale.

"For the first time I examined the homemade cannon. It was an extraordinarily long piece with a very small bore. There was no rifling, but it was breechloading and had homemade shells that threw a solid ball. It was, in short, a sort of mammoth early American squirrel rifle mounted on a pair of small locomotive wheels. The gunner was an American named Carpentier, an almost dainty little chap who wore a pair of new kid gloves."

Sporadic rifle fire died away during the night, and dawn came, bringing with it a breeze with a "sweet, clean smell." Juárez, changing color with the angle of the sun, was peaceful. Then a shot was fired and the town erupted once again with the popping of small arms. Carpentier got ready to fire the virgin round from Madero's only piece of artillery. The first shot missed Ciudad Juárez altogether, sailing harmlessly over El Paso. Carpentier and his Mexican loaders lowered the long muzzle and fired again. "We felt sure something had happened," said Turner. Later they found out what it was. Most of the federal troops were fortified in the town *cuartel*, an adobe fortification built around a large patio. In the center of the patio stood an elevated water tank, and it was through the wooden sides of this tank that the second shaft of solid metal passed. The federal soldiers inside the *cuartel* were showered with the only drinking water available to them, and their suffering from thirst grew intense as the late-morning sun blazed down.

Carpentier's gun was soon out of action. With the third round, the breechblock exploded, putting the artillerists out of the action.

The battle for the narrow streets of Juárez lasted for thirty-six hours. Hungry, thirsty, with no escape route open or needed care for the wounded, the troops under General Navarro staked their arms in the courtyard of the *cuartel* and surrendered.

On May 21 Porfirio Díaz agreed to vacate the power and the

glory of the National Palace. Five days later he boarded a train for Veracruz, where he embarked on the German liner *Ypiranga*. Díaz died in Paris four years later, almost a forgotten man.

While Woodrow Wilson campaigned vigorously against Taft for the Presidency he closely followed the fortunes of Francisco Madero, who had ridden into Mexico City on a white horse at the head of an army of insurrectionists, scruffily uniformed and randomly armed. On May 25, 1911, Madero formed a provisional government under Francisco León de la Barra, who had been Foreign Minister, and on November 1 Madero himself was freely elected Mexico's new President. Madero's promises to Mexico— and to the world—to secularize education, to separate church and state, to achieve land reforms, to disband the revolutionary armies, to unfetter the press and guarantee free elections henceforth, were heartening. It seemed that for the first time since the days of Benito Juárez, who was President from 1861 to 1872, that a liberal and truly democratic Mexico was in the making. Madero dreamed of a Mexico that would eventually rival the United States economically, politically and socially. He looked forward to uncounted years of service to the suffering masses. He was a messiah, a redeemer of forgotten pledges.

Madero lasted fifteen months.

His failure to parcel out the great haciendas disillusioned General Emiliano Zapata, the great land reformer, whose peasant army had fought the Díaz troops south of Mexico City. Zapata refused to disband or disarm. General Pascual Orozco was angered by Madero because the new President had rewarded him with a minor post instead of the governorship of the state of Chihuahua. There was a garrison revolt at Veracruz, then bloody fighting broke out all over again in Mexico. Madero watched helplessly as the capital was threatened from nearly every side. In desperation he called for help from General Victoriano Huerta, a stolid-faced Aztec Indian, a saloon tough addicted to brandy whose black eyes glittered like a snake's. Huerta crushed the Orozco rebellion and kept Zapata's army away from Mexico City.

But Huerta, who had been a friend of Díaz's, had only contempt for Madero, whom he considered an idealistic, ineffectual weakling. Huerta plotted with other generals and on February 9, 1913, downtown Mexico City was turned into a battlefield in the struggle to oust Madero from the National Palace. Civilians, desperate for food, were caught in cross fires and killed in the streets. After ten days the fighting stopped. Huerta had won. He ordered the arrest of Madero and his Vice-President, José María Piño Suárez. Huerta immediately sent a telegram to President Taft that was a marvel of brevity and braggadocio: "I have overthrown the Government, therefore peace and order will reign."

Huerta promised Madero and Piño Suárez to spare their lives if immediate resignations were forthcoming. Helpless, locked in a room in the National Palace, the victims gave in. A whimsy of Mexican law then produced the shortest term ever held by a President. The resignations were accepted by the Chamber of Deputies at 7 P.M. on February 19, and at 7:01 the Minister of Foreign Affairs, Pedro Lascurain, automatically became provisional President. Lascurain appointed Huerta the new Minister of Foreign Affairs, and forty-five minutes later Lascurain resigned; Huerta automatically succeeded him, was sworn in as provisional President of Mexico and there the matter rested. The deputies did not even bother to leave their seats in the interim.

Madero's wife appealed to the U. S. embassy to cable President Taft requesting sanctuary for her husband either inside the embassy or across the border in Texas. No answer came. Members of the Texas Legislature sent petitions to the lame-duck President asking that something be done to save Madero's life. The petitions went unheeded. On the night of February 22 Madero and Piño Suárez were taken from the National Palace to the penitentiary on some pretext. The cars pulled up at the rear of the prison; the two were told to get out and were shot to death. The assassins sped away, leaving the bodies slumped on the ground by the prison wall. Huerta's explanation to the world: "Shot while trying to escape."

Ten days later Thomas Woodrow Wilson was inaugurated as the nation's twenty-eighth President. "Mexico," he said, "will never become a peaceful and law-abiding nation until she has been permitted to achieve a permanent and basic settlement of her troubles without outside interference." As to the character of the government settled upon the fifteen million Mexican citizens, Wilson called it "none of my business." But in the months to come, Wilson bent nearly every energy toward getting "that unspeakable Huerta" out of office.

Wilson's first problem was to deal with the American ambassador to Mexico, Henry Lane Wilson, a leftover from the Taft Administration. Ambassador Wilson, a lean corporation lawyer who parted his hair in the middle and cocked his head to one side like a parrot when listening to others, had played an unprecedented role in Mexican internal affairs. Wilson was one of the last of the "dollar diplomats," and a strong supporter of Huerta. During lulls in the fighting for the capital Wilson was seen riding around in the embassy automobile tightly gripping a large American flag that flapped in the breeze, visiting Huerta aides and Senate leaders known to be in favor of getting rid of Madero. Members of the diplomatic corps believed that the leaflets urging support of the attacking generals were cranked out by a secret printing press in the basement of the U. S. embassy.

On the night of Madero's arrest Ambassador Wilson had held a meeting at the embassy, a black-tie affair that included members of the diplomatic corps, Victoriano Huerta, General Félix Díaz (Don Porfirio's nephew) and other plotters against Madero. Wilson introduced Huerta as Mexico's provisional President, then read from a list the names of the new government officials—a list that had been prepared in the embassy. The ambassador then embraced Huerta and proposed a toast to the new government of law and order.

In a lengthy letter dated March 12, 1913, Ambassador Wilson urged Secretary of State William Jennings Bryan to persuade President Wilson to recognize the Huerta regime immediately, calling Huerta "a soldier, a man of iron mold, of absolute courage, a sincere patriot [who] will cheerfully relinquish the responsibilities of office as soon as peace in the country is restored and financial stability reestablished." The ambassador prophesied "that unless the same type of government as was implanted here by Porfirio Díaz is again established, new revolutionary movements will break forth and general unrest will be renewed." He wanted active support of Huerta's government "without being especially concerned as to whether its character is in accordance with our ideas of general democratic institutions."

President Wilson was also pressured for quick recognition of Huerta by spokesmen for the American colony in Mexico and by representatives of banking houses, railroads and oil concessionaires; they all saw in the new dictator another Díaz who would protect vested interests, whatever the methods, whatever the cost.

Woodrow Wilson stubbornly refused. "I will not," he said privately, "recognize a government of butchers."

However, sixteen other nations did recognize Huerta, including Great Britain, whose Royal Navy depended almost entirely upon the flow of oil from Mexico. Germany's Kaiser Wilhelm II sent a congratulatory note to Huerta, calling him "a brave soldier who will save his country with the sword of honor."

Miss Brenner recalled that while Huerta allowed the national treasury to be plundered from within, he "sat every day dispatching state business from behind a cognac bottle in his favorite bar, the Café Colón, a place with conveniently furnished dining rooms backstairs. In the evenings the Government moved to his 'rabbit hutch' outside the city. 'I always found him,' said Rodolfo Reyes, the Minister of Justice, 'in strange company, eating national dishes, singing, and acutely alcoholic.' Every night the police trusties conveyed oppositionists, or people who knew something, or were in somebody's way, or had the wrong women, in cars to the suburbs, and there ended the ride."

Wilson's distrust of his namesake in Mexico City was such that he refused to communicate with the ambassador, although the other Wilson continued sending long notes to Secretary Bryan pushing Huerta's cause. By-passing the ambassador, Wilson sent a journalist and former Episcopal clergyman, William Bayard Hale, on a secret, fact-finding mission to Mexico City. Hale, as the President had hoped, reported back that Huerta would never be able to pacify the country or to weld it together again economically. On July 17, 1913, Henry Lane Wilson was recalled from Mexico and dismissed.

President Wilson next sent John Lind, former governor of Minnesota, to Mexico City to act as embassy adviser and to present a note to Huerta's Foreign Minister, Federico Gamboa. The note explained that "the Government of the United States does not feel at liberty any longer to stand inactively by while it becomes daily more and more evident that no real progress is being made toward the establishment of a government at the City of Mexico which the country will obey and respect." Wilson was at pains to point out that "we act in the interest of Mexico alone, and not in the interest of any person or body of persons who may have personal or property claims in Mexico. We are seeking to counsel Mexico for her own good . . ."

To Wilson, a "satisfactory settlement" of Mexico's internal

affairs was conditioned upon a cessation of fighting throughout Mexico, assurance of early and free elections in which Huerta would promise not to be a candidate, and agreement by all factions to abide by the results of the election and to co-operate "in the most loyal way in supporting the new administration."

Gamboa rejected Wilson's conditions, calling them "humiliating and unusual." Gamboa expressed the opinion that Wilson was "laboring under a serious delusion" as to the conditions that prevailed in Mexico. He revealed his astuteness when it came to answering Wilson's request that Huerta eliminate himself from any presidential election. "Aside from its strange and unwarranted character, there is a risk that the same might be interpreted as a matter of personal dislike. This point," Gamboa stressed, "can only be decided by Mexican public opinion at the polls."

Wilson drafted a new note, a shortened version of the first one, but with an important—and astonishing—addition: there was a hint that if Huerta went along with Wilson's conditions, the U. S. government would use its influence with American bankers to effectuate an immediate loan in order to make it possible for the Mexican government to meet its financial obligations. Gamboa rejected this bribe out of hand. "Mr. Confidential Agent," Gamboa replied to Lind, "precisely because we comprehend the immense value of the principle of sovereignty which the Government of the United States so opportunely invokes in the question of our recognition or non-recognition—precisely for this reason we believe that it should never be proposed to us to forget our own sovereignty by permitting a foreign government to modify the line of conduct which we have followed in our public and independent life. If even once we were to admit the counsels and advice (let us call them thus) of the United States of America, not only would we forgo our sovereignty but we would compromise for an indefinite future our destinies as a sovereign entity, and all the future elections for president would be submitted for veto of any President of the United States of America."

Gamboa said that the offer of a loan seemed to be "moved by petty interests," adding that "When the dignity of the nation is at stake, I believe that there are not loans enough to induce those charged by the law to maintain it to be lessened."

Wilson received this latest reply from Gamboa on August 26, and the next day he went before a joint session of Congress to explain what his confidential agent had tried to accomplish in Mexico, as well as giving them the benefit of Gamboa's tart riposte. Henceforth, Wilson explained, the United States would pursue a policy of "watchful waiting." It was a clear admission of almost total tactical defeat.

Huerta, having won the first round in the confrontation with the "Puritan from the North," now added outrage to Wilson's discomfiture. On October 10, 1913, he fell upon the Chamber of Deputies and arrested one hundred and ten political leaders known to be sympathetic to Maderista philosophies. The election held afterward made the transition from de facto dictator to de jure President ripple-free.

On November 24 Secretary Bryan sent a note to the American chargé d'affaires in Mexico City, Nelson O'Shaughnessy, which stated Wilson's attitude in no uncertain terms. "The present policy of the Government of the United States is to isolate General Huerta entirely; to cut him off from foreign sympathy and aid and from domestic credit, whether moral or material, and to force him out."

To this end, Wilson now moved.

Although Huerta was firmly in control of Mexico City and its environs; although his troops were in solid possession of Veracruz, the major seaport on the Atlantic; although he could count on approximately eighty thousand federal soldiers to help keep order in the central part of the nation; although he was sure there were no incipient revolts brewing inside the National Palace; although he had managed to stave off active American intervention, his grip on the country was far from secure. Only days after the overthrow of Madero in February 1913, new banners of revolt had unfurled in the north, in the states of Coahuila, Sonora and Chihuahua. Chief among the malcontents was Venustiano Carranza, the governor of Coahuila, a white-bearded patriarchal figure with his eye on the President's chair. Carranza, a large landowner, had been a senator in the days of Porfirio Díaz; he was haughty, stubborn and egocentric, and believed that only he was capable of acting as Mexico's savior. Carranza assembled a sizable army, which he called "Constitutionalist," and proclaimed himself First Chief. He held absolute control of the northeast of Mexico in early 1913, and he intended to fight his way south and occupy Mexico City as quickly as possible, killing every Huerta supporter who got in his way.

Ostensibly allied with Carranza, but operating his campaigns in Chihuahua as he saw fit, was the bandit Francisco Villa, whose rise to military chieftain in the northeast had been meteoric.

He was born on June 5, 1878, in the small village of Río Grande in the state of Durango to Agustín and María Arango, simple peons. He was named Doroteo, and his father proudly claimed that he weighed twelve pounds at birth. At the age of seventeen he joined a bandit gang led by Ignacio Parra that preyed upon cattle roaming the unfenced ranges in Durango and Chihuahua. The younger Arango changed his name to Francisco Villa, but the apt nickname, "Pancho," remained with him for life.

Villa's eyes belied an otherwise benevolent expression. Newspaperman Timothy Turner observed that they were "full of energy and brutality . . . intelligent as hell and as merciless." Villa never drank, seldom smoked, but was notorious for his love of women, often promising to marry on the spur of the moment in order to get them to bed. Like most Mexicans, Villa was extremely fond of small children, but he could shoot down a man point-blank, showing no more emotion than if he were stepping on a bug.

Villa was a natural leader. He had an overabundance of *macho*. What *corazón*, heart, is to contemporary Puerto Rican street gangs, *macho* is to the Mexican male. A man has *macho* if he accepts a challenge to fight a bigger man with his fists, or any man with knives or pistols; a man has *macho* if he dares to steal another man's girl. It requires *macho* to become a truly great matador. The quality of *machismo* has always been a blessing and a curse to the Mexican male; without it he has no pride and is without soul and an outcast, and with it he inevitably gets into trouble. *Machismo* was partially responsible for Villa's later defeats. But it was this quality that elevated Villa to commander of the Parra gang when Ignacio Parra was killed during an attempt to hold up a stage carrying a mining company's payroll.

As a bandit leader Villa became a popular folk hero, the subject of endless ballads and poems, the friend of the poor, the Robin Hood of the nation. He rustled cattle and gave meat to the hungry; he looted great haciendas and distributed the spoils among the needy; he rode into the city of Chihuahua one Sunday afternoon and shot down a betrayer who was strolling with his sweetheart in the crowd on the Paseo Bolívar. In 1909 Villa married a plump, dark woman named Luz Corral and retired from banditry to open a butcher shop in Chihuahua City. Years of open-air slaughtering of stolen cattle qualified him in the trade, and the profit margin was unusually large in the new shop because the majority of the carcasses he put on the block were provided by livestock vigorously rustled by his own men.

When the revolution against Porfirio Díaz began in 1910, little persuasion was required to lure Villa away from the butcher shop and into the field as head of a guerrilla cadre. Villa was actively recruited by a wealthy landowner, Abrán González, who was the vice-presidential hopeful under Madero. Villa entered the field as a captain commanding fifteen men, and by the time of the seizure of Juárez he was a colonel, but a not very subservient one. On June 4, 1912, General Huerta had Villa thrown in jail on the charge of insubordination. Villa was actually standing before an open grave in front of a firing-squad wall when reprieve came through the intervention of Madero's brother, Raul. Villa afterward spent six months in prison in Mexico City, where he learned the rudiments of reading and writing. One day in December he strolled out of the main gate wearing no more disguise than a pair of dark glasses, and for a while managed to hide out in an obscure rooming house near the tracks in south El Paso. An enterprising reporter from the El Paso *Times* discovered his whereabouts, but Villa, "armed with two revolvers and a large dirk," declined to talk for publication.

Madero's murder in February 1913 sent Villa into a rage. One night in early April, Villa and four companions with scanty provisions slipped across the river to begin a counterrevolution against Huerta. Within thirty days he had recruited three thousand men and was driving Huerta's soldiers out of one town after another. By early fall only three major centers were left to Huerta in northern Mexico: the cities of Torreón, Chihuahua and Juárez. Villa's Division of the North took Torreón on October 1, 1913, after stiff fighting, and on November 5 Villa launched an assault on Chihuahua City, almost three hundred miles farther north. Probing attacks and one of his famous charges were bloodily repulsed. Unlike the later Villa, this one realized the difference between a rash display of *machismo* and tactical daring. He called off the attack against Chihuahua City, withdrew the bulk of his army a safe distance southward and planned a surprise attack against Ciudad Juárez, two hundred miles to the north. The operation became a classic not equaled during the Revolution.

It is doubtful in the extreme that Villa had ever heard of *The Aeneid,* but his plan for the capture of Juárez was almost pure Virgil in concept. Villa chose about two thousand infantry, and late on the night of November 13, led them in a semicircle around the city to get across the railroad that connected Chihuahua City with Juárez. A federal troop train puffing its way south was halted and seized without a fight. Leaving the captured federals under guard, Villa loaded his men into the boxcars and backed up to the small station at Moctezuma. There he sent a telegram to the commander of the Juárez garrison, a general named Castro, saying that the engine had broken down, that he needed a new locomotive and five additional boxcars. Villa signed the name of the train commander, then waited for results. Late in the day a train chuffed into the station from Juárez and was quickly taken over by the Villistas. Villa then sent a second telegram: "Large force of rebels approaching from south. Wires cut between here and Chihuahua. What shall I do?"

General Castro, who of course believed he was dealing with his own subordinate, wired back: "Return at once." Villa loaded his brigade safely out of sight in the boxcars and ordered the engineer to make speed for the border. This Trojan horse boldly entered Juárez at midnight on November 15, the boxcar doors slammed open, and the Villistas swarmed out and swept through the heart of town. Dozens of astonished federals were killed while still in their underwear, and by sunrise the garrison gave up; their duped general had run away.

Eight days later Villa crushed a federal counterattack south of Juárez, and on November 29 the demoralized federal garrison at Chihuahua abandoned the city. Villa triumphantly entered the state capital on December 8 at the head of thousands of bandoleered troops eager to carry the fight to Mexico City. He proclaimed himself governor of the state of Chihuahua, a position he would not have dreamed of a few years earlier. To the peon, the ragged soldier, the barefoot child, the old woman patting *masa* for tortillas, Pancho Villa was "the Friend of the Poor," "the Invincible General," "the Centaur of the North," "the Inspirer of Courage and Patriotism," "the Hope of the Indian Republic."

. . .

Equally vigorous as a revolutionary campaigner for Carranza was the "plump and agreeable" Álvaro Obregón, a shrewd ex-mechanic and farmer. Obregón commanded thousands of Mexico's most feared warriors, Yaqui Indians—Obregón's tool with which to forge an altogether new Mexico. Obregón's theater of operations was north of Mexico City, below Villa's domain and above that dominated by the still-untamed Zapata, whose guerrillas were giving sleepless nights to Huerta, even as they had to Díaz and Madero. These bands pushed relentlessly toward Mexico City, taking what they needed as they went along. Unwilling providers were the hated Spaniards and the rich Americans, who watched helplessly as guns, ammunition, food, clothing, rope, kerosene and horses were casually looted. There were now no *rurales* to protect them; those police in dove-gray outfits had either all been killed or shucked their uniforms to join in any of the myriad revolutionary bands that roamed the country.

Like revolutionists everywhere, the Constitutionalists were motley. For uniforms they wore whatever was at hand and armed themselves with what they could steal or retrieve from the battlefields. Wives, girl friends, boys and dogs traveled with the fighting men inside of and on top of boxcars. The women often joined in the fighting, and were as reckless as any. It was this reckless quality among those who had very little to lose except their lives that enabled the Constitutionalists to defeat federal troops in one bloody no-quarter battle after another. By the spring of 1914 they had wrested three fourths of Mexico from Huerta and were eager to pounce on the rest.

To Woodrow Wilson, "the Constitutionalists" was a phrase that rang sweetly in his ear. And were they not followers of the Madero doctrine that promised democracy for all? "My passion," Wilson said during these days of crisis, "is for the submerged eighty-five percent who are struggling to be free." In Carranza, he of the erect figure and prophetlike countenance, Wilson saw a weapon with which to rid Mexico and his own psyche of Huerta, as well as a stalwart to right wrongs in a ravaged land. Wilson, in late November of 1913, drafted a proposal to Carranza that was little short of astounding: in exchange for allowing Wilson to guide the Carranza rebellion along lines pleasing to Wilson he would actively abet the Constitutionalists in their fight to take over the nation and the government. Wilson would send battleships, would blockade the ports and strangle Huerta, would send American cavalry and infantry into Mexico, station them at strategic points to protect foreign lives and property. The action would be kept unilateral by invoking the Monroe Doctrine.

The proposal was presented to Carranza at a meeting in Nogales, Arizona, between the First Chief and Wilson's emissary, William Bayard Hale. Wilson had no more luck with Carranza than with Huerta; Carranza rejected Wilson's scheme out of hand, saying in effect that the Constitutionalists wanted guns, not guidance, and that if American troops sought to enter Mexico they would be met with force. Carranza went back to the Revolution, and Hale returned to Washington still stinging from the rebuff. Wilson sulked into the New Year, then decided that a Carranza victory without Wilsonian guidance was better than no victory over Huerta at all. On February 3, 1914, the arms embargo, in force since March 14, 1912, was lifted and the flood of munitions resumed its flow across the Rio Grande.

Explaining the sudden move, Secretary Bryan pointed out that "settlement by civil war carried to its bitter conclusion is a terrible thing, but it must come now whether we wish it or not, unless some outside power is to sweep Mexico with its armed forces end to end; which would be the beginning of a more difficult problem."

The German ambassador to Mexico, Admiral Paul von Hintze, had been waiting for the United States to make some move that would commit the Americans to one revolutionary faction or the other; now that Wilson had thrown his support to Carranza the Germans would counter by aiding Huerta. Von Hintze paid a call on Huerta and offered a deal: the Germans would supply Huerta with needed war matériel if Huerta would deny the British Navy oil should Germany and England go to war. Huerta quickly agreed. Von Hintze cabled Germany, and in Hamburg less than a week later, 200 crated Maxim machine guns and 15 million rounds of ammunition were put on board the ubiquitous *Ypiranga*, bound for Veracruz. In her wake sailed the freighter *Bavaria*, loaded to the gunwales with another 1.8 million cartridges and more than 8,000 rolls of barbed wire. This was not the last time that Imperial Germany would seek to guide the destiny of revolutionary Mexico.

. . .

Wilson had hoped that the fresh infusion of munitions to the Constitutionalists would allow them to blast Huerta out of the National Palace with little delay. But two months after the lifting of the arms embargo Wilson's *bête noire* still clung to power. Then one of those trivial incidents occurred that so often in history have permitted rulers to pursue a course of action rooted in expediency while pretending to uphold some lofty principle.

On the morning of April 10, 1914, a U. S. Navy paymaster named Charles W. Copp and eight sailors set out in a whaleboat from the U.S.S. *Dolphin*, then lying at anchor off the city of Tampico. The *Dolphin* was one of several U. S. naval vessels stationed in the Gulf of Mexico, manifestations of gunboat diplomacy and useful in providing haven for Americans fleeing the carnage wrought by opposing armies throughout the country.

When Copp pulled ashore near the Iturbide Bridge and climbed out with five of the sailors to pick up cans of gasoline for the *Dolphin*, he and his small detachment were arrested by a squad of Huerta troops under the command of a captain. He explained that the whaleboat had landed in a military zone, Tampico then being held by the federals but under siege by the rebels. While the sailors and their officer were being marched up the street under the curious stares of the citizens of Tampico, a federal officer dashed up and ordered the captain to return the Americans to their boat. A message had arrived from the commander of the Tampico garrison, General Ignacio Morelos Zaragoza, apologizing to the Americans for the arrest and ordering their release. Copp got his men and the gasoline loaded aboard the whaleboat and returned to the *Dolphin*, where he routinely reported the incident.

Admiral Henry T. Mayo, commanding the American squadrons lying off Tampico, was livid when he learned of the arrest of the *Dolphin* sailors. Without bothering to refer the incident to anybody in Washington, Mayo fired off an ultimatum to Huerta not only demanding further apologies but ordering Huerta to "publicly hoist the American flag in a prominent position on shore and salute it with twenty-one guns." Mayo gave Huerta twenty-four hours in which to comply. The next day Huerta sent a formal apology to Mayo through Nelson O'Shaughnessy, but he refused to offer a salute to the flag. Not unreasonably, Huerta wondered why the United States demanded a salute from a government it did not recognize and whose collapse it was doing its best to bring about.

When news of Mayo's high-handed action reached Secretary of the Navy Josephus Daniels, he was deeply disturbed. Daniels "felt strongly that inasmuch as the Admiral was in easy reach of Washington by wireless and telegraph he should not have issued an ultimatum without authority of the government." However, Daniels found precedents for the admiral's behavior—action taken by the Navy at Tripoli and Tunis in 1805 and "the old-time Naval practice which guided Perry in Japan"—and decided that he "could not let Mayo down."

Wilson half-heartedly agreed with Daniels, and although he was extremely vexed with Mayo, he felt that "the only course left open was to enforce Mayo's demand." The ultimatum stood, but at the hour of its expiration, no American flag had been hoisted in Tampico, no salute fired. President Huerta was spending Easter Sunday at the race track.

Wilson called a conference with leading members of the Senate Committee on Foreign Relations, and afterward reported that the talks were satisfactory to him, that the committee was ready to back him to the limit. According to Daniels, the senators were hot to avenge the handful of sailors who had, at worst, been kept idle for ninety minutes on a pleasant spring morning, an incident that was now inflated to the status of a grievous national insult. Daniels recalled the senatorial bombast: "I'd make them salute the flag if we had to blow up the whole place," said William Chilton. "If our flag is ever run up in Mexico it will never come down," said William E. Borah, and added, "This is the beginning of the march of the United States to the Panama Canal!"

Wilson told the members of his Cabinet that he had the right to act without specific authority of the Congress but that he preferred to ask for the authority, anyway. He cited the American bombardment of Greytown, Nicaragua, in 1854 as an example of presidential authority, and Senator Henry Cabot Lodge pointed to the Boxer Rebellion as an instance of a President acting to protect American lives and property—ignoring the fact that American lives and property were not the issue at Tampico. Wilson now presented an ultimatum of his own, calling upon Huerta to accede to Mayo's demands by 6 P.M., April 19, or he would lay the matter before Congress "with a view to taking such action as may be necessary to enforce the respect due the national flag." But Huerta's batteries remained silent.

Before both houses of Congress, which had given Wilson carte blanche to "use the armed forces in such ways and to such extent as may be necessary to enforce its demand," Wilson then issued another of those statements which were at such variance with the train of action that had been set in motion. "There can be no thought of aggression," he said in his address. "The people of Mexico are entitled to settle their own domestic affairs in their own way." Less than twenty-four hours later, however, armed blue-jackets and United States marines would be streaming ashore at Veracruz to seize the town.

The sequence began at two-thirty in the morning on April 21 when the telephone rang in Joseph Tumulty's bedroom, bringing the President's private secretary out of a sound sleep. At the other end was William Jennings Bryan with upsetting news: the *Ypiranga*, loaded with munitions for Huerta, was due to dock at Veracruz at ten o'clock that morning. President Wilson and Josephus Daniels were quickly brought on the line via a four-way hookup, and with everybody still in pajamas, an impromptu high-level-policy dialogue began.

BRYAN: I recommend that the Navy act to prevent the landing of arms.

WILSON: Of course you understand, Mr. Bryan, what drastic action might mean in our relations with Mexico?

BRYAN: I thoroughly appreciate this, Mr. President, and fully considered it before telephoning.

WILSON (distressed, hesitant): What do you think should be done, Daniels?

DANIELS: I do not think that the munitions should be allowed to fall into Huerta's hands. I can wire Admiral Fletcher to take the customs house and prevent the shipment being landed. I think that is the proper course to pursue.

WILSON: Have you considered all the implications?

DANIELS: Yes, Mr. President. If the munitions reach Huerta it will strengthen his hand and will add to the loss of life in Mexico. They may even be turned against American soldiers if Huerta's power is increased.

WILSON (after a long pause): Daniels, give the order to Fletcher to take the customs house at Veracruz.

The receivers clicked, and Daniels promptly sent off the following telegram: "Seize customs house. Do not permit war supplies to be delivered to Huerta government or to any other party."

The U. S. landings at Veracruz on the morning of April 21 began without warning to the Mexican commander ashore, General Gustavo Maass. A few minutes past eleven o'clock, Admiral Frank Fletcher watched as more than seven hundred marines and rifle-carrying bluejackets made their way toward shore in small boats, backed up by the guns of the battleships *Florida* and *Utah* and the gunboat *Prairie*.

Maass, who had no orders covering an American invasion, did several things in succession. He wired the authorities in Mexico City, asking them whether he should withdraw or offer all-out resistance. Then he began handing out hundreds of rifles to civilians who had gathered at the armory clamoring for guns with which to repel the Yankees. He released the military prisoners, armed them, then ordered his six hundred regulars to stand by for any eventuality. While waiting for a reply from Mexico City, he decided to prepare for the worst and sent about a hundred of the regulars toward the dock area with orders to fight.

Mexico City was quick to reply: Maass was ordered to withdraw his forces from Veracruz, apparently to leave the forty thousand inhabitants to their fate. Maass hurriedly loaded the remaining five hundred troops aboard a waiting train that began chuffing away at about the same time that the marines and sailors set foot on Mexican soil. It was eleven-thirty in the morning.

At first it seemed that the seizure of Veracruz would be bloodless. Shortly after the landing, the dockside buildings and the U. S. consulate buildings were taken without a shot being fired. Then crowds gathered, shouting "Death to the invaders! Down with the Yankees! Vengeance! Vengeance!" Marines, moving to the end of Independence Street to occupy the cable office, were pelted with stones hurled from rooftops, then came under rifle and pistol fire from behind a makeshift barricade. While the marines fell prone in the gutter to return the fire with their Springfields, a machine gun set up at the other end of the street fired over their heads into the barricade, killing everyone there. The marines removed ten bodies from behind the barricade when they occupied the town's communications center.

In advancing toward the railway station, another detachment of marines came under viciously accurate sniper fire that pinned them down. Several men were hit before the sharpshooter was spotted firing from inside the tower of the library. A message was semaphored to the *Prairie,* and soon 5-in. shells screamed overhead, reducing the library tower to rubble, burying the solitary sniper beneath its ruins.

The post office fell, then the railway station. Two hundred yards distant lay the customs house, the object of Daniels' telegram. The bluejackets and marines who moved toward the building were fired upon from every street corner, from every balcony, from every roof. Americans who sought cover in the corners of houses were driven away by scalding water poured on them by women. After nearly an hour of inching their way forward, the attackers gained a stronghold in the customs house. Sailors beat down the doors of a nearby store with their rifle butts and dragged out sacks of flour, rice, coffee and beans to form breastworks inside the customs house. They lay there, panting from the exertion in the humid and oppressive atmosphere of Veracruz while corpsmen looked after the wounded and counted the dead.

At twelve-thirty, while the fighting raged ashore, the *Ypiranga* steamed into Veracruz harbor and dropped anchor. A U. S. Navy launch was sent over and an American officer described the situation to the German captain, who was warned that he could off-load the munitions ashore—for seizure by the Americans—but that he would not be allowed to leave Veracruz with them aboard. Menaced by the big guns of the battleships, the German could only comply. (Two days later the *Ypiranga* slipped out of Veracruz, ostensibly destined for Germany, but she went down the coast instead and put ashore at Puerto México, and off-loaded the guns and ammunition, which were put on trains and trundled inland, bound for Huerta's army.)

It was apparent to Fletcher that crushing the resistance house to house would result in unacceptable casualties among the landing force, and he refused the option of shelling Veracruz to bits. He radioed Tampico for reinforcements and ordered the men ashore to stay put until help came. Shortly after midnight more battleships, cruisers and supply ships began arriving at Veracruz, packed with marines and bluejackets eager for action. Among the marines' most colorful officers was Major Smedley D. Butler, "the Fighting Quaker." Butler had enlisted in the Marine Corps when he was sixteen by lying about his age in order to "whip the dastards who blew up the *Maine*."*

"All day long we fought like hell," Butler recounted. "At daylight we marched up the street, peppered from the roofs by snipers. Mexicans were using the houses as fortresses, and the marines rushed from house to house searching for those who had fired on us. Just as two of my men were smashing in one door they were mysteriously shot in the stomach from below. The house was deserted, but from the angle of the bullets the Mexicans were obviously under the floor. We poured a volley through the floor and then ripped up the boards. There we found two dead Mexicans dangling between cross beams. The sailors who marched up the street were badly shot up, not only by the Mexicans but in at least one instance by their own men.

"The Marine plan was to station a machine gunner at one end of the street as lookout, then we advanced under cover, cutting our way through the adobe walls from one house to the other with axes and picks. We drove everybody from the houses and then climbed up on the flat roofs to wipe out the snipers. The marines lost only two killed and five wounded."

By early morning of the second day of fighting Admiral Fletcher had more than four thousand men ashore, and the *Prairie*, *Chester* and *San Francisco* were pouring shells into the town. One shot struck the huge clock in the center of the Municipal Palace, stopping the hands at 7:12. Marines came under fire from civilian snipers posted in the annex of the Hotel Diligencias, but again the machine guns and carefully aimed rounds from Springfields drove the Mexicans to cover. Ten more bodies were dragged from the hotel to the street to await burial.

The greatest drama was played out in front of the naval acad-

---

* When Butler's father learned that his son had given a false date of birth, the old Quaker said, "If thou is determined to go, thou shalt go, but don't add another year to thine age, my son. Thy mother and I weren't married until 1879." Josephus Daniels later had Smedley Butler's enlistment papers corrected.

emy, attended by boys seeking careers in Mexico's minuscule navy. The school, an imposing two-story structure surrounded by a stone wall, appeared deserted to the fourteen hundred sailors and marines who marched in column up the street to occupy the buildings. When the point of the column was a hundred yards from the main gate, rifle barrels slid through the windows of the buildings and a ragged volley greeted the Americans. Then a machine gun opened up, largely overshooting but causing casualties. The column was ordered into line of skirmishers that tried a flanking movement, but they were pinned down by the spirited fire of the cadets.

The attackers, knowing neither the strength nor the composition of the defenders, called for bombardment of the school. In fact, the academy was held by no more than seventy cadets, most of them in their early teens, commanded by Commodore Manuel Azueta, who had aroused his students to a fighting stance on the morning of the first day.

A Mexican journalist, César Reyes Aguirre, described what happened next: "The shells of the [U.S. Navy] guns practically converted the building into a sieve. At this time there occurred an act so wonderful that in attempting to describe it one feels his heart swell and his eyes fill with tears of gratitude for those who know how to die defending the dignity of their nation. The sentry at the main gate was a twelve-year-old boy named Colín. When the invaders began their attack upon the building, the boy closed the gate and opened fire upon the assailants from the embattlements of the guardroom over the entrance. A shell burst through the door frame, demolishing part of the guardroom. Colín fell to the floor in a cloud of dust and debris. His companions thought he had been killed, but with astonishment they saw him pick himself up, grab his rifle and again begin to defend his post. A few moments later a new shell accomplished the infamous work which the first failed to do, and this time the sentinel Colín was killed.

"The war vessels were firing from a distance of less than 800 yards and threatened the utter destruction of the school. Commodore Azueta, realizing that to remain there longer would mean useless sacrifice, ordered a retreat. Corporal Uribe, sixteen years of age, remained alone to cover the retreat of his companions and kept up the fight until he fell mortally wounded. Dying and covered with blood, he dragged himself to his bed, where, two hours later in the face of the Americans, his loving native land gathered him in her arms. This sacrifice was not useless, for it enabled his comrades to abandon the school without further harm."

The town of Veracruz was declared secure at five o'clock that afternoon. Burial parties went through the streets and houses collecting the dead. The bodies of one hundred and twenty-six Mexicans were counted, but it is certain that more than that had been killed. In one instance, recovered Mexican corpses were stacked like cordwood and burned. Another hundred wounded Mexicans were looked after by both Mexican doctors and U.S. naval surgeons. Seventeen Americans had been killed, and sixty-three wounded.

The Stars and Stripes was run up over Veracruz, but no Mexicans stood to salute it, as had been Wilson's desire. "Even Nature protested," commented Aguirre, "for there were no breezes to support it and it fell in languid folds."

CHAPTER

3

Recognition and Revenge

Reaction to the American seizure of Veracruz was not what Wilson had expected. Violent anti-American demonstrations erupted throughout Latin America, and U. S. citizens still living in Mexico feared for their lives. Although the American occupation of Veracruz was a blow against Huerta, robbing him of a million pesos a month, Carranza did not see it that way. He fired off a stiff note to Wilson the day after the city fell: "The invasion of our territory and the permanency of your forces in the Port of Veracruz are a violation of the rights that constitute our existence as a free and independent sovereignty and will drag us into an unequal war which until today we desired to avoid." The note ended with Carranza's demand that Wilson immediately withdraw American forces from Mexican soil. Twenty-four hours later, however, the 5th Brigade, U. S. Army, sailed from Galveston, Texas, to begin what was to be a seven-month occupation of Veracruz.

From Tampico came a frantic telegram signed by the American consul: "Practically all Americans have been brought out of this Consular district. Two thousand have been sent to Galveston. Vast oil properties and interests have been totally abandoned, wells are left running wild, millions of barrels of oil in storage completely at mercy of natives. Other foreign interests safe. Interests abandoned by Americans have valuation of not less than two hundred million dollars."

In Washington the military planners drew up march routes and outlined logistical support for the contemplated drive on Mexico City. The battleships, seven of them, and the command ships and the cruisers and the colliers then lying off Veracruz, were alerted for imminent action that would secure the rest of Mexico's ports. Wilson had engineered a situation that seemed almost certain to plunge the nation into war. Then came the reprieve. Envoys from the "ABC Powers"—Argentina, Brazil and Chile—offered to mediate the crisis on neutral ground. Wilson clutched at the straw, and the conference opened on the Canadian side of Niagara Falls on May 20.

The talks between American and Mexican representatives see-sawed back and forth and ultimately proved only that Wilson had learned nothing about the Mexican mind and little about the nature of a revolution that had been tearing Mexico apart for the past four years. After the fall of Veracruz the Constitutionalist armies were everywhere poised to deliver the final blows against Huerta's battered federals; complete military victory was within Carranza's grasp. Yet Wilson, through his representatives, now insisted that the fighting be stopped—something the Carrancistas were not about to agree to. Further, Wilson insisted that a provisional government be formed. Of course, neither Carranza nor Villa would be acceptable to Wilson as head of that government. With the throne inside the National Palace beckoning, perhaps only weeks away, Carranza found Wilson's stipulation childish and unrealistic. Carranza's representatives at Niagara Falls made it clear that the Constitutionalists wanted no part of Wilson's schemes to guide the Revolution along American lines, pointing out that they "were entitled to fight out their own fight in their own way, just as the United States had settled the question of slavery without the intervention of foreign powers." The Niagara conference, mediated in name only, adjourned on July 2. Although war had been averted for the moment, the talks could only be interpreted as yet another diplomatic defeat for Wilson.

Once again an arms embargo was clamped down all along the Rio Grande, but the flow of weapons continued as border smugglers came out of partial retirement and waxed fat from the profits. The Revolution would run its bloody course despite anything Wilson could do.

Since late spring 1914, Huerta's troops had been penned inside several of the larger towns and state capitals of central Mexico; the option of movement was no longer his, it belonged solely to the armies of Obregón, Villa and Zapata. On May 13 Tampico fell to the Constitutionalists, and with it the precious oil revenue. The remaining centers of federal resistance fell quickly afterward. The mountain city of Saltillo, capital of Coahuila, was taken by Francisco Villa on May 21, and moving his army over two hundred miles southwest, he captured the city of Zacatecas a month later. After General Álvaro Obregón—and he *was* a general—stormed into the city of Guadalajara on July 8, the way was clear for a straight thrust on Mexico City, less than three hundred miles away.

On July 15 Victoriano Huerta handed in his resignation to the Mexican Congress, after making provisions for a successor by appointing Francisco Carvajal, a respected lawyer, to the office of Minister of Foreign Affairs. Huerta took the opportunity to fire a final salvo at Woodrow Wilson in his farewell address: "I abandon the Presidency of the Republic, carrying with me the highest sum of human wealth, for I declare that I have arraigned at the bar of universal conscience the honor of a Puritan whom I, as a gentle man, challenge to wrest from me that possession." Huerta entrained for Puerto México and boarded the German ship *Dresden*, bound for exile in Spain.*

During Villa's spectacular campaigning in the north, Carranza had refused Villa logistical support, leaving him more or less to his own devices to procure fighting supplies. Publicly Carranza said that Villa was "insubordinate," but privately he sulked because Villa made the headlines and was immensely popular with the masses. Following the capture of Zacatecas, there was nothing to keep Villa's Division of the North from storming Mexico City except a critical shortage of ammunition and an almost total lack of the coal needed to run his troop trains. Villa demanded supplies from Carranza's vast stores, but the First Chief saw a chance to humble his field commander and refused to give him a single cartridge, a solitary bucket of coal; instead he reprovisioned Obregón's army corps at Guadalajara and ordered him to move swiftly upon Mexico City before Villa could somehow get there

* Eight months later, on April 13, 1915, Huerta arrived in New York City to plan a counterrevolution against Carranza. He was heavily subsidized by the German government, which hoped to embroil the United States in a war with Mexico and thus drain off war matériel then being sold to the Allies. But Huerta never saw his homeland again. He was arrested in New Mexico on June 27, 1915, was imprisoned at Fort Bliss for a time and died of a liver ailment in El Paso on January 14, 1916.

first. Enraged, Villa helplessly watched as Obregón entered the city on August 15. Insult was added to injury when Carranza, who had been proclaimed First Chief in charge of the Executive Power, made a point of not inviting Villa's forces to join the mammoth victory parade in the capital. Open warfare between Villa and Carranza now threatened.

Wilson rushed a new envoy to Mexico to see what could be done. He chose a New York lawyer named Paul Fuller, who conferred with the two antagonists. Both Carranza and Villa agreed to a convention which would draw together the revolutionary chiefs and their followers with a view to coming up with a workable solution to the problems of governing the prostrate land. Villa and Zapata wanted Carranza to retire; Carranza wanted Villa and Zapata to disband, and later have himself elected President; Wilson hoped that the Villistas would dominate the convention; Villa hoped that one of his generals, Eulalio Gutiérrez, would become the new President.

The wrangling went on for a month at Aguascalientes (literally, "hot waters") with the end result that Gutiérrez was elected interim President, and Villa and Carranza declared war on each other. On November 19 Obregón evacuated Carranza's forces from Mexico City and moved them to Veracruz, where they would be built up for the coming battles. The last U. S. soldier at Veracruz stepped aboard the Quartermaster Corps transport *Sumner* on November 23, ending the occupation and leaving the city for Carranza to use as the seat of his provisional government.

In December, Villa and Zapata met just south of Mexico City. There, in the dreamy atmosphere of Xochimilco, where canopied boats and floating gardenias drifted on lagoons, the two guerrilla leaders planned the destruction of Carranza's scattered forces. Villa boasted to Zapata of his forty thousand soldiers, his well-equipped troop and hospital trains, his seventy-seven pieces of field artillery, the millions of rounds of ammunition at his disposal. Zapata modestly admitted to command some twenty thousand men—good fighters but short of cartridges and barren of artillery. Villa promised Zapata guns and ammunition.

"Carranza is a scoundrel," Zapata said.

"He is an insolent person who has come from God knows where to turn the Republic into an anarchy," Villa added. "His followers do nothing but massacre and destroy. Those are men who have always slept on soft pillows—how could they be friends of the people, who have spent their whole lives in suffering?"

"They're all a bunch of bastards," Zapata said. "I am going to fight on, even if they kill me and all of those who follow me."

After the meeting at Xochimilco, Villa and Zapata returned briefly to Mexico City to tour the huge National Palace. Villa, looking as though he had been stuffed into his unaccustomed dark blue uniform of a Mexican general, plumped himself down onto the gilt-and-plush presidential chair to pose for the photographers. He grinned broadly. Zapata, seated to his left, clutched an enormous new sombrero resting on his knee, his face enigmatic. At that moment victory lay within reach, but it would quietly slip away.

Zapata moved his army on Puebla, seventy-five miles southeast of the capital, and captured the old colonial town in the middle of December. The surviving Carranza forces fled and headed for Veracruz. Now was the time for both Villa and Zapata to launch a two-pronged drive for the coast, there to scatter the retreating Carrancistas and push them into the sea. Instead Zapata stayed on at Puebla, moving nowhere. Villa, by thrusting quickly, could have driven on to Veracruz alone and crushed Obregón's army a-building, but he dallied too long in the capital; when he did move he marched to the north, toward territory he already largely controlled. Obregón, with the precious gift of time, reassembled an army financed and armed by the Germans through the port facilities of Veracruz. In January 1915 he was able to mount attacks against the Zapatistas, driving them back into their home state of Morelos, and by early spring Obregón was ready to engage the main enemy, Villa's Division of the North.

The stocky, powerful, energetic Obregón chose the small candy-making town of Celaya, one hundred and thirty miles northwest of Mexico City, as the anvil upon which to break Villa's back. Obregón had avidly followed the course of the war on the Western Front and it did not escape him that the French infantry—with its great élan and almost inhuman courage, but commanded by generals with no common sense—was being wasted in furious attacks against prepared positions. Obregón set his troops to work digging zigzag trenches in front of Celaya, sandbagging drainage and irrigation ditches that crisscrossed the town, and filigreeing the whole with aprons of tautly strung barbed wire. Helping

Obregón site the artillery was an experienced Imperial German Army officer named Maximilian Kloss. The cavalry was kept mounted and under cover, and reserves of infantry were broken into attack groups, ready to be flung in where needed. Obregón gave special attention to his machine guns, siting them for interlocking fire and cupping them with tightly packed bags of earth. Thus prepared, Obregón waited for Villa.

The first elements of the Division of the North made contact with a screening force of Obregón cavalry late in the morning of April 6, 1915. Villa's own "golden cavalry," the famed Dorados, drove the enemy inward, and followed by yelling infantry, charged for the town. They were cut down in droves by methodical machine-gun fire that traversed their ranks, and by rifle bullets fired by men who were well dug in. Units were thrown in piecemeal as soon as men reached the zone of combat, only to be stopped by the wire and by the machine guns, which seemed to be firing from every quarter. Hundreds of Villista dead carpeted the approaches to town. The Villistas tried to bulldog their way into Celaya through the afternoon and into the night, sustaining heavy casualties but doing little damage to Obregón's defenses. Villa renewed the attack the following morning, but was routed by a cavalry charge that rolled up his flanks, driving the Villistas from the field of battle. Obregón wisely pulled his cavalry back into town, tended to the wounded and gratefully received another million rounds of ammunition sent by Carranza from Veracruz.

A week later, on the morning of April 13, Villa tried again. Under cover from a barrage of 75-mm. shells, Villa drove his Dorados forward again and again. These men, superbly uniformed and superbly mounted, had been victorious in a hundred battles and skirmishes. They were the cream of guerrilla cavalry and were not accustomed to defeat. They plunged across the hard earth in a great curving wave, but were simply mowed down. Those who were not killed by shrapnel fired by Kloss's artillery were raked by machine-gun fire. The few Dorados who managed to reach the forward trenches were caught in the barbed wire, and the horses were torn open. They kept coming, mounting charge after charge, heedless of life, heedless of loss.

But it was not war.

While the Dorados, their mounts slavering and glassy-eyed with fatigue, pressed forward in one final assault, they were struck left and right by Obregón's fresh cavalry that swept them aside to crash into the infantry lagging behind. Villa's foot soldiers, bloodied, exhausted and dispirited, threw away their rifles and ran for their lives. Obregón's infantry swarmed out of the trenches to finish the kill. When the Villistas could run no farther, they raised their arms in surrender. Obregón claimed 8,000 prisoners, 4,000 killed. Villa admitted to 6,000 dead or captured.

To Villa, defeat was unthinkable—especially at the hands of "the banty rooster, Obregón." Villa wired his brother Hipólito in Ciudad Juárez to ship more arms and ammunition.* On June 2 Villa's division attacked Obregón near León, sixty miles northwest of Celaya, and again it was disaster for Villa. He left thousands dead on the field, including most of the remaining Dorados, who were spent in useless attacks against machine guns.

Obregón was standing on a rooftop watching the battle when a Villista shell tore off his right arm. "When I came to," reported Obregón, "I found that members of my staff already had taken my watch and my pocketbook."

Three times defeated by Obregón, Villa gathered the remnants of his army together and marched them to the final stronghold in Chihuahua.

In October 1914, shortly after the split between Villa and Carranza, a force of fifteen hundred men loyal to Carranza had entrenched themselves in the small town of Naco in the state of Sonora. They were immediately besieged by a superior force of troops under the command of General José Maytorena, governor of Sonora and loyal to Villa. Naco in Mexico was separated from Naco, Arizona, only by a wide dirt street; except for the usual sights and smells of a poor Mexican village there was little to differentiate one town from the other. Maytorena dug in half a mile from the border, and from there launched waves of fierce Yaqui Indians supported by an astonishing variety of weapons, including, as an American officer observed, "small arms, three-inch shells, shrapnel, Hotchkiss revolving cannon, rockets, land mines, bombs, bugle calls and epithets."

---

* Villa spent prodigiously of his loot to equip his Division of the North. During one three-week period in 1914, Villa paid $180,056.60 for ammunition alone, mostly .30-30 Winchester and 7.62-mm. cartridges for lever-action rifles and for Mausers bought from the Germans.

Elements of the 10th U. S. Cavalry stationed at Naco were quickly reinforced by troops from the 9th Cavalry, the rest of the 10th Cavalry and a machine-gun troop. A line of red flags was placed all along the border, and the Americans either dug in or took shelter behind U-shaped bales of hay with corrugated iron roofs. Homes and hotels were made as bulletproof as possible, but during the long siege no fewer than fifty-four Americans were killed or wounded from the deluge of fire being poured into Naco by Maytorena's men. One trooper of the 10th was killed and eighteen were wounded; yet these regulars, Negroes all, obeyed orders and did not return the fire. After the 10th's commander, Colonel William C. Brown, had seen his headquarters tent punctured four times by Mexican bullets, the troops were pulled back a mile north of town, leaving the line defended by two troops of cavalrymen standing to inside deep bombproofs.

Brigadier General Hugh Lenox Scott, sixty-one, a veteran Indian fighter who had held border command until his recent appointment as Chief of Staff, received a telegram informing him that an American civilian had been shot through the heart while on the way to the Naco post office. In a rage, Scott broke into the office of Secretary of War Lindley M. Garrison and shouted, "I can't stand this any more! If Mr. Bryan won't do anything, I'll go down there and drive those Mexicans away myself!" The idea caused Garrison "much merriment." Later, however, that is almost exactly what happened. Scott bitterly complained, "Whenever a telegram was received by the War Department with the information of the killing of our own people, a copy would be hurried right over to the State Department, but for all the attention it received it might as well have been put into the fire." Passengers aboard the Golden State Limited on the way to and from California learned to duck whenever the train approached Naco; many of the coaches bore scars of the siege, from bullets exported into Mexico and fired right back.

Finally the State Department acted. On December 10, after two months of siege, Bryan sent a note to Carranza demanding that the fighting stop. If not, Bryan warned, "positive measures" would be taken by the United States to ensure the safety of American lives in Naco. As usual, Bryan was vague as to what, exactly, the United States proposed to do in case Carranza refused to stop the fighting, but Carranza sensed that Bryan was threatening invasion by U. S. cavalry. Carranza rejected Bryan's note out of hand, suggesting that civilian casualties were caused by "the imprudent curiosity of the American citizens." Carranza said that if the United States used force to stop the fighting at Naco it would be considered an act of hostility and a breach of Mexican sovereignty.

Next, Wilson sent Hugh Scott to Naco to see if he could make good his boast to Garrison and "drive those two armies away." Scott quickly got the Carranza generals at Naco to agree to stop the fighting—they were reeling anyway—but Maytorena stubbornly refused. He told Scott that more than eight hundred of his men had been killed and that he "was not going to ignore that sacrifice." Besides, Maytorena added, he had the Carrancistas exactly where he wanted them. Stalemated, Scott sent a telegram to Villa in Mexico City requesting a meeting in Ciudad Juárez to settle the Naco dispute.

On January 9, 1915, Scott and Villa sat down at a table and, as Scott said, "locked horns there like two bull elk for two hours, swaying now this way, now that." Villa told Scott that he could send eight thousand fresh troops to Naco "and end the whole business in eight hours." Scott replied that this could only result in more American lives lost and that "they could not fight for eight minutes." In the end Villa agreed to Scott's proposal: both sides would evacuate Naco; Maytorena would be given a port of entry at Nogales, while the Carrancistas could use Agua Prieta, opposite Douglas, Arizona, and nearly one hundred miles east of Nogales. Villa sent a formal order to Maytorena telling him to sign the agreement. At first Maytorena obstinately refused, then he "seized the pen roughly, signed the paper and threw the pen on the floor with all his might, breaking into tears of rage and mortification."

Later, while Scott and Villa were driving through the streets of Juárez in Villa's car, Villa told the American general that only two weeks previously he had been approached by a Japanese naval officer in Mexico City who asked him what Mexico would do in case Japan attacked the United States. "I told him," Villa said, "that if Japan makes war on the United States she would find that all the resources of Mexico would be used against her." Villa also assured Scott that "there can never be another cause of friction on this border if you and I can get together, and I will come up from Mexico City any time you send for me." Relieved,

Scott boarded the train and started the long trip back to Washington.

Wilson did not have to depend solely on Scott's evaluation of Villa's attitude and temper. In December 1913 a special emissary named George C. Carothers had been appointed by Wilson to ingratiate himself with Villa and act as both agent and liaison officer. Carothers, unlike the other agents previously selected by Wilson, knew something about Mexico. He had been a consular officer for thirteen years, lately at Torreón, and a sideline grocery business had brought about a fluency in Spanish and a knowledge of the workings of the Mexican mind. Carothers, a stocky, cherub-faced little man with glasses, was warmly accepted by Villa and often went with Villa's headquarters staff while in the field. Carothers was impressed by Villa's simplicity and his lack of ambition to become President, a position which Villa felt he was "not qualified" to fill. Carothers' reports, combined with Scott's first-hand observations, prompted Wilson to remark that "Villa was perhaps the safest man to tie to."

William Jennings Bryan had referred to Villa as "a Sir Galahad" and as an "idealist" because Bryan had learned that Villa did not drink.* Villa's flamboyancy and reputation for helping the poor made him a popular figure in the nation's press—and hence with the American public in general. Even the staid *New York Times* referred to Villa as "the Robin Hood of Mexico." In early 1915 there was every chance that Wilson could have guided the Revolution along lines acceptable to his conscience had he thrown full support to Villa when Carranza and Obregón were at their weakest. Villa's choice to replace Huerta was his own divisional artillery chief, General Felipe Ángeles, educated at the École Polytechnique in Paris, a man respected by the various Mexican factions and with an affinity for America. Hugh Scott believed that Ángeles was prime presidential material, calling him "the most cultivated and loyal gentleman I have known in the history of Mexico." But the moment passed, and after the spring battles of Celaya and León, Wilson's options had run out. By the time he was thirty-seven, Villa's star was descending.

---

* Bryan, a lifelong teetotaler, earned the jibes of diplomatic society by serving only grape juice at a formal dinner for retiring British Ambassador James Bryce in April 1913. Commented London's *Pall Mall Gazette:* "Official life in Washington under the Wilson-Bryan regime holds out little prospect of gaiety."

Adding to Wilson's agenda of indecision were the manifold problems created by the rising tempo of the war in Europe. On May 7, 1915, the *Lusitania* was sunk by a U-boat with the loss of more than eleven hundred lives—one hundred and twenty-eight of them American. Wilson's note to the German government was, to Bryan, shocking in its severity; where Wilson chastised and demanded, Bryan sought only restraint and arbitration. Propped up by his advisers, Wilson remained firm, and Bryan handed in his resignation. He was quickly replaced by Robert Lansing, an unemotional, precise individual with wide experience as an international lawyer. One of Lansing's first problems was to handle a delegation representing the American mine and smelting operators with extensive holdings in Chihuahua. Villa had demanded a loan from them of $300,000 in order to re-equip his army and carry on the fight against Carranza. With some trepidation the Americans had refused the loan, and now they were afraid that Villa would confiscate or destroy the mines, still worth millions. Lansing sent for Scott and asked for assistance. "I will help you very soon, Mr. Secretary, if you want to invade Mexico," Scott said.

"You know we can't do that," Lansing replied.

Scott explained that Villa was a "wild man who needed funds for his operations and was going to take them as all the other belligerents were doing."

"Those mining men are on my back," Lansing complained. "I can't get them off and I don't know what to do. Won't you *please* go and talk to Villa?" Scott said he would see what he could do.

On August 10 Scott and Villa met again, in El Paso. After a friendly preamble they got down to business and Villa agreed not only to rescind his demands made on the American miners but to return other U. S. and foreign property worth $6 million which he had previously confiscated. "I had no equivalent to offer," Scott said later, "not even promises. He gave all this up only because I asked him to." The mine owners were so grateful that they presented Villa with a thousand tons of free coal.

Two months later Wilson recognized Carranza as President of Mexico, the man he had complained was "impossible to deal with on human principles." Wilson did not confide his reasons for the sudden act either to the nation or to his intimates. Robert Lansing, however, wrote the following in his diary:

"Germany desires to keep up the turmoil in Mexico until the

United States is forced to intervene; *therefore we must not intervene.*

"Germany does not wish to have any one faction dominant in Mexico; *therefore we must recognize one faction as dominant in Mexico . . ."*

Lansing also noted that future dealings with Mexico would be governed by U. S. relations with Germany, since these were of paramount consideration.

Wilson once again utilized his now-famous elastic embargo, this time shutting off Villa from supplies but leaving channels open for Carranza. Badly in need of some kind of port of entry for smuggled goods, which were getting more expensive and harder to come by, Villa decided to attack the isolated Carranza stronghold at Agua Prieta. With a force of fifteen thousand men, short on matériel but long on faith, Villa pushed across the vastness of northern Chihuahua, determined to crush the Carrancistas who had been holed up there for months and who could not send for reinforcements, or so Villa believed, because Villa controlled all of the lines of communication in the state. In an extraordinary move—unknown to Villa—President Wilson allowed a regiment of heavily armed Carranza troops to enter the United States, board American trains and get off at Douglas. From there they simply stepped across the border and began augmenting the trench system at Agua Prieta, backing the barbed-wire aprons with additional machine guns. Villa flung the Division of the North against Agua Prieta on November 1 and was astonished at the volume of fire that poured from the town. He fought all that afternoon with no other result than heavy casualties, then an hour after midnight sent his men rushing forward under cover of darkness. They were suddenly blinded by explosions of light pouring from powerful searchlights located behind the town, powered by American current. His closely packed men starkly illuminated were slaughtered by the hundreds. The attackers broke and fled across the desert, hounded by quick-firing artillery. Villa salvaged ten thousand men and moved south toward Hermosillo, capital of Sonora and one hundred and sixty miles from Agua Prieta. His soldiers, demoralized by defeat, were again bloodily repulsed at Hermosillo in a Western Front–style battle that Villa could not master.

The remnants drifted to the north, toward Nogales, where they spilled their rage by shouting insults at the American cavalrymen patrolling on the other side. Words were not enough; the Villistas opened fire—and were greeted in return with accurately aimed shots from Springfields. There were rumors that Villa planned to ask for asylum in the United States, but these were forgotten when his band—it was no longer an army—appeared at Juárez and hotheads among them sniped into the railway yards across the river, killing an El Paso trainman. Then Villa and a few hundred fighting men vanished into the winter bleakness of Chihuahua. It seemed that 1916 would begin with peace in Mexico, the fiery border damped by Villa's defeat. President Wilson began to believe that his various policies had triumphed after all.

Five years of revolution had brought Mexico to the brink of economic ruin. From a 1912 production high of 5 million tons of baser metals and ores, less than 800,000 tons were produced in 1915. The gold and silver yield in 1912 amounted to more than 32 million ounces, but by 1915, production of these precious metals had dropped to less than 6 million ounces. With Villa apparently out of the way, Obregón believed the time was ripe to start luring American miners back into northern Mexico to renew the taxable flow of silver, copper, lead, zinc and gold. Obregón realized, however, that Americans would, understandably, be leery of returning to the interior of a country where nearly three hundred of their countrymen had been killed by members of one faction or another since 1910.

One of the most grisly disasters to befall Americans living in Mexico had occurred during the first week in February 1914. A bandit chief named Castillo, an enemy of Villa's, wrecked the much-used Cumbre Tunnel in Chihuahua by running flatbed cars loaded with burning lumber into its interior. A passenger train came along and rammed into the flaming debris, killing everybody aboard. The charred bones of fourteen Americans were recovered from the wreckage, including those of a Mrs. Lee Carruth and her five children. In Tepic on December 10, 1911, an American plantation owner named Frank Gillette had been murdered by bandits while his wife, tied to a tree, was forced to watch. Near Veracruz an oil-field worker named W. H. Waite was taken by bandits on April 4, 1912, robbed of his boots, watch and cash, and then beheaded. A young rancher named Charles Austin got into a dispute with Carrancista soldiers near Matamoros on August 7, 1914, and was shot to death; his father was murdered the following year.

Despite the toll of dead, Obregón now convinced the officials of the American-owned Cusi Mining Company that it was safe to reopen the mines at Cusihuiriachic, sixty miles southwest of Chihuahua City. The government, Obregón said, offered "full protection" to Americans traveling in northern Mexico. During the first week in January 1916, the mine's general manager, Charles R. Watson, and seventeen experienced American miners left El Paso and journeyed to Chihuahua City, where they changed trains for Cusi. The Americans were all in one coach and about twenty Mexican miners occupied another. When the train entered the cattle station of Santa Isabel on January 10, halfway to the mine, it was stopped by a large band of Villistas commanded by Colonel Pablo López, whom Villa had ordered to stop the train and seize the payroll. One of the Mexican workers, José Sánchez, told how the Villistas "rifled our pockets, took our blankets and even our lunches. López then called out, 'If you want to see some fun, watch us kill these gringos!' "

The unarmed Americans tried to save their lives by fleeing from the train and running for the hills nearby. One man was shot while still in his seat, another killed at the step. Watson and a miner named Thomas B. Holmes escaped from the coach and ran about a hundred yards toward some brush by the side of a stream. Watson was hit once, fell, got to his feet and was hit again. His body rolled into the water. Holmes dived into the brush and played dead. The survivors were lined up on the railway embankment with their hands in the air, listening to a violent argument between the bandits as to which among them would act as executioners. López chose two men, and a few seconds later the helpless miners lay dead in the cinders. Their bodies were stripped of shoes and clothing and left nude where they were. When the bandits had gone, Holmes crawled from the brush and lived to report details of the massacre.

Villa was later to deny any responsibility for the deaths of the seventeen Americans at Santa Isabel, but Columbus was only sixty days away.

4

Wilson Acts

The grim details of Villa's attempted sacking of the little town of Columbus reached Washington shortly after nine o'clock in the morning, nearly three hours after Villa was driven across the border by Tompkins and the troopers of the 13th Cavalry. No action was taken that day, no orders given, but the next day, Friday, March 10, the telegraph and telephone wires were kept humming.

One of the first long messages to come through was sent by the commander of the Southern Department, U. S. Army, fiery little Major General Frederick Funston, fifty, from his limestone headquarters building at Fort Sam Houston in San Antonio. Funston, who stood only five feet five and weighed little more than a hundred pounds, was a hero of the Philippine campaign and had been promoted to brigadier at the age of thirty-six. His father, Edward Hogue Funston, had begun the family military career with an Ohio regiment during the Civil War and later became known as "Foghorn" Funston while a member of Congress from Kansas. Freddy Funston, however, had no political ambitions; he was a soldier's soldier who held the respect of subordinates and superiors alike. His bantam figure, in a neatly cut uniform, gleaming boots that encased tiny feet and the well-groomed Van Dyke beard, was a familiar sight to the permanent guests of the old Menger Hotel in San Antonio, where Funston preferred to have his late-afternoon juleps. His most recent experience with Mexico had been as military governor of Veracruz when the army was sent to occupy that unfortunate town.

Funston's reaction to the Columbus raid was expressed in the telegram sent to the War Department early Friday: "It is the opinion of Colonels Dodd and Slocum, in which I concur, that unless Villa is relentlessly pursued and his forces scattered he will continue raids. As troops of the Mexican Government are accomplishing nothing and as he can make his preparations undisturbed, he can strike at any point on the border, we being unable to obtain advance information as to his whereabouts. If we fritter away the whole command guarding towns, ranches and railroads, it will accomplish nothing if he can find safe refuge after every raid." Funston advised immediate pursuit lasting until Villa was run to earth.

Secretary of State Lansing sent a message to a pair of his special agents in Mexico, John R. Silliman and John W. Belt. Lansing wanted the agents to stress to Carranza that "this appears to be the most serious situation which has confronted this Government during the entire period of Mexican unrest and that it is expected that he will do everything in his power to pursue, capture and exterminate this lawless element which is now proceeding westward from Columbus."

Carranza referred Agent Belt to his Minister of Foreign Affairs, Jesús Acuña, who seemed to be almost gloating. Belt later reported that Acuña's first remark was, "The fact that Villa and his forces have entered United States territory is evidence of the strength of the de facto Government's forces." Belt pointed out to Acuña that Villa's fear of the Carranza troops was not the point in question. Rather, Washington wanted to know if Carranza had been aware that Villa's band was where it was prior to the attack, and what did Carranza propose to do about the outrage?

Carranza's reply was routed via Acuña to Secretary Lansing through Agent Silliman. Carranza acknowledged that he was "pained to hear of the lamentable occurrence at Columbus"; then he pointed out that twenty-five hundred men under General Luis Gutiérrez had been sent into Chihuahua to deal with Villa long before the raid and that the bandits "doubtless made this move because they were driven to it by the persistent pursuit conducted by the said command of General Gutiérrez." Then Carranza launched into a lengthy historical digression in order to lead up to an essentially useless request of his own.

Carranza, almost as though reminiscing, mentioned Indian raids into Sonora and Chihuahua in the 1880s. He recalled the time when Geronimo and his braves had crossed the border and "committed murders and depredations, taking the lives and property of Mexican families." He described a series of invasions of Chihuahua by the Apaches from 1884 to 1886. He pointed out that thirty years previously both governments had agreed that armed forces of either nation might freely cross into the territory of the other in order to pursue and chastise the bandits.

Carranza added that he wanted to wipe out the horde led by Francisco Villa as soon as possible, and concluded by asking that "the Mexican forces be permitted to cross into American territory in pursuit of the aforementioned bandits led by Villa, upon the understanding that, reciprocally, the forces of the United States may cross into Mexican territory if the raid effected at Columbus should unfortunately be repeated at any other point on the border."

While waiting for the American reply, and with invasion of Mexican territory apparently a foregone conclusion, Carranza sent telegrams to General Gutiérrez in Chihuahua and to General Agustín Millán, commanding at Veracruz. To the former, Carranza said: "At the proper time I will communicate to you the attitude you should take if it is confirmed that American forces are going to cross the border." And, remembering 1914, the First Chief ordered General Millán to "take all precautions against a landing of American marines, which you will resist."

Carranza prepared the long-suffering Mexican people for further trials by a public notice in the newspapers. An extra edition of the Querétaro *La Opinión* hit the streets at eleven o'clock at night on March 12, advising the people to be prepared for any emergency. Carranza warned that the Constitutionalist government "will not admit under any circumstances and whatever may be the reasons advanced and the explanation offered by the Government of the United States about the act it proposes to carry out, that the territory of Mexico be invaded for an instant and the dignity of the Republic outraged.

"I am sure," Carranza added, "that I am voicing the national sentiment and that the Mexican people will worthily perform their duty, no matter what sacrifices they may have to undergo in the defense of their rights and sovereignty." Then he cautioned the people to exercise prudence in order to guarantee the safety of North American citizens still living in Mexico.

The First Chief urged Eliseo Arredondo, his ambassador-designate in Washington, that "the Department of State should be made to understand that it would be unjust to attribute to the Government and the people of Mexico the responsibility for the acts committed by a band of brigands which this Government has placed beyond the law, and that there would be no justification for any invasion of Mexican territory by an armed force of the United States . . . It is inconceivable that the Government of the United States would resort to such means to capture Villa, as the only result would be to facilitate his impunity to leave the country and to bring about a war between the two countries, with the numberless loss of life and property, without such loss serving to avenge the crimes which the American government is endeavoring to punish. Such a war would be the most unjust which modern history would record . . . and furthermore would only serve for the American Government to satisfy the deliberate purpose of Francisco Villa and the reactionaries who have induced him to commit the crimes he did at Columbus, as his only aim was to provoke armed intervention by the United States in Mexico. Francisco Villa and the other traitors who are seeking the above results will avoid the struggle; and the only ones who would go to it would be honest Mexicans who have in no way provoked it." Carranza ended the note by saying that he had nothing more to add on the subject because "the right and justice of our side is so clear." Carranza's message to Arredondo and the text of the newspaper proclamation were delivered to Secretary of State Lansing late on Sunday, March 12. It was perfectly clear that Carranza wanted no American troops chasing Villa because of Columbus, that violation of Mexican territory would be looked upon as an act of war.

To anyone not familiar with the internal workings of the State Department, it would appear that the U. S. government was seeking permission from the Mexican de facto government before mounting an invasion of the state of Chihuahua, that a workable protocol was being arrived at. This was not the case at all: concrete plans to enter Mexico in force had been made within less than twenty-four hours after the raid. On Friday morning, March 10, President Wilson had called a Cabinet meeting, where it was unanimously decided that Villa must be brought to account for the murders at Columbus, not to mention the killing of the mining engineers at Santa Isabel. The public was thoroughly aroused by now and the cry for revenge was echoed in nearly every American newspaper editorial. And, of course, 1916 was an election year.

When the Cabinet meeting broke up, the throng of correspondents hovering outside the door were handed copies of a statement composed by the President. Because of the confusion that was later to arise over the wording, the statement is worth quoting in full. It read: "An adequate force will be sent at once in pursuit of Villa with the single object of capturing him and putting a stop to his forays. This can and will be done in entire friendly aid of the constituted authorities of Mexico and with scrupulous respect for the sovereignty of that republic." Thus the *New York Times* the next morning was able to report to the world that America had decided to pursue Pancho Villa and make him prisoner.

Formulating the plans was the job of old General Hugh Scott and Wilson's brand-new Secretary of War, Newton Diehl Baker, who had accepted the post only three days before Villa struck Columbus. At forty-four, Baker was the youngest Cabinet member and was as unlikely a choice for Secretary of War as Bryan had been for Secretary of State. Baker was a small, bland-looking man with a large head characterized by a straight, strong nose pinched by a rimmed pince-nez just like Wilson's. A West Virginian, Baker had graduated from Johns Hopkins, where he earned an enviable record as a classical scholar. He was fluent in German and collected books, pewter and razors. He had been mayor of Cleveland from 1912 through 1915, when he fought for three-cent streetcar fares, three-cent utility rates, and fish to retail to the housewife for three cents a pound. Inevitably, Baker was known in Cleveland as "the Three-Cent Mayor." He shined his own shoes with a kit he kept in his office, and detractors claimed he had an icy, aloof personality. Not only was Baker lacking in martial mien, but he was an avowed pacifist and freely admitted as much. However, Baker's pacifism was structured upon a realistic base. On the day he took office as Secretary of War, he proclaimed, "I believe in peace and in the proper enforcement of the laws of peace—by force if necessary."

Immediately after Wilson's statement was handed to the press, Baker found his way to General Scott's office to see about sending the U. S. Army after Villa. Baker had tremendous respect for the gruff old general, and the day that they first met he had told Scott, "I am going to look up to you as a father and I am going to do what you advise me—and if either of us have to leave this building I am going first."

Baker sat down in front of Scott's desk and said, "I want you to start an expedition into Mexico to catch Villa."

"Mr. Secretary," Scott replied, "do you want the United States to make war on one man? Suppose he should get on the train and go to Guatemala, Yucatán or South America. Are you going to go after him?"

"Well, no, I am not," Baker replied.

"That is not what you want, then," Scott pointed out. "You want his band captured or destroyed."

"Yes, that is what I really want," Baker said.

The two men put their heads together and drafted a telegram for Wilson's approval before sending it to General Funston in San Antonio. Funston was ordered "to organize an adequate military force of troops . . . to proceed promptly across the border in pursuit of the Mexican band which attacked the town of Columbus, New Mexico, and the troops there on the morning of the ninth instant. Those troops will be withdrawn to American territory as soon as the de facto government of Mexico is able to relieve them of this work. In any event the work of these troops will be regarded as finished as soon as Villa's band or bands are known to be broken up."

There was no mention of capturing Villa, which is what the President had promised the public only that morning. However, Wilson approved the orders as drafted and they went out the same evening, March 10. This done, Wilson retreated to the sanctuary of the presidential yacht, the *Mayflower*, for the rest of the weekend.

Wilson returned to Washington to find that the capital was inflamed with talk of an impending war with Mexico. He learned why when he was able to catch up on the messages that had been flying back and forth between Carranza and the State Department. He had barely had time to digest all this when a new telegram arrived from Agent Belt informing Lansing that Mexico's Foreign Minister had said to Belt. "Should war result over the Columbus affair, the position of the United States would be that of assisting the reactionaries as against the Constitutionalist Government." By "reactionaries" the Foreign Minister meant Villa. But Villa was the very man Wilson had ordered the U. S. Army to punish—or capture, depending upon which official statement one was reading. Nothing seemed to go right. First Veracruz, then Haiti,* and now this.

The key to the problem concerning Carranza's attitude lay within easy grasp of both the President and the entire State Department. That is, the penultimate paragraph of Foreign Minister Acuña's original note of March 10, in which Carranza agreed in principle to reciprocity of hot pursuit of bandits on either side of the border if the raid effected at Columbus "should unfortunately be repeated" elsewhere along the border. There it was for all to see: an agreement for the future, not for the present.

The meaning of the Mexican note was disregarded, as well as Carranza's subsequent warnings, and preparations for the invasion went forward until the evening of March 14, when a telegram arrived from Columbus with the disturbing news that the Carrancista commander at the border town of Palomas had declared that he would resist the crossing of any American troops. Did he mean it? Nobody could be sure. The first strike column of the Punitive Expedition was poised, ready to enter Mexico at noon the next day, Wednesday, March 15.

That morning in Wilson's office Joseph Tumulty begged the President to proceed as planned, reminding him of the forthcoming election. Wilson's reply so impressed Tumulty that he hurried back to his desk to write it all down.

"Tumulty," Wilson began, "you are Irish and therefore full of fight. I know how deeply you feel about this Columbus affair. Of course, it is tragical and deeply regrettable from every standpoint, but in the last analysis I, and not the Cabinet or you, must bear the responsibility for every action that is to be taken. I have to sleep with my conscience in these matters and I shall be held

---

* For several years the United States had sought ways to seize control of Haitian customs houses and to obtain a naval base at Môle-Saint Nicolas. One bloody coup d'état after another threatened American investments in Haiti and virtual anarchy reigned. Invoking the Monroe Doctrine, Wilson sent U. S. Marines and sailors ashore on July 28, 1915. The "pacification" resulted in more than two thousand Haitian dead before the tiny country came under total U. S. domination. The American occupying forces were not withdrawn until nineteen years later.

responsible for every drop of blood that may be spent in the enterprise of intervention. I am seriously considering every phase of this difficult matter, and I can say frankly to you, and you may inform the Cabinet officers who discuss it with you, *that there won't be any war with Mexico if I can prevent it*, no matter how loud the gentlemen on the Hill yell for it and demand it.

"It is not a difficult thing for a President to declare war, especially against a weak and defenseless nation like Mexico. In a republic like ours, the man on horseback is always an idol, and were I considering the matter from the standpoint of my own political fortunes, I should at once grasp the opportunity and invade Mexico, for," Wilson continued with fine perverse logic, "it would mean the triumph of my administration. But this has never been in my thoughts for a single moment.

"The thing that daunts me and holds me back is the aftermath of war, with all its tears and tragedies. I came from the South and know what war is, for I have seen its wreckage and terrible ruin. It is easy for me as President to declare war. I do not have to fight, and neither do the gentlemen on the Hill who now clamor for it. It is some poor farmer's boy, or the son of some poor widow away off in some modest community, or perhaps the scion of a great family who will have to do the fighting and the dying. I will not resort to war against Mexico until I have exhausted every means to keep out of this mess. I know they will call me a coward and a quitter, but that will not disturb me. Time, the great solvent, will, I am sure, vindicate this policy of humanity and forbearance. Men forget what is back of this struggle in Mexico. It is the age-long struggle of a people to come into their own, and while we look upon the incidents in the foreground, let us not forget the tragic reality in the background which towers above this whole, sad picture. The gentlemen who criticize me speak as if America were afraid to fight Mexico. Poor Mexico, with its pitiful men, women and children, fighting to gain a foothold in their own land! They speak of the valour of America. What is true valour?"

Wilson had earlier given his definition of valor to members of the Gridiron Club, and Tumulty added the President's remarks to his remembrance of the conversation. "Valour," Wilson said, "is self-respecting. Valour is circumspect. Valour strikes only when it is right to strike. Valour withholds itself from all small implications and entanglements and waits for the great opportunity when the sword will flash as if it carried the light of heaven upon its blade."

This was fine rhetoric delivered with atypical passion. Tumulty remembered that Wilson's "eyes flashed," and that his "lips quivered" during the lengthy unburdening. Wilson rose from his chair and stood before the study window, gazing across the Potomac toward the hills of Virginia. He told Tumulty that some-day he would tell the American people why he hesitated to inter-vene—that is the word he used—in Mexico. Germany was anxious to have the United States embroiled in a war with Mexico so as to have American minds and energies taken from the war raging in Europe. Wilson said that it looked as if war with Germany was inevitable, that the American people must have patience a little longer and await the development of the whole plot in Mexico.

Not long afterward another telegram came from Columbus. The Carrancista commander at Palomas had changed his mind. He would not resist a border crossing by American troops. In fact, he said, he and his men were eager to join the chase.

For the moment, the threat of war evaporated.

CHAPTER

5

Pershing's Swift Sword

The War Department had chosen precisely the right man to command the Punitive Expedition. After discussing the matter for
a few minutes on the morning of March 10, General Hugh Scott
and his Deputy Chief of Staff, Major General Tasker H. Bliss, un-
hesitatingly picked fifty-five-year-old Brigadier General John
Joseph Pershing. Needed was a soldier who could not be provoked
into rashness but who could fight hard; a disciplinarian with the
respect of subordinates; a man with tactical experience against
an armed enemy in guerrilla warfare; a general who knew the
book but was flexible in exercising options; and above all, a
soldier who placed military duty above political ambition or
expediency, but with a knowledge of political machinations.
Pershing was the only general in the U. S. Army who met all of
these qualifications. Moreover, he had held a command at Fort
Bliss in El Paso since April 25, 1914, and had developed a feel for
what was happening across the border. Pershing was as baffled
over Wilson's and Bryan's actions as anybody else. On June 2,
shortly after arriving in El Paso, Pershing forwarded an appraisal
of the situation in Mexico to Tasker Bliss, then commander of the
Southern Department:

"Mr. Bryan and the President are undoubtedly throwing their
influence toward Carranza and the Constitutionalists. I hope they
will let them go on to Mexico City and fight it out. That is the only
way we can have even the prospect of peace, it seems to me.

"The Constitutionalists are anxious to have ammunition,"

Pershing continued, "and [Special Agent] Carothers is in favor of it. It does look rather one-sided. Why should we allow Huerta to get in several million rounds of ammunition and still block Carranza and his people, especially when we actually want Carranza to win? That does not look logical to me. We desire to create the impression with the Constitutionalists that we are friendly to them, and that we are anxious to see them succeed, but we sit here and enforce an embargo which may prevent them from succeeding.

"There would be little if any danger in allowing the Constitutionalist Army to have ammunition so far as the possibility of its use against us is concerned. They waste ammunition so fast that there would soon be none left. The principal danger in lifting the embargo would be that all these small bands along the border such as Quévado's and Orozco's and the rest would get it, and so would the worthless element of Mexicans on both sides of the border."

Later that summer Pershing received both Villa and Obregón at his headquarters at Fort Bliss. Villa was impressed with the cavalry and field artillery drills Pershing staged for the visitors' benefit, and was delighted with Pershing's command of Spanish. Villa thought that the American general was *muy simpático*, while Pershing found Villa a genial, rough-and-ready sort, not unlike some of the guerrilla chieftains he had fought against in the Philippines. Before Villa and Obregón returned to Juárez late that afternoon they all posed for photographers on the International Bridge; Obregón stiffly correct in military uniform, Villa in a Norfolk jacket, white shirt and bow tie, his round hat pushed back on his head, Pershing exhibiting one of his rare broad grins.

Pershing was born on September 13, 1860, in the small town of Laclede, Missouri. His father, John Fletcher, started out as a section foreman on the Hannibal & St. Joseph Railroad and was a sutler during the Civil War. In the postwar years he became a prosperous store and land owner, and postmaster of Laclede, until the depression of 1873, when he lost practically everything he owned. The Pershings were of pure Alsatian stock, the name Anglicized from Pfoershin to Pershing via Pfershing. At the age of thirteen young John was a farm hand, the champion cornhusker of Linn County. He attended the local Methodist church every

Sunday. Although not especially military-minded, Pershing competed for entrance to the U. S. Military Academy at West Point in order to secure an education his father was unable to provide. Pershing entered West Point in 1882 and graduated thirtieth in a class of seventy-seven. He was a dedicated if not brilliant student who consistently scored higher in military discipline than in academic subjects. "He was the leader of our class," Pershing's roommate, Charles Walcutt, commented "not in his studies but in everything else." Pershing received his diploma from the hand of General William Tecumseh Sherman and was posted to the 6th Cavalry at Fort Bayard, New Mexico.

While on the Western frontier, Pershing took part in the Army's final campaigns to subdue Geronimo's Apaches in New Mexico and Arizona, and later helped quell the last Sioux uprising in Nebraska. Pershing not only fought Indians, he studied them; although he had been a poor student of languages in the West Point classrooms, he quickly mastered several of the difficult Indian dialects while campaigning. In 1891 he took a post at the University of Nebraska teaching military science to undergraduate cadets, who learned that if he was severe in discipline, he was always just and never played favorites. During his four-year stay in Lincoln the unmarried girls discovered that Pershing had a great fondness for the company of women; he attended nearly every dance the university held. But, although past thirty, Pershing had yet to be seriously interested in any one female.

At the outbreak of the Spanish-American War in 1898 Pershing was first a lieutenant teaching tactics at West Point. In May of that year he received orders to join the 10th Cavalry (after leaving Nebraska, he had served with this all-Negro regiment in Montana for two years—an association which led to his nickname Black Jack) and arrived in Cuba in time to help storm San Juan Hill. His commanding officer later told him that he thought Pershing was "the coolest man I ever saw under fire in my life." Then he recommended him for the Silver Star.

Two years later Pershing was in the Philippines on what the U. S. government called a mission of "pacification." Commanders interpreted this in various ways, most of them agreeing that the only way to bring the warring Moro (Spanish for "Moor") tribes to heel was, in the words of a popular song, to "civilize 'em with a Krag." Occasionally Captain Pershing found it necessary to do

so—he once flattened the Moro fortress of Bacolod when the
Moros refused to hand over their weapons—but he preferred
reason to bloodshed. He learned the Moro dialect, gained an understanding of their Moslem ways and beliefs, and thus was able to
talk many chieftains out of combative moods. He became so popular among the Moros that he was elected an honorary chieftain,
then was asked by the Sultan of Bayan to be an adopted father
to the sultan's wife—an honor no other officer in the U. S. Army
was ever accorded. "Some of the Moros will do anything for me,"
Pershing commented.

In 1903 Pershing was transferred to Washington and eagerly
entered the social whirl open to staff officers in the capital. He
was a favorite of President Theodore Roosevelt, who introduced
him to Senator Francis E. Warren of Wyoming, then chairman of
the Senate Military Affairs Committee. Warren's daughter, recently graduated from Wellesley, caught Pershing's fancy and
after a year's courtship she agreed to marry him. Pershing was
forty-five, Helen Frances Warren twenty years younger. To
Pershing, she was "the dearest girl in all the world." They were
married in the Church of the Epiphany on January 26, 1905, in
a ceremony attended by more than five hundred guests, including
Teddy Roosevelt, who thought it was "a bully match."

The Pershings spent the next eight years in the Far East. As
military attaché in Tokyo, Pershing went to Manchuria to observe
the fighting between the Russians and the Japanese. After six
months, when the war was over, Pershing returned to Tokyo. In
September the following year he was presented with a daughter
and some startling news: he had been promoted to brigadier general in an order signed by the President. The sudden jump from
captain to brigadier—over the heads of eight hundred and sixty-
two senior officers—aroused heated comment, especially among
those who had been jumped. They were quick to point out that
Captain Pershing was, after all, a senator's son-in-law. Teddy
Roosevelt was as quick to point out that the promotion was due
to his work in the Philippines and that Pershing was the stuff out
of which superior field commanders were made.

The new brigadier was assigned to the Philippines, now as
commanding officer of Fort McKinley. In 1908 he made a fact-
finding tour of Europe, accompanied by his family, which had
been augmented by a second daughter. After a few months in

America in 1909, during which time his son, Warren, was born while the Pershings were on leave at the senator's home in Wyoming, he returned to the Philippines as commander of the Department of Mindanao and Governor of Moro Province. The Pershings rented a large house at Zamboanga, swam in the sea and took long horseback rides in the late afternoons.

Although Pershing, as Governor of Moro Province, achieved good results in bringing the majority of the warring tribes to terms with the U. S. government, there remained a die-hard corps of fighting Moros to be dealt with while the general was still in the Philippines. These men, whom Pershing described as "some of the most notorious cattle thieves and murderers that ever infested the island," had established a jungle stronghold atop Mount Bagsak on Jolo Island. Not even Pershing's personal diplomacy could persuade them to lay down their arms. "The only principle for which they fought," Pershing commented, "was the right to pillage and murder without molestation from the government."

Pershing moved his troops against Mount Bagsak on the morning of June 11, 1913. In the tangled jungle growth and up the steep slopes, the fighting was close and bloody. The battle was fought with Krag and Mauser rifles, machetes, bayonets, pistols, fists and boots. Like Lee at the battle of the Wilderness, Pershing was right up there with the privates during the final critical hours of the fight. Junior officers and noncoms were amazed to see the middle-aged general standing calmly while directing squad and even individual movements this way and that, oblivious to the broad-bladed barongs and spears that were hurled at him from the Moro stronghold. Pershing's men—captains, sergeants, privates, all—were so impressed with the general's personal courage at Bagsak that they gathered testimonials and affidavits and sent them to the Adjutant General in Washington, asking that Pershing be awarded the Congressional Medal of Honor. Pershing learned of this and wrote his own letter, explaining why he did not deserve the medal: "I went to that part of the line because my presence there was necessary." He was awarded the Distinguished Service Medal instead, and this he accepted.

Pershing's service in the Far East had been long, satisfying and arduous. He was filling with years and with soldierly contentment. Frances was still "the dearest girl," his children were growing and healthy. But malaria and the rigors of living in tropical climate had thinned him, aged him. There were no regrets when, in the fall of 1913, he was ordered back to the United States to command the 8th Infantry Brigade at the Presidio in San Francisco.

There the Pershings were given the best quarters the government would afford the new commanding general: a rickety two-story frame structure with a long wooden veranda, a house easily condemnable by any fire marshal. When war with Mexico loomed at the time of the Veracruz crisis in April the following year, Pershing was ordered to take the 6th and 16th Infantry of the 8th Brigade to Fort Bliss. By the following year it became apparent to Pershing that border conditions would keep the brigade at El Paso permanently, so he arranged for new quarters at Fort Bliss for his family. But only a few days before he expected his wife and children to arrive, half of his world turned to ashes.

Before dawn on August 27, 1915, Pershing was roused from sleep to receive a terrible message: fire had gutted the house at the Presidio, killing every member of his family except one. Gone were his wife and his daughters Helen, Anne and Mary Margaret. Only Warren, aged six, was alive, pulled to safety by Johnson, the Negro servant. Pershing buried his family at the Warren plot in Wyoming and returned to duty along the Rio Grande. Outwardly he was still the same hard-boiled brigadier; but in private, several weeks later, he admitted just how crushing the blow had been. He confided to a friend that he did not understand how he had managed to live through the tragedy thus far, that he "should never be relieved of the poignancy of grief at the terrible loss." He wrote that he could "not see that time makes the slightest difference. It is just as it was on the dreadful morning when the telephone message gave me the heartbreaking news." Somehow enduring the unendurable, Pershing stayed busy keeping his brigade combat-ready, but he complained of shortages in such things as wagon parts, tent flies and helves, straw for bedding, blacksmith coal, mule and horse shoes, and khaki shirts and pants for his men.

Once the order to pursue Villa was given, Pershing faced serious problems. The larger enemy was the sprawling, partially convoluted terrain of Chihuahua, more than 94,000 square miles of country that offered featureless plains scoured by the sun, lush valleys blooming with peach trees and wax-leafed live oaks, and

above all, the seemingly endless chain of the Sierra Madre
Occidental—soaring mountains running southward to the Gulf
of California. Water for the animals and for the men, Pershing
knew, would be scarce. Even in a good year, Chihuahua would
have only twenty inches of rain, and that usually fell in the high
plateau country, 3,000 and 4,000 feet above the valley floors where
the cavalry would have to march. Moreover, the hard clay sub-
strata of Chihuahua rejected the rains soon after they fell, and the
water rushed away in torrents. Where the soldiers would be going
the rains usually began in early July, but this was March. In places
the grass would reach high above the fetlocks of a horse, but the
stuff was brittle and offered no nutrient at that time of year.
Grazing would be time-consuming and nearly profitless.

There were no roads, or hardly any, and the quartermaster
would be severely handicapped because Washington had made
it clear that the U. S. Army could not use the Mexican railroads.
How easy it would have been to load the regiments aboard trains at
El Paso and send them straight down to Chihuahua City, let them
get off two hundred miles to Villa's rear, then ride through the
wide cut south and west and get behind the brigand somewhere
below the town of Guerrero. Also, since the tracks branched
sharply westward, plunging through narrow valleys in the Sierras,
other regiments could flank fleeing Villistas in that direction. Villa
would be boxed in, his escape routes to the south cut off, and lives,
time and horses might be saved. But this was theoretical, wishful
thinking; there would be no American rolling stock on Mexican
rails unless Carranza so agreed, which was unlikely. Pershing
would have to supply his people with wagons and, when he could
get them, with trucks. Columbus was to be the base from which
all things flowed, at five to ten miles per hour through rutted
wastes one, three or five hundred miles into the interior—or however far it would take to bring Villa to bay.

As Pershing knew, one of the delights on any campaign was
the expectation and the savoring of hospitality of towns and cities
along the route of march. This had been true ever since men
began warring against one another, but it would not be so for
the troops engaged in the Punitive Expedition. Washington absolutely forbade the use of any Mexican town either as base camp,
temporary stopping place or as recreational site; there must be
no indication that the U. S. Army was "occupying" any part of

Mexico, no echoes of Veracruz. Pershing made this clear in a statement to the El Paso *Morning Times* two days before he crossed the border: "It is no time to indulge in idle theories about invasion. I give the Mexican people too much credit for common sense to think that they will not gladly accept our aid in eliminating an international outlaw."

Still another nettlesome question was how the Carranza troops would react once the Americans were actually inside Mexico by the thousands. An armed clash with the de facto government was the last thing Wilson wanted. In a field order dated March 14, General Funston stressed again that "the greatest caution will be exercised after crossing the border that fire is not opened on troops pertaining to the de facto Government of Mexico." He warned that "the greatest care and discretion will have to be exercised by all." Although full co-operation between Carranza's regulars and American cavalry in running Villa down was the ideal, it was only that. While Villa was still at large his followers might cause vexations to Carranza, but after his crushing defeats at the hands of Obregón, Villa was no longer a threat to the Constitutionalist grip of power in Mexico; Carranza felt, rightly, that he did not need U. S. intervention in dealing with Villa definitively. And if it turned out that the Americans and not Carranza forces captured Villa, it would cause loss of face for the Mexicans, who, whether high born or low, are proud to a fault of being Mexican. It is an attitude of *machismo* melded with a natural disinclination to cherish a larger, much richer and condescending neighbor. Still rankling in many Mexican minds were the defeats at the hands of General Zachary Taylor in such places as Palo Alto, Resaca de la Palma, Monterrey and elsewhere during the Mexican-American War, which began in the spring of 1846, over now these seventy years. And, of course, Veracruz was still an open wound. Within living memory, and beyond that, Americans had come to Mexico as investors or conquerors only and it was unreasonable to expect that they, in the mass, would receive traditional Mexican hospitality.

Personal relationships along the border had never been worse. Ceaseless raids by small bands of cattle thieves and looters who casually murdered generally peaceable Texas ranchers and farmers getting in their way had incurred an understandable hatred for Mexicans from across the river which indiscriminately applied equally to peaceable Mexicans who lived and worked on the Texas side of the Rio Grande. Texans still remembered the Alamo—while forgetting that some of its defenders were named Abamillo, Esparza and Espalier, and that the arch-hero, James Bowie, was married to a striking girl named Ursula Veramendi, one of Mexico's finest. Mexicans in Texas who acted "suspicious" were often shot out of hand. On October 18, 1915—to cite one example—a gang of bandits had crossed the Rio and rode six miles north of Brownsville, where they stopped a passenger train and robbed the occupants of watches, wallets and jewelry. The Texas Rangers shortly afterward laid hands on four Mexicans whom they suspected of having taken part in the daring brigandage. The captives were not brought to trial but hustled into the brush and killed. Obviously no records of such summary executions were kept, but the number of victims of this kind of border justice have been estimated at between two and three hundred during the years when border raids were common. Passions on both sides were as high as they were irrational. It was not a time for reasoning or for euphemisms: men were "greasers" or "gringos," and enmity ran deep.

What help, then, could Pershing's command expect from the ordinary Mexican peon, storekeeper or vagabond? Very little. His statement in the El Paso *Morning News* having to do with common sense on the part of the Mexican people in accepting aid to eliminate an international outlaw was not founded in reality, and he must have known it. To the poor of Chihuahua, Villa was a hearthside hero of truly magnificent proportions, a righter of wrongs; a stealer of horses for his men, perhaps, but a promiser of land and the proven enemy of the *rurales* or those who might take their place. Going into Chihuahua to lay hands on Villa was like the Sheriff of Nottingham entering Sherwood Forest expecting the peasants to help him hang Robin Hood. Pershing could not count on idolaters to help him catch the idol.

From as far east as Fort Oglethorpe, Georgia, and as far west as Fort Huachuca, Arizona, the Punitive Expedition assembled. Pershing's choices of combat troops were severely limited, considering the magnitude of the task that lay ahead. At the time, the United States Army consisted of 170 regiments of coast artillery, which were useless, and 6 regiments of field artillery, but only 31 regiments of infantry and 15 of cavalry, the arm needed for operations in Mexico more than any other. A regimental complement called for 24 officers and 786 men, but reliance on the volunteer system failed to fill the quota and it was not unusual for a regiment to be below the required strength by a hundred men. The bulk of the U. S. Army was permanently garrisoned in such places as the Philippines, Hawaii and the Canal Zone, leaving only 24,602 men in what was known as "the mobile forces" within the entire continental limits, and this figure included support troops and medical men, who did not contribute to fire power.

From what was most readily available, Pershing chose the 7th, 10th, 11th and 13th Cavalry, and the 6th and 16th Infantry Regiments. To this he added two batteries of the 6th Field Artillery. The artillery in question amounted to eight guns, 2.95-in. Vickers-Maxim mountain guns, howitzers with a maximum effective range of fifty-five hundred yards. It required four mules to carry one gun, disassembled, plus another six mules to carry the ammunition; thus, to transport one gun required ten animals, which needed shoeing and forage, plus a dozen men to look after the mules as well as assemble and fire the gun. Sergeant Mack Emerson of the 4th Field Artillery commented, "A good crew could get off eight rounds per minute, but we were so short of ammunition we never got enough practice." In fact, the total ammunition available for the guns in early 1916 amounted to fifty-eight hundred rounds, or about three minutes' worth in combat in the hands of the Army's six regiments of artillery. The infantry was better off; there were four days' worth of reserve rifle ammunition available in various armories throughout the nation.

Supporting the combat arms of this Provisional Division were two companies of Army engineers, an ambulance company and field hospital, two wagon companies of 27 wagons, 112 mules, 6 horses and 36 men each, and a Signal Corps detachment operating the primitive field radios scrounged all up and down the Rio Grande. Finally, there was the 1st Aero Squadron, upon which he pinned great hopes.

In all, Pershing had 4,800 men and 4,175 animals with which to begin the pursuit of Villa, and General Funston promised him reinforcements as soon as they could be shipped to the border. One of the blessings was the fact that the troops under Pershing's command were all regulars, many of them seasoned in the Philippines, and outfits like the 13th, 10th and 7th Cavalry comprised veterans of service along the border who were wise in the ways of life in that harsh land. They were used to the heat, the dust, the "gyppy" water, and knew enough to shake their heavy field shoes upside down every morning to dislodge any scorpions that might have found a cool, dark place to sleep. The ranks contained a liberal sprinkling of immigrants—Germans, Irish, Italians, Poles and Scandinavians predominating—and literacy in any language was not high, but a good percentage of the men "spoke Mex" and were familiar with the more elemental aspects of Latin life. They were shorter than today's soldier—averaging five feet nine—and could route-march or ride very long distances with heavy packs and fueled only with hardtack, bacon and coffee. The loosely cut olive drab shirts and baggy, flared O.D. breeches provided no vestige of military chic, but the men lavished care on their horses and their .30-06 Springfield rifles, and after the long boredom of border watching and parade-ground drills they were spoiling for a fight. For the job at hand they were the best soldiers Pershing could ask for, better than the Prussian Guards or anybody else.

The Expedition entered Mexico in two columns, twelve hours and fifty miles apart. The first column, with Major Frank Tompkins of the 13th Cavalry at the point, left Columbus and stirred up the dust down the straight road leading to Palomas. The regimental colors crossed the international boundary shortly after noon on March 15. The infantry deployed as skirmishers while the cavalry galloped through the small adobe town. The precautions were unnecessary; the Carrancista commander had fled with his troops, leaving the place deserted. Only a ragged elderly couple were left to watch as the Americans set about erecting pup tents in a precise line between the town and a small stream nearby. When the sun dropped, it became bitterly cold. Fires were lit and the troopers wrapped themselves in blankets against the chilled earth, and still they shivered. Few slept, and when they rose from the ground at five the next morning, they found the water in the canteens frozen solid.

Pershing crossed into Mexico on horseback with the western column thirty minutes past midnight on March 16. The crossing was made from Culberson's Ranch, forty miles south of the town of Hachita, New Mexico, where the brigade had formed. The border gate was undefended, ahead stretched only the darkened sweep of unfamiliar terrain. Pershing's destination was the town of Nueva Casas Grandes, more than seventy-five miles distant, where the other column would rendezvous with his. From there, Pershing would make field decision as to how best to divide the command in an effort to box Villa in. He wanted to get to Casas Grandes as quickly as possible and begin the hunt. Villa's trail was now a week old.

Without pause the column pushed on under the stars. The country was flat, and for the first few hours men, mules and horses suffered only the usual discomforts of a forced night march under heavy loads. But the country quickly changed, became broken, rutted, uneven. It had not rained in northern Chihuahua since the preceding July, nine months previously, and choking clouds of white alkaline dust was whipped up by the passage of so many feet and hooves. The mule packtrain soon fell behind despite the cursing and blows directed at the beasts by the mule skinners, whose nostrils were as clogged and irritated as those of the animals. The train was stopped, and the mule skinners tied rags across the muzzles of the animals to help keep the nostril membranes moist; they had already pulled their own neckerchiefs up beneath their gritty eyes and knew how the mules felt. Then they started off again; by the pale light of a fading moon they looked like some ghostly legion of highwaymen driving gray beasts of burden laden with loot. It wasn't until the next day that they caught up with the rest of the column.

The cavalry plodded slowly through the dust followed by the infantry, whose only advantage over the cavalrymen was that because they were working harder, they suffered less from the biting cold. The long march that lay ahead could not be mitigated by the prospects of glory; everyone knew that this was a cavalry campaign and that the infantry was brought along to guard the line of communication and the camps. The foot soldiers would be stuck in this seemingly uninhabited desert for weeks, perhaps even months, forbidden even to seek what diversions the drab, flea-bitten little Mexican villages might offer. Already they regretted leaving behind the rowdy pleasures they had so recently enjoyed in the gamier sections of El Paso: the cold beer, the girls with the dark eyes, the cockfights where a man could wager a few silver dollars. Well, now that they were in Mexico, a private's pay

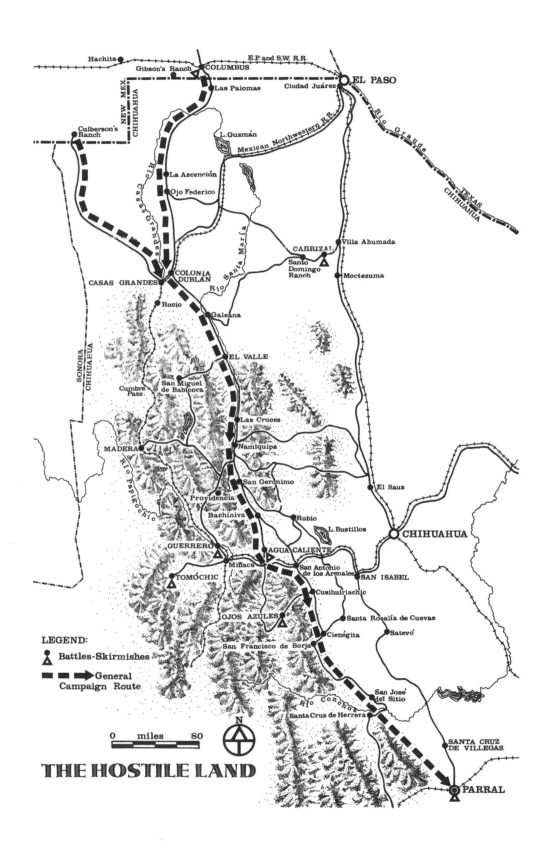

THE HOSTILE LAND

LEGEND:
▲ Battles-Skirmishes
▬▬▶ General Campaign Route

0 ___ miles ___ 80

N

jumped from $15 a month to $18—but where, they asked, could they spend it?

Kicking through the soft dust, the infantryman became painfully aware of the load that bore down on his shoulders and hips. He could shift the nine-pound Springfield rifle from one shoulder to the other, or place it like a yoke behind the neck with hands grasping either side—as though re-enacting the Crucifixion—but the rest of the burden was strapped firmly in place. Around the waist and across the chest hung web belts and bandoleers of rifle ammunition in five-round clips. From the cartridge belt dangled a bayonet and scabbard, first-aid pouch, canteen and cover, machete and scabbard. The noncoms also carried the heavy Colt .45 automatic pistol in a leather holster, which was attached to the cartridge belt with prongs through brass eyelets—and these prongs dug cruelly into a man's hip. In the pack dragging at the shoulders were stuffed a can of bacon, a can of condiment, a mess kit with spoon and knife, a blanket, water-repellent poncho, a cake of soap, two pairs of socks, an extra pair of drawers, a towel, a toothbrush, spare undershirt, rifle cleaning gear, a "housewife" (needle, thread and spare buttons), and whatever else a man thought he might need, usually dice, cards, prophylactics, a copy of Company Orders No. 1, an indelible pencil, a few post cards, spare "makins" for smokes. After exhausting hours of slogging across alien terrain in an effort to keep pace with the insouciant cavalry, and eating their dust, the men of the 6th and 16th Infantry felt themselves no better than the poor pack mules struggling along behind them.

Pershing drove his troops for six hours. They marched until dawn, when they reached a place called Geronimo's Rock, twenty-five miles south of the border. After seeing to the animals and brewing coffee, they flung themselves down to sleep, letting the suddenly hot sun bake away the chill and fatigue. The men were on the road again at noon and had covered another thirty miles by sundown. They pushed on at seven o'clock the next morning, and twelve hours and thirty minutes later reached the Mormon colony at Colonia Dublán, only a few hundred yards north of the town limits of Nueva Casas Grandes. All around were cultivated fields, and a stream of fresh water ran nearby. Few Mormons were left at Dublán now but they were all Americans, and Pershing felt that there was less likelihood of creating an incident by bivouacking there than in the Mexican village of Casas Grandes. Even the troopers of Pershing's column, aching in every muscle, hoped that the men in the first column would take their time in getting there; every day at Dublán would be a day of respite.

The first column, which had more ground to cover and was slowed by having to tolerate the crawling progress of the wagon companies, did not arrive at Dublán until early afternoon of the twentieth, having been five days on the march. There was little of significance the commander, Colonel James Lockett, could report to Pershing: they had seen no Carranza troops, were not sniped at by bandits, and when they passed through the town of Ascensión, the fifteen hundred or so inhabitants came out only to stare apathetically. Twenty miles south of Palomas, on the second day of the march, they discovered the body of a man the surgeon estimated had been dead for a week. Wearing only drawers and a shirt, the man was still blindfolded. He had been shot in the head, and his shoes and wallet were gone. There was no identification, but they guessed he was an American. He was buried deep enough to discourage the coyotes, and prayers were said before the column moved on.

When the troops crossed the border at Columbus, word quickly got to Carranza, who was then at Querétaro, northwest of Mexico City. Carranza dictated a note to Secretary Lansing expressing mock astonishment. The note, dated March 18, was handed to Acting Secretary of State Frank L. Polk: ". . . the Chief Executive of Mexico is in receipt of reliable information that without the knowledge of or advice to the nearest civil or military authorities, and without any intelligence between the Government of the United States and my Government, an expedition described as punitive, for the purpose of pursuing Villa and his band, has entered Mexican territory via Palomas." Carranza harked back to the note of March 10, pointing out that formal protocol regarding reciprocal pursuit had yet to be worked out, and that until such time as the terms were fixed, the note of March 10 "should and must not be understood as tolerating or permitting any expeditions into the national territory."

This was embarrassing to the State Department, especially since only that morning Acting Secretary Polk had wired Special Representative James L. Rodgers in Querétaro to request that

Carranza issue special orders to authorities in Chihuahua to permit the use of the Mexican Northwestern Railway to supply Pershing's Expedition. "You will remind General Carranza," Polk said, "of this Government's courtesy to him in repeatedly allowing his forces to use the railroads of this country."*

In his official reply to Carranza, dated March 18, Polk apologized for the misunderstanding, pointing out that "no time was to be lost if the pursuit was to be effective," and that American military commanders had explicit instructions to respect scrupulously the sovereignty of the Mexican government. In conclusion Polk said that the United States would welcome any suggestions the Mexican Government cared to make to cover operations of troops "under these particular conditions."

"Suggestions" were not long in coming. Eliseo Arredondo, Carranza's representative in Washington, that afternoon handed Polk not suggestions but a fifteen-hundred-word draft agreement divided into fifteen articles, obviously drawn up some days previously. In essence, acceptance of the agreement would immediately nullify the Punitive Expedition and make any other expeditions farcical. Carranza stipulated that crossings be made only in unpopulated or isolated parts of the border, that is, at least ten kilometers from any towns or military camps, and, he specified, only between the Colorado River, where Arizona and California join, and the Mexican town of Piedras Negras, opposite Eagle Pass, Texas. (Exclusion of the territory east of Piedras Negras would mean leaving more than three hundred miles of common border along the Rio Grande at the mercy of the bandits.)

Carranza wanted a zone sixty kilometers wide on either side of the border beyond which no troops could penetrate. No more than one thousand troops would be allowed inside the zone, and they could stay for five days only. Moreover, only cavalry would be allowed to cross; infantry, artillery and airplanes were excluded. (Only the naïve would fail to see that what Carranza really wanted was no punitive expeditions at all—certainly none that his own forces could not control.)

While the State Department was studying this remarkable document, a reaction was received to Polk's request of the

* Polk was referring to the use of American rails to reinforce the Carranza garrison at Agua Prieta in 1915. Villa never forgot the "courtesy," but Carranza chose to ignore it.

eighteenth for use of the Mexican Northwestern Railway, although there was no direct mention of the railway anywhere in Carranza's note. Instead, he said that Polk's message "caused great surprise to the Mexican Government, for it had not until now received any official notice from the Government of the United States that American troops had crossed into Mexican territory or that they were at or near Casas Grandes . . . much more distant from the boundary line than any other point which, under previous treaties, has been the extreme limit in cases of pursuits." Then Carranza called upon the United States to provide "information as to the circumstances under which the passage of American troops into Mexican territory was effected at El Paso, their number, the branch of service to which they belong, the name of the officer in command, the place where they are, and the causes which occasioned their crossing."

Carranza knew very well the causes which occasioned the crossing of American troops, and the information he was after came under the heading of military intelligence. Polk told Carranza what he must have known in any case, that the Expedition consisted of cavalry, infantry and artillery and was commanded by Pershing. "Their location at the present time cannot be stated with preciseness," Polk hedged. Then he set about getting some military intelligence of his own. On March 22 he sent telegrams to all American consuls on the Mexican border: "Ascertain and telegraph immediately number and location infantry, cavalry and artillery forces now stationed along border in your district; also number cannon. Have forces in your district increased since March 10; if so, to what extent? Keep Department promptly informed of proposed and actual changes of these [Mexican] forces."

When Polk was informed that the Carranza garrisons at Matamoros, Juárez and elsewhere along the border had been "materially reinforced during the past two weeks," he sent a rather naïve telegram to Special Representative Rodgers at Querétaro. "You will," he requested, "most discreetly sound de facto authorities as to truthfulness of these reports, expressing the hope that they are untrue and that all available forces will be sent to join the pursuit and capture of our common enemies, Villa and his followers." To ask Carranza to reduce the strength of his garrisons along the border in order to help Pershing chase Villa was, to say the least, unrealistic. Of course Carranza did no such thing.

. . .

Meanwhile Pershing was not idle. Natives of Casas Grandes reported that Villa was somewhere in the vicinity of San Miguel Babícora, where the vast William Randolph Hearst ranch was located, about sixty miles south on a high plateau deep in the Sierras. Villa was trading worn horses for fresh, gathering new recruits. Although the hard-marching 7th and 10th Cavalry had been at Dublán for only a few hours, Pershing ordered them roused from brief rest to prepare for further trials almost immediately. He was not, after all, going to wait for the first column to arrive from Columbus.

The 10th Cavalry had been almost constantly on the move since March 10, covering the two hundred and fifty-two miles from Fort Huachuca, Arizona, to Dublán via Hachita, and the horses were sagging with fatigue. Pershing decided to send the 7th on ahead to Babícora, but the 10th would go by rail from Dublán to Madera, thirty-five miles south of Babícora, and thus block Villa's retreat in that direction. The 7th Cavalry, twenty-eight officers and six hundred and forty-seven men under the command of Colonel James B. Erwin, dragged out of Dublán at three o'clock in the morning on March 18. A few hours later Pershing sent a telegram to the general manager of the El Paso & Southwestern Railroad ordering a locomotive and at least a dozen cars. Pershing did not have permission to use Mexican rails, but then, he had not received orders not to use them, either. The train chuffed into Dublán the following morning, but delight at seeing so many cars turned to rage when it was discovered that almost all of the cars needed overhaul of one kind or another. Engineers went to work cutting holes in the sides of the boxcars to provide ventilation, and wheel bearings were laboriously repacked. The cattle cars were ventilated, but many of them in the wrong places: legions of hobos had built fires on the flooring, burning large holes through the wood that exposed the roadbed below, holes that horses might step through and break their legs. Planking had to be found to patch these holes, and abandoned corrals were torn down and chopped into firewood for the locomotive. It wasn't until late in the day that the men and horses of the 10th Cavalry could be loaded aboard the cars and dispatched to the high mountains.

The long train crawled slowly upward through lofty valleys flanked by barren slopes until late that evening, when the supply of wood was nearly exhausted. There followed a frustrating wait in the cold for several hours while the engine was sent on ahead with some men to seek more firewood and return. At four o'clock in the morning on the twentieth, the engine was recoupled and the train started off again, reaching the little town of Rucio, twenty-eight miles south of Dublán, barely halfway to Babícora. Here Colonel William C. Brown off-loaded a squadron, two hundred and seventy-two officers and men, and struck off on horseback through the rugged Sierras. The other squadron stayed aboard to continue the slow journey to its destination at Madera.

There were frequent stops along the way for more wood and water for the locomotive, and it wasn't until early in the morning on March twenty-first that the contingent reached Cumbre Pass, still a day's ride from Madera. While the train crawled up the Cumbre switchback, two cars loaded with horses jumped the rails and plunged down a steep embankment. The black troopers of the 10th Cavalry riding on top of the cars went crashing down among the rocks and brush. Cries of the injured mingled with the screams of terrified horses. Eleven badly hurt men were pulled from the wreckage, one of whom later died. When the debris was sorted out, the wounded loaded aboard the caboose, gear loaded on other cars and the injured horses unsaddled and shot, the train started off again and struggled upward a little farther, to Música, where the squadron commander, Major Ellwood W. Evans, decided that he had had enough of trains. He ordered his troopers to mount up and start riding to Las Varas, twenty-six miles away.*

Colonel Brown's squadron reached Babícora only to learn from the Hearst ranch manager that Villa had not been near the place. At Las Varas, Carrancista Colonel Maximiliano Márquez told Evans that Villa and his band were not up in the high country at all, but at Namiquipa, forty miles to the east across the mountains

---

* The empty train went on to Las Varas, where the injured cavalrymen lay for three days. Mexican officials there refused to allow them to ride the train on its way back to El Paso. An American cattleman, a Hearst employee, loaded the injured aboard a handcar and pumped them through the mountains all the way back to Casas Grandes, where they arrived on the twenty-seventh. Commented Major Frank Tompkins: "The vagaries of Mexican authorities are beyond comprehension."

and down in the next valley. During the following week Brown and Evans drove their men up mountains, through deep canyons and across parched valleys, covering between them more than four hundred miles of wild and inhospitable terrain, goaded on by false leads given them by civilians and de facto troops alike. They could have expected little else; Namiquipa, for instance, was one of the most revolutionary towns in Mexico, the birthplace of Candelario Cervantes, one of Villa's chief lieutenants. Many of Villa's men had been recruited from the search area of the Santa María River valley, and it was not likely that friends or relatives would put the Americans on the scent of those who had joined Pancho Villa.

"Several Mexicans frankly said that they would consider it a national disgrace if the Americans should capture Villa," Major Tompkins observed. "Nor was this attitude entirely confined to native Mexicans. Most foreigners, including some Americans with interests in Mexico, hoped we would not succeed, believing that the expedition would be withdrawn if we did."

Where was Villa?

After the attack on Columbus, Villa had led the four hundred-odd survivors due south of Palomas, east of the Sierras and into arid but generally flat country where the horses could make faster time. They paused at El Valle, at the entrance to the lush Santa María Valley, and here Villa sent his men to gather the towns-people to hear an impassioned speech. Among the ragged crowd who stood in awe before this legendary hero was a young Mexican named Modesto Nevares, who recalled that "Villa asked for volun-teers to help him fight the Americans who, he said, were in our country and who would probably be here that day." Apparently about forty men stepped forward, but not including Nevares, who added: "He then asked the rest of us if we were not going to join, and when we refused he stood us in line, dismissed the old men and took the rest of us prisoner under guard."

Villa pushed straight down the Santa María Valley for thirty-five miles, arriving at the secluded town of Namiquipa on March 18.* The next day his scouts rushed into town and told him that a force of Carranza troops was bearing down on Namiquipa, so

* The day after Pershing arrived at Casas Grandes, more than seventy miles to the northwest.

Villa hurriedly left town with his men. But they had ridden only a few miles when Villa realized that he outnumbered his pursuers, so he wheeled around and gave battle to two hundred de facto troops. The Carrancistas were routed, losing a hundred horses and a pair of machine guns to Villa. He marched out of Namiquipa on the twentieth (four days before Colonel Brown's squadron arrived) and struck southeast over the mountains for the town of Rubio, thirty-five miles away. He paused at Rubio on the twenty-fourth and twenty-fifth to organize his band for an attack on the city of Guerrero, a Carrancista stronghold buried in the middle of the Sierras.

Villa's army was now a very small one indeed, top-heavy with ranking officers. Colonels found themselves commanding as few as thirty men, less than the strength of an American infantry platoon presided over by sergeants. Villa's staff and escort, the remnants of the illustrious Dorados, amounted to sixty men, while the four hundred fighting men included no fewer than three generals and four full colonels.

On the night of March 26 Villa's army slipped quietly out of Rubio, bound for Guerrero.

Of the men dispatched by Pershing from Dublán, the detachment of 7th Cavalry dogged Villa's elusive trail the hardest. Pershing had appointed an old Indian fighter, tough, rangy, cigar-chewing Colonel George A. Dodd, as provisional commander of the flying columns. Dodd attached himself to the 7th, and although the regiment was commanded by Colonel Erwin, it was Dodd who gave the orders. Dodd was sixty-three years of age, but was one of the most aggressive regimental commanders then at Pershing's disposal. He reflected the spirit of Custer's 7th "Garryowen" Cavalry, but only to a point; there was none of Custer's recklessness that brought on disaster at the Little Big Horn.

Dodd pushed the 7th down the Santa María Valley in Villa's wake, and by March 25 was leading his cavalry up the sides of the Sierras, across the Continental Divide, lashed by freezing winds and snow flurries. Guided more by military instinct than by conflicting reports from Carranza officers and natives as to which direction Villa had taken after leaving Namiquipa, Dodd wound the column south and westward through the mountains, past thickly planted stands of pine, oak, cedar and juniper trees. By

March 28 Dodd was at Bachíniva. There, a Mexican civilian partial to Carranza volunteered the information that Villa had moved westward over the mountains and was at that moment at Guerrero, only thirty-six miles to the south.

One of the 1st Aero Squadron's airplanes, seen only infrequently by the ground troops so far on the campaign, flew in from the north and landed. Lieutenant Herbert A. Dargue, the pilot, climbed out of the Jenny with a message from Pershing: the 11th Cavalry had now joined the chase, and Dodd was to lead the 7th back to Namiquipa to recuperate, turning over his pack animals to the fresher troops. But having come this far, and believing that Villa could be struck a blow at Guerrero, Dodd declined to turn the command around just then. He wrote out a message for the pilot to take back to Pershing: he intended to proceed deeper into the Sierras and attack Villa if he could. Dodd watched the flimsy Jenny take off and fly down the valley out of Bachíniva, wishing that the poor airplane could fly over those forbidding peaks to the west so that he might have some accurate information about the unknown terrain for a change. But that was quite impossible; the peaks between him and Guerrero topped 11,200 feet above sea level. Dodd would have to get through the maze of canyons and arroyos on his own, seeking a way to get at Villa.

Villa struck at Guerrero at four o'clock, before dawn on the morning of March 28. The garrison there was caught asleep in the barracks, no sentries were posted, and the place fell without a shot being fired. Part of Villa's force had been diverted from the Guerrero operation to pounce on the little village of San Isidro, just across the valley, but here Carrancista General José Cavazos and his men were more alert and put the attackers to flight. The Carrancistas poured after the fleeing Villistas all the way to Guerrero, whereupon a vicious fire fight broke out. Modesto Nevares, whom Villa had forced to "volunteer" at El Valle, recounted:

"When we reached Guerrero, Villa gave us arms and a small amount of ammunition so that we could take part in the fight against the Carranza forces. During the progress of the fight we were lined up in an arroyo facing the Carrancistas."

The men in the arroyo watched Villa and his staff bound forward on foot toward the enemy. Nevares saw one of the unwilling volunteers raise a rifle to his shoulder and aim it directly at Villa's bobbing figure. He squeezed the trigger, the rifle blammed, and the prisoners yelled when they saw Villa's big figure lurch and fall heavily. "It was our intent," said Nevares, "to kill him and go over to the Carrancistas, but just as Villa was shot the Carrancistas gave way and ran, leaving us with no possible way to escape. So we again assumed the pretense of loyalty and declared that if he had been shot by any of us, it was purely accidental.

"Villa was shot with an old-fashioned Remington [.44 caliber] rifle, which takes a very large lead bullet. The bullet entered his right leg from behind, just opposite the knee joint, coming out through the shinbone about four inches down. The bullet made a big hole where it went in and a much larger hole where it came out. The shinbone was badly shattered and I afterwards saw them pick out small pieces of bone from the hole in front."

Nevares described how Villa's wound was dressed, then the leg put in splints. Nevares was picked out from the El Valle "volunteers" to serve as the driver of a wagon in which Villa would travel to Parral, more than one hundred and thirty miles to the south, where the wound would be given time to heal. Villa was gingerly loaded into the wagon, and one hundred and fifty of Villa's men mounted up as escort. Sometime after midnight on March 29, Nevares snapped the reins and the wagon started south out of Guerrero.

Colonel Dodd moved the three hundred and seventy officers and men of the 7th Cavalry out of Bachíniva after sundown on March 28. He badly wanted to make his strike at Guerrero no later than dawn on the following morning, catching the Villistas unprepared. But the poor maps at his disposal did not indicate any trails that would lead his command through the awesome mountains that lay between him and the town. The civilian guide attached to the 7th, J. B. Barker, told Dodd that although he had been to Guerrero some years before, he had entered the town from another direction and had little idea of how best to reach Guerrero from Bachíniva. Grilling of local Mexicans failed to produce any usable information.

Dodd headed south down a plateau 7,500 feet high, then swung west and entered the Sierras. It was dark and bitterly cold. The column accordioned its way up rocky slopes, down gulleys and through arroyos, steadily climbing. There were frequent halts while the point blundered ahead, seeking passable terrain. Men lay down on the icy ground, reins in hand, and slept during these halts, rising to find breath frosted on facial hair. Dodd pushed the column, and by six-thirty the 7th was in a position from which an attack could be made, but they were still three miles south of Guerrero and facing terrain that made a sudden, sweeping mounted charge impossible. To the east of town, precipitous bluffs rise, cut by deep arroyos running far back into the upper plain. To the west, Guerrero is backed up against bluffs rising up to the mountains. To the south, where the 7th had paused, there are no bluffs but the ground is corrugated, cut by ravines leading from the river that runs past the town. By the time Dodd had divided the squadrons for separate assaults it was eight o'clock and the sun was well over the mountains behind Guerrero. Of course the Mexicans were now aware that the Americans were getting ready to invest the town; all were up and many were mounted, ready to flee. Villa had not ordered Guerrero defended to the death.

Dodd sent a squadron of cavalry across the river to get behind the town and block the escape of Villistas to the east while the rest of the cavalry fought its way into Guerrero. The combat opened everywhere at once. E Troop got behind the town and engaged in a hot fire fight with Villistas who wanted to escape in that direction. Machine-Gun Troop opened up on the town from a range of a thousand yards, firing from across the river. Horses splashed through the river, came under fire, and the troopers dismounted to return it with Springfields. Private Arthur C. Fleenor, a Headquarters Troop messenger, spurred his horse up the riverbank, but the horse lost its footing and fell backward, crushing Fleenor's ankle. Fleenor hopped back on the horse and kept going with his message. Mounted Villistas galloped out of town and across the river, seeking safety by climbing up an arroyo leading through the bluffs on the eastern bank. They were stopped by Lieutenant Colonel Selah R. H. "Tommy" Tompkins (Frank Tompkins' brother) and C Troop. In the fighting that followed, Private T. P. Brown was shot three times, twice in the body and once in the face, but picked up his rifle after each hit and kept firing until he passed out from shock. Some of the Villistas managed to reach the cover of an arroyo, where they were pinned down. Tommy Tompkins ordered a mounted charge to wipe out the pockets of resistance, but the troop was stopped by a barbed-wire fence. Sergeant Daniel Heaton, who had just ridden up with I Troop, jumped from his horse and ran toward the wire with cutters. Bullets plucked at his clothes, but he cut a path through the wire, then remounted and joined in the charge up the arroyo.

North of Guerrero, Lieutenant Pearson Menoher watched as a squadron of Mexican cavalry rode calmly out of town and up a ravine. The rider at the point was carrying a large Mexican national flag. The Americans thought they were witnessing the exit of Carranza cavalry and nobody fired. Thus escaped intact a large body of Villistas.

Scattered packets of mounted Villistas fled the town and managed to cross the river, seeking to escape eastward toward San Isidro. They gained the gulleyed eastern bluffs, paused to pour fire at the pursuing Americans, then continued the difficult retreat. Dodd ordered a mounted pistol charge, but it was abandoned when the American horses began to falter. Spurrings and shouted exhortations were unable to move the exhausted mounts faster than a limping walk; the horses had covered nearly fifty-five miles since leaving Bachíniva and were done in. The Mexicans scattered and vanished, pursued only by long-range rifle fire.

Guerrero fell.

Five Americans were wounded, none killed. Fifty-six Villistas were killed, thirty-five were wounded, but no prisoners were taken. However, the 7th did capture thirteen horses and twenty-three mules, animals the cavalry was glad to have. By any standard Villa had been dealt a severe blow, and had it not been for a vengeful rifle bullet fired by an impressed irregular the campaign might have ended that morning, two weeks after it began instead of almost a year later.

But Congress was thrilled, and when the account of the fight at Guerrero was read on the floor the members cheered. Wilson nominated Dodd for a Silver Star, and a few days later the old Indian fighter was confirmed as brigadier by a grateful Senate.

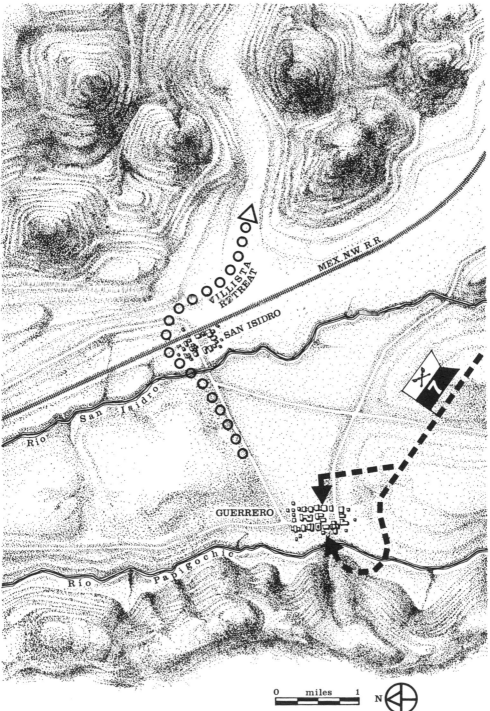

MEX. N.W. R.R.

VILLISTA
R<u>E</u>TREAT

SAN ISIDRO

Río San Isidro

X
7

GUERRERO

Río Papigochic

0   miles   1

N

INTO THE VALLEY
28 MARCH 1916

6

No Eyes for the General

Guerrero could have been attacked earlier in the day with greater success had Colonel Dodd been provided with aerial reconnaissance before starting the forced march over unknown ground to charge an ill-defined target using animals fatigued from unnecessary travail. But the aircraft to do the job simply were not available. Pershing had opened the campaign with eight tired airplanes, and within thirty days only two remained. In Europe, Western Front commanders could call upon a variety of planes to perform reconnaissance, photomapping, artillery regulation— using air-to-ground wireless—and bombardment missions. British, French and German planes could reach speeds exceeding 110 mph, and climb higher than 15,000 feet. They carried machine guns firing through the propeller. But Pershing served a government totally indifferent to history's lesson then being taught at such cost to others, and as a consequence he would remain virtually blind throughout the campaign.

The 1st Aero Squadron was organized early in 1914 at North Island, near San Diego, California. It then consisted of five pilots, thirty enlisted men and three Martin T biplanes. The squadron was commanded by thirty-four-year-old Captain Benjamin Delahauf Foulois, a lean, long-jawed, pipe-smoking dedicated soldier who believed in the future of air power. Foulois had risen from the rank of private to lieutenant in nine years and became this country's first dirigible pilot. He had received rudimentary flying instruction from Orville Wright but was largely self-taught as an aviator. From late in November of 1909 to the spring of 1911, Foulois was this nation's only pilot and navigator in the U. S. Army's heavier-than-air division. Foulois learned to fly at a time when fatalities averaged one for every hundred hours spent aloft by students in training.

In the summer of 1915 Foulois was ordered to move the 1st Aero Squadron from California to Fort Sill, Oklahoma, to see what could be accomplished utilizing the new Curtiss JN-2 "Jennies" in artillery liaison work. When the factory-fresh airplanes were uncrated and assembled on Fort Sill's parade ground, the pilots looked on them with distrust: the Jennies were ungainly, underpowered, the tail surfaces seemed too small and were fitted with cumbersome shoulder harnesses that actuated the ailerons. To force a bank to the left or right, pilots leaned into the harness to flip the ailerons in the desired direction. It was an inexact procedure which produced jerky changes in attitude in all but the most stable of airplanes—and the JN-2 looked far from stable. The pilots' suspicions were confirmed during the squadron's first trial of the new Jenny when Lieutenant R. B. Sutton lost control of the plane near the ground and crashed to his death.

The JN-2s were given a chance to prove their worthiness in field operations only a few days after delivery at Fort Sill. Foulois was ordered to detach four pilots and two Jennies for border patrol duty along the lower Rio Grande valley in Texas. The planes were crated and shipped by rail to Brownsville and were first used on August 26, 1915; they proved to be nearly unmanageable. Lieutenants B. Q. Jones and J. C. Morrow were at 1,100 feet in rough air when the airplane suddenly dropped nearly two hundred feet in a vicious sideslip that required Jones to exert every effort of control. He got the machine to 4,500 feet, looking for calmer air, but again the plane slipped wildly out of control. Fearful for their lives, the fliers nursed the JN-2 back to the ground. Twice pilots aborted routine daylight search missions, criticizing the plane's handling characteristics. Then tragedy occurred on September 5 when Lieutenant Morrow took an enlisted man up on patrol. Morrow, one of the more skilled and experienced pilots in the squadron, climbed to 200 feet and started a turn to the left. The Jenny immediately fell into a steep spiral that ended with fatal impact for both men.

Back at Fort Sill, news of the disasters at Brownsville not only caused deep gloom among Foulois and the other pilots but it resulted in a mutinous attitude on the part of the artillery officers assigned to the squadron as artillery spotters. Risking courts-martial, they refused to fly, and told Foulois that "only in time of war and in case of absolute necessity would they be willing to fly in the Curtiss JN-2 airplane."

Alarmed, the Army requested that wind-tunnel tests be run on the JN-2 model sent to the aeronautical engineering department at the Massachusetts Institute of Technology. Exhaustive testing only proved what the 1st Aero Squadron pilots already knew: the JN-2 was unstable under any conditions other than absolute straight and level flight in calm air. The craft's designer and builder, Glenn Curtiss, hurried to Washington to see what modifications would satisfy the Army.

Meanwhile Foulois was ordered to move the squadron from Fort Sill to San Antonio for permanent duty. Perhaps to restore public confidence in the hated JN 2s, Foulois was ordered to move the squadron through the air and not by rail on the four-hundred-and-fifty mile jump to Texas. The six planes got airborne on November 19. Two stops and three days later the Jennies came down at Waco without mishap. Foulois took the opportunity afforded him by the Waco Rotary Club to address the nation on the subject of U. S. air power. Following a luncheon in the pilots' honor, Foulois said, "We have been several years building fifty-three airplanes for the Army. Our active squadron now on the way to San Antonio totals six. To show the insignificance of such a force, more than that number are destroyed every day in the European war."

Using maps supplied by the U. S. Post Office Department—the only ones Foulois could find—the pilots left Waco on November 23 for Austin, only ninety miles to the south. In haze and fighting an easterly wind, the formation became widely scattered. Only two pilots landed in Austin on time; the others put down at different fields as far as fifty miles northwest of the intended rendezvous point. Finally, all six Jennies landed on the broad greensward of the cavalry drill ground at Fort Sam Houston late in the morning of the twenty-sixth. It had taken seven days to make the trip, but Foulois was thankful that nobody had crashed.

Less than four months after the discouraging cross-country flight, Foulois received orders to take the 1st Aero Squadron into combat with the Punitive Expedition—still using the same untrustworthy JN-2s. Modifications suggested by Curtiss—larger control surfaces, a different wing design, a more powerful engine —added so much extra weight to the JN-2 that engineers were back at the drawing boards trying to solve the problem of how to create a workable airplane for the armed forces of the nation that had presented the world with the airplane in the first place. The fault did not lie with American industry; the United States produced some of the best aeronautical minds of the new century: Glenn Martin, W. Starling Burgess, Grover C. Loening, Thomas Morse, Glenn Curtiss, and others. American pilots were making names for themselves as serious contenders for altitude, distance and speed records, and as showmen. The public was dazzled by aerial Barnums like Lincoln Beachey and John Moisant, who provided educational thrills for thousands of Americans paying to see cow-pasture "circuses" staged throughout the country.

The U. S. Army's attitude toward aviation was summed up in a single sentence in its *Annual Report for 1913:* "Aviation, which may be considered a sport by the people of the country at large, is to the Army a vital necessity." This was pointed toward the Congress more than anywhere else; yearly requests for increased expenditures for the Army's air arm were met with driblets of money instead of the torrents needed to elevate the nation to a par with the rest of the world. In the five-year period 1908 to 1913 the U. S. government appropriated a total of only $453,000 for aeronautics. Germany, on the other hand, realized the potential of the new weapon and spent $28 million during the same period. France spent nearly as much, and even Tsarist Russia allocated $12 million for aircraft and dirigibles. At the beginning of 1914, the United States ranked fourteenth—behind feudal Japan even— among nations in air power.

Ironically, had not the outbreak of war in Europe intervened, revolutionary Mexico would have possessed an air arm four or five times the size of that of the United States. Not long after Huerta assumed the Presidency of Mexico, he sent thirty-one officers of the Escuela Militar de Aspirantes, Mexico's West Point, to the pilot training school run by Louis Blériot, near Paris. Huerta placed a tentative order for thirty Blériot monoplanes to be returned with the graduating pilots. But after August 1, 1914, France needed every airplane the factories could produce and the order was never filled. Two of the new Mexican pilots stayed on in

France to fly with the Service Aéronautique, and the others returned home.

A comic sort of aerial warfare had been waged in Mexico nearly three years before the Punitive Expedition crossed the border at Columbus. In January 1913 a Mexican colonel named Moreno visited the Glenn L. Martin hydroplane school near Los Angeles, California, and hired one of Martin's instructors to fly for Obregón. The instructor, Didier Masson, managed to smuggle a Martin biplane across the border near Nogales, Arizona, and shipped it by wagon and by rail to the interior of Mexico. After endless difficulties in securing needed parts, Masson performed his first combat mission for Obregón's rebels. On May 10, 1913, Masson attacked the federal gunboat *Guerrero* lying off the port of Guaymas on the Gulf of California. Masson's bombs were homemade: foot-long pipes three inches in diameter filled with 40 percent dynamite. From an altitude of 5,000 feet Masson circled the *Guerrero* while his passenger, Gustavo Salinas Camina, tossed the bombs over the side.

Masson admitted that the bombs did no damage to the gunboat, but reported that "the moral effect was considerable. I watched as the *Guerrero* hurriedly moved from one place to the other in the Gulf while the crew plunged into the water." When Masson and Camina ran out of bombs they dropped propaganda leaflets on the federal encampments at Guaymas urging them to come over to the side of the Constitutionalists.

Pancho Villa tried to organize an air strike force for his Division of the North and hired a Holyoke, Massachusetts, pilot named Edwin C. Parsons to teach a few of his rebels to fly. After watching Parsons crash-land one of Villa's five aging Wright "L" biplanes, the students fled. Parsons, like Masson, had returned to the States long before American forces under Pershing entered Mexico.* Carranza forces captured the remaining Villa Wright biplanes, and although Carranza established his own flying school and the so-called "National Aviation Shops" in November 1915 at Balbuena, near Mexico City, the first Mexican-built airplane wasn't produced until nearly a year later. The little warp-winged, 60-hp biplane was an even worse contraption than the JN-2. Foulois

---

* Both Parsons and Masson later had distinguished records as volunteer fighter pilots with the Lafayette Escadrille in France in 1916–17. They had never met in Mexico.

and his pilots did not have to face opposition in the air either from Villa or from the de facto government, but the obstacles they faced at the beginning of the campaign were nonetheless formidable.

The 1st Aero Squadron's service with the Punitive Expedition began on March 11, 1916, when Secretary of War Newton Baker ordered General Funston to attach Foulois and his men to Pershing for the duration of the campaign. Funston and Foulois discussed the wisdom of sending the enlisted men and the trucks ahead while the pilots actually flew the Jennies to Columbus, a distance of five hundred and twenty miles. Recalling the recent flight from Fort Sill to San Antonio, Funston decided it would be best to disassemble the airplanes and ship them by rail. The planes were crated, and the following day Foulois, ten pilots, eighty-two enlisted men, one civilian mechanic and two hospital corpsmen boarded a Southern Pacific train and left for the "front."

One of the pilots, Lieutenant Edgar S. Gorrell, recalled that the squadron "was in horrible shape. The [eight] airplanes were not fit for military service, especially along the border. Hunsacker, then in charge of aeronautical engineering at the Massachusetts Institute of Technology, had just reported that these airplanes had only four horsepower over and above the amount necessary to fly at sea level. The squadron had no machine guns, no bombs and none of the utensils of warfare later known to World War I flyers. Some of us carried pistols. Two flyers had high-powered .22 rifles. It wasn't until sixty days after reaching Columbus that we got our hands on about sixteen machine guns which represented, according to Captain Walsh, the Ordnance Officer, about 50 percent of the total number of army machine guns then in existence.

"The bombs arrived in April and were but three-inch artillery shells and nobody knew how to use them. They were sent, not for use, but so that certain authorities in Washington could tell the newspapers that we were equipped with bombs."

The first tentative sortie by the squadron was a test hop across the border. Foulois and Townsend F. Dodd wanted to see what effect the higher altitude would have on the Curtiss engines. The pilots were aloft for less than an hour and returned to Columbus from their twenty-five-mile trip with the news that altitude seemed to have no effect on the airplane's performance. For their purposes, this was a meaningless report. The mean altitude that far south of Columbus is only 4,000 feet above sea level. The country is generally flat and featureless, offering only one hill rising gently to 7,900 feet off to the right, and a sprawling dried salt lake to the left. Past the fifty-mile mark, however, the country begins to change radically. Peaks reach 10,000 feet, and an hour out of Casas Grandes the valleys narrow into seeming trenches while the rugged tops of the Sierra Madre climb nearly 12,000 feet into the sky.

On Sunday afternoon, March 19, Pershing wired Foulois from Casas Grandes "to proceed here at once for immediate service." Although Foulois knew that it would be five o'clock at the earliest before all of the pilots and planes were ready and that they could not possibly traverse the ninety miles to Casas Grandes before dark, he nonetheless took Pershing's "at once" literally and ordered the squadron to get ready for takeoff. The pilots were dismayed.

"In the whole corps," reported Gorrell, "only Lieutenant Dodd had ever flown at night. The rest of us had never been off the ground after dusk. We had no idea where Casas Grandes was. We had no maps, only blueprints which someone thought was a representation of the country south of the border. We had no reliable compasses, and such as they were, each airplane was equipped with a different type. There were no lights on the planes and when the sun went down we could not see any of the instruments.

"Telegraphic information that the landing field would be lit by fires reached us just before we took off. The height at which we were to fly was not set for us; our orders were to follow the airplane ahead of us so that if one got lost, *all* got lost. We were simply to follow the man ahead of us."

With such vagueness, coupled with the decision to risk the squadron on a night mission over unknown ground, Foulois invited a fiasco. It did not seem to occur to Foulois to wait until dawn to make the flight by daylight, which, even for the JN-2s, would have posed only the problem of keeping the engines running for two hours at a stretch. To arrive at Casas Grandes at night would in no way help Pershing.

At five-fifteen the first plane took off; the great mission began.

Lieutenant Walter G. "Mike" Kilner barely managed to clear a wire fence stretched at the end of the field when his engine started dropping revs on the long takeoff roll. He could not nurse his Jenny up more than a few hundred feet, so he turned around and landed back at Columbus to change engines. The remaining seven Jennies flew on in a bobbing, straggling formation of follow-the-leader. Dusk soon fell and the pilots groped ahead by following the murky silhouettes and the exhaust flames of the planes in front of them. Afraid of midair collision, the pilots Gorrell, Robert H. Willis and Joseph E. Carberry, all flying at the tail of the aerial column, climbed a thousand feet above the others. By six o'clock the earth was visible only as a purple smudge and Foulois realized the wise thing to do was to set down. Only three of the pilots noticed his descent to follow him down for a safe landing at Ascensión, halfway to Casas Grandes. The others kept flying and were soon separated and on their own in the alien sky.

Carberry, seeing the lights in Janos, ten miles beyond Ascensión, glided down for a landing on the road going through town. Gorrell flew on, oriented by the stars overhead and by a faint orange glow on the horizon. Gorrell assumed it came from the signal fires lighting the landing field at Casas Grandes and made directly for this welcome beacon. He almost collided with Willis, whose airplane swept in front of his, heading west. Willis disappeared into the darkness. Gorrell dropped lower but was confused by lights on both sides of the hills shielding the valley where he thought he was supposed to land. Then he realized that he was flying over a forest fire and not the field at Casas Grandes. He pulled up the nose of the Jenny and managed to turn around in the narrow canyon.

"I saw only four things," Gorrell remembered. "The mountains below me, the full moon, the North Star and the darkness. I realized the only thing in the world that made any difference to me then was how I was going to land. With little more than an hour of fuel remaining, I knew I could not get back to the United States. Whether I was east or west of the line of troops I did not know. I felt that if I could only get down safely somehow, I could take off in the morning and find the lines of communication. I had no idea whether I was drifting east or west, but I pointed the nose of my plane towards the North Star, determined to keep to that course until I ran out of gasoline.

"I passed over small shacks and could see the occupants stick their heads out of the lighted doorways, but there was no place to come down. Finally I began to smell the familiar odor of an engine burning up because of lack of oil. Just as it dawned on me that I was about to ruin the engine, it spit once or twice and the propeller stopped. There stretched ahead of me a silver ribbon which I hoped was water. I headed down in a series of steps—nose over, level off, nose over, level off. On one of these leveling-off times I leveled off tangent to the ground. The plane seemed to roll less than twenty feet. I climbed out of the cockpit and discovered that I had landed in a few acres of bunch grass. I heard the barking of dogs. Ahead were a few adobe huts, but because all of us believed the Mexicans were unfriendly I intended taking no chances of falling into their hands.

"I took out my pistol, canteen of water, emergency rations and blueprint map from the cockpit. I was dressed in khaki, with a full-length blue overall suit over the uniform. I wore a leather flying coat, a pair of wool-lined flying gloves and a sort of football helmet. I thought I saw some men come out of the adobe houses to stalk me. With this, I started walking north, holding to the reliable North Star, which was still visible. Later, as I thought these men were coming closer, I dropped to my stomach and started to crawl."

Back in Columbus the mechanics worked most of the night to install a new engine in Kilner's JN-2. At dawn Kilner took off; he flew steadily without incident and landed at Casas Grandes two hours later. He was the first to report. A few minutes later Carberry swooped down the wide valley and landed. He had spent a cold night guarding the airplane near Janos, but was unhurt. A little later Foulois and the other three pilots who had stayed overnight at Ascensión arrived at Casas Grandes. This left Willis and Gorrell unaccounted for. Foulois reported to Pershing and was ordered to make a reconnaissance flight south toward Cumbre Pass to locate American cavalry moving in the direction of Babícora.

With Dodd as pilot and Foulois as observer, the first mission for Pershing got under way shortly before noon. After little more than an hour the Jenny returned to Casas Grandes, having penetrated no farther than twenty-five miles into the desert. Foulois explained to Pershing that they were unable to get the underpowered Jenny over the tops of the foothills of the Sierra Madre in order to enter the pass; he complained of "terrific vertical currents of air" that made controlling the aircraft difficult. Lieutenant Thomas S. Bowen stepped forward and suggested that the Jenny might be able to negotiate the hills with only one man in it, and he volunteered to try.

The others watched as Bowen ran up the engine and started down the field in strong, gusty winds. The Jenny was no more than fifty feet off the ground when it slipped off on one wing and plunged to the ground. The plane was smashed beyond repair, but the pilot was pulled from the cockpit suffering from nothing worse than a broken nose and lacerations. Thus ended the first day's effort to utilize American air power as the eyes of the Army.

It wasn't until late the next day that Willis arrived at Casas Grandes—on foot. After his near-collision with Gorrell he had kept flying until the engine ran out of fuel, and he attempted a landing (as it turned out) about twenty miles southeast of Casas Grandes. The terrain he chose was rugged and the plane's landing gear was ripped off when he put the Jenny on the ground. Willis, like Gorrell, guided himself by the North Star and started walking out. Ten miles south of Pershing's headquarters, a Mexican astride a mule pointed the way to Casas Grandes. Later when a troop of the 13th Cavalry located Willis' plane they found it hacked to pieces, with every instrument ripped out. The Mexicans had apparently not managed the engine and left it in its mounts. The plane was abandoned to rot in the desert.

Meanwhile, Foulois and the other pilots wondered, *Where is Gorrell?*

When Gorrell started crawling away from his imagined pursuers, he was followed by a herd of cattle and horses. Later, Gorrell could laugh at his predicament, but at the time he was terrified. "As I crawled forward the herd came after me; when I stopped crawling, the herd stopped. When I started crawling again, the cattle and the horses would start forward, and eventually they came so close their lowered heads and horns almost touched my heels. I had heard many stories about herds of animals stomping to death things they did not like on the ground. I jumped up and ran as hard as I could towards the stream of water. The herd started running, too. I jumped into the stream, hoping it was not too deep. Fortunately it wasn't and I waded through it, leaving the animals on the other side."

Gorrell headed for the crest of a mountain, which he reached after seven hours of steady plodding. He lay down and slept on the cold mountain top until dawn. To the east and west, desert stretched as far as the eye could see. To the north were the mountains, and to the south lay the valley. Gorrell guessed that he had drifted east in the last hours of his flight and decided to strike out westward, hoping to come across the Army's line of communication between Columbus and Ascensión. At six o'clock he started walking.

Lashed by dust and sand driven by furnace winds, Gorrell walked through the desert until four that afternoon, seeing no sign of life. He remembered that he had not eaten since the previous afternoon, but he had no desire for food. His pint canteen was already half empty and he craved water. Since he realized that he would probably die of thirst before getting help, he reluctantly decided to return to the stream where he had landed.

Rationing himself to one tablespoon of water per hour, Gorrell wearily retraced his steps until darkness fell. The fierce heat of Chihuahua did not diminish and Gorrell was reduced to gargling with what little water remained, then spitting it back into the canteen. His mouth was so parched that he could not close it and his tongue stuck to the roof of his mouth. A number of times he lost consciousness and fell. He lost track of time and direction. He stumbled forward and was beset with hallucinations. "My mouth was a supply depot and I seemed to be carrying headquarters on my back; the two would not coordinate." He passed out again and lay there for hours.

When Gorrell came to, it was still night. Ahead, not fifty yards away, was the stream. He was suddenly racked with convulsions, and when these had passed he got up and made his way to the stream and lay down in the water, painfully drinking his fill. He put his emergency ration into his canteen cup to dissolve, but his throat was so swollen that he was unable to get down anything semisolid. He slept, then arose before dawn and walked upstream until he reached the airplane. He found it untouched. The horses were still there, grazing in the sparse grass. Gorrell decided to steal one and ride out of the valley.

"I picked out the horse I wanted," Gorrell recounted, "and led him out of the herd by the ears. Intending to make a bridle, I began tearing strips out of my overalls with one hand while holding the horse by one ear with the other. Before I could finish, a Mexican

on horseback appeared about seventy-five yards away, riding
straight for me and yelling his head off. I let go of the horse's ear
and ran for the nearest adobe shack. While the Mexican circled
the house I went from window to window, pointing my pistol at
him. I shouted '*Amigo!*' several times, then stepped outside."

The other man was unarmed and Gorrell explained his plight
in halting Spanish learned at West Point. He offered the Mexican
eight silver dollars—all he had—if he would lend him a horse
and lead him to the nearest Americans. The sight of the silver,
and Gorrell's cocked .45, convinced the Mexican and they rode
together to the corral. Gorrell was suspicious of every move and
took cover behind some trees while the Mexican saddled a horse.
When the Mexican returned with the horse he was accompanied
by an elderly *pacífico* (nonrevolutionary) who offered Gorrell a
jug of fresh milk. "I refused," Gorrell said, "as I feared it was
poison. Such were the tales we had heard."

The Mexican rider set out for Ascensión, about twenty miles
away, covered every step of the way by Gorrell's pistol. However,
the American's guide was far more fearful of being seen by Villistas than he was of Gorrell. As the day wore on, the Mexican
fretfully observed what Gorrell described as "smoke signals" rising
from the tops of the distant hills. The guide told Gorrell they were
signals from one band of Villa's men to another, and he was
terrified of being caught while helping an American. The lure of
silver in that destitute land was great, however, and the guide
led Gorrell almost to the outskirts of Ascensión. A troop of cavalry
bore down on them and Gorrell kicked his tired horse into a feeble
trot to meet the Americans. They surrounded him with drawn
pistols. Gorrell, "angry and surprised," raised his hands. Then he
realized that he looked like a bandit: grimy, unshaven, his oily
blue coveralls torn to shreds, helmetless and wearing only one
glove. The only military thing about Gorrell was his West Point
ring and he held it up for the troopers to see. He gave his guide
four silver dollars and said he would get the other four the next
morning, when he was to lead Gorrell back to his airplane.

In camp Gorrell was doctored and told to rest in bed. Lieutenant
Courtney H. Hodges,* 6th Infantry, tried to persuade Gorrell to
eat, but the food would not go down.

* Hodges later attained the rank of lieutenant general; commanded the
U. S. First Army in Europe during World War II.

Gorrell borrowed the 6th Infantry's regimental Ford sedan, eight gallons of gasoline and a gallon of oil, and the next morning started back for his airplane. He could not find his guide, but Ascensión's town chief provided a replacement and the Army provided a driver. The airplane was just as Gorrell had left it. He filled the radiator from the stream, fueled the tanks and made a successful takeoff despite a sudden rain. Buffeted by winds, Gorrell's Jenny staggered thirty miles eastward to Ojo Federico, where he had to refuel. A truck convoy returning to Columbus stopped and Gorrell was able to fill his tanks from a gasoline drum carried by one of the trucks. He enlisted the help of several of the truckers to hold the wings and tail while he got maximum revolutions from the engine. The truckers let go and the Jenny shot forward. Just as the wheels left the ground one of the lower wings smashed against the empty gasoline drum, which had been left standing upright by the side of the narrow field.

Climbing for altitude, Gorrell had been in the air only a few minutes when he noticed that a large piece of the rear wing spar was missing. Tacks "began jumping out of the wing," and the linen covering started to shred in long flapping ribbons. Gorrell fought the plane around, and after landing safely back at Ojo Federico, disgustedly climbed out of the airplane. He hitched a ride with a truck convoy on its way to Casa Grandes and reported to Foulois what had happened. Two days later he returned to Ojo Federico, patched up the Jenny and flew it back to the squadron. Gorrell's odyssey lasted for seven days, and he need not have endured it had not Foulois decided to fly by night.

While Gorrell was still trying to make his way back to Casas Grandes, Foulois attempted to comply with Pershing's requests for reconnaissance missions. On March 22, two Jennies took to the air to locate American cavalry moving south alongside the Mexican Northwestern Railroad tracks. They managed to reach the northern end of Cumbre Pass, but as before, could not get the 90-hp airplanes over the mountains. Vicious crosscurrents and sudden downdrafts nearly wrested control away from the pilots, who reported that the Jennies were driven within twenty feet of the treetops. They were forced to retreat down the valley and return to base.

Foulois immediately drafted a lengthy memorandum to Pershing asking for total re-equipment for the 1st Aero Squadron. He requested two each of five different kind of airplanes manufactured by Martin, Curtiss, Sturtevant, Thomas and Sloane, with engines ranging from 125 to 160 hp, complete with spare engines, wings, landing gear, radiators and magnetos. He suggested that the order be telegraphed and the new planes shipped by express. Pershing forwarded Foulois' memo to Funston, who endorsed it and sent it on to Washington. Secretary of War Baker replied that it was impossible to fulfill the request because "all airplanes available for service were already with the Pershing Expedition."

Among the correspondents following Pershing's mobile headquarters was Bryon C. Utecht of the New York *World*. Utecht, with a keen eye for the dissatisfaction among the pilots, encouraged the fliers to vent their feelings. Incautiously, they did, and on April 3 the *World* headlined: HANDICAPPED BY OFFICIALS HERE, AVIATORS IN MEXICO TELL WORLD. The article quoted Foulois in the subhead: "Risking Lives Ten Times a Day but Are Not Given Equipment Needed." Utecht quoted Lieutenant Dargue as saying it was "criminal to send men up under such conditions." According to Utecht, the pilots had told him that "they have failed to receive cooperation in their service in the present campaign [because] the aviation system has been badly bungled in Washington." Utecht reported that the pilots blamed "politics, personal ambition and utter lack of knowledge of aviation" on the part of higher authorities as being responsible for the dangerous plight of the 1st Aero Squadron.

Reaction to this broadside was not long in coming. Incensed, Secretary of War Baker sent a copy of the newspaper article to General Funston demanding to know if the pilots had really uttered such treasonable remarks and if the dispatch had cleared the field censors. Pershing's inspector general descended upon Foulois and the other pilots, all of whom expressed shock that anybody would think they had said such things; they denied ever having given Utecht an interview. Then the IG learned that Utecht had foresightedly not submitted his story for the censor's pencil. Utecht was labeled untrustworthy and his accreditation to the Punitive Expedition was withdrawn, forcing him to leave Mexico. However, the truth was out. Which was probably what the pilots had intended all along.

. . .

Congress passed what it called the Urgent Deficiency Act, which provided $500,000 for the Air Service, part of which was for the purchase of twenty-four new airplanes, but Secretary Baker ruined the hopes of the pilots by pointing out that "There is no intention of buying twenty-four machines outright. The first thing will be to buy eight machines and experiment with them to get the best type we can . . ."

Denied the use of Foulois' planes in the critical role of air intelligence, Pershing could use them only as couriers plying back and forth between Columbus and the various field headquarters serving the cavalry pursuit columns. In this role the Jennies performed surprisingly well; they were not called upon to surmount Chihuahua's rugged peaks, but only to putter along in broad daylight over the wide valleys. They flew as many as nineteen missions in a single day, hampered only by sudden snow or hail squalls, carrying mail and dispatches from one command to another. Even a record of sorts was established—one of the few things Foulois could boast about in his war diary—when Dargue and Gorrell made an aerial sweep from Columbus, beyond Pulpit Pass in Sonora, over Ascensión and back, covering three hundred and fifteen miles in less than five hours. Noted Foulois: "American aeroplane record for non-stop flight with two men."

But the effectiveness of the squadron steadily deteriorated. On April 6 Lieutenant Kilner damaged another of the unit's dwindling supply of aircraft when a wheel sheared off during landing. The plane ground-looped, ripping off a lower wing and snapping several longerons in the fuselage. Kilner climbed out unhurt, but Foulois was forced to condemn the Jenny and have it destroyed, like some faithful horse.

The next day Foulois was ordered to carry dispatches from Pershing to the American consul in Chihuahua City, Marion H. Letcher. The city was then firmly in control of the Carrancistas, but Foulois decided to take no chances: he had the messages duplicated, the originals to be flown in by himself and Lieutenant Dargue, the copies to be carried by Dodd and Carberry in a second airplane. Foulois and Dargue landed north of town at about the same instant that Carberry put his Jenny down on the southern outskirts. Foulois told Dargue to fly the Jenny over there and join Carberry and Dodd while he, Foulois, delivered the pouch to Letcher in person.

Just as Dargue had taken off, Foulois was startled by a sudden burst of rifle fire. Down the road to the city a squad of Carranza soldiers were trying to shoot down the airplane. Foulois ran toward them waving his arms and shouting. The firing stopped, but Foulois was arrested and marched toward town covered by guns. By this time a mob of several hundred men and small boys which had gathered followed Foulois and his captors through the streets of Chihuahua City. Foulois spotted an American civilian standing on the street and called out to him, "Tell Consul Letcher that I have arrived!" Foulois was marched directly to the city jail and kept under guard. While Foulois waited for somebody to come and have him released, he wondered what had happened to the others.

Dargue got away without being hit and landed safely on the other side of town beside the other plane. Then Dodd took the duplicate messages and set out for town to deliver them to Letcher, leaving Dargue and Carberry to guard the aircraft. A large crowd of barefoot natives, Carranza soldiers and officers surrounded the Jennies and began taunting the aviators. The pilots watched help-lessly as civilians reached over with lighted cigarettes and burned holes in the wings of Dargue's Jenny. Knives flashed out, slicing into the fabric, and small boys amused themselves by unscrewing various nuts and bolts from both planes. Menaced by the crowd, Dargue and Carberry wisely decided not to attempt to use their revolvers but to fly the Jennies to safety at an American-owned smelter six miles away.

Carberry got away first, the propeller blast keeping the crowd at bay. But when Dargue started his takeoff run he was followed by a shower of rocks. He had barely gotten into the air when a large piece of the fabric aft of the cockpit ripped away and be-came tangled in the stabilizer. He managed to land the Jenny with-out crashing, but once again found himself surrounded by the mob. Rescue arrived in the form of an armed guard rushed to the scene following the intervention of Letcher, who had also ar-ranged for Foulois' release. The Americans patched up the van-dalized Jennies and flew out of Chihuahua City the next day.

. . .

With American cavalry columns pushing farther into the interior of Chihuahua, Pershing's need for daily, sometimes hourly,
aerial reconnaissance became greater. The squadron moved its
operating bases south with the cavalry four times during the
month of April in an attempt to keep up with the commanding
general's requirements and seeking terrain to match the capabili-
ties of the JN-2s. But the effort was doomed from the start. After
Foulois returned from Chihuahua City on April 8, the 1st Aero
Squadron had only twelve days' usefulness left.

Seek the Devil

At Dublán, Pershing motorized himself by renting a Dodge touring car from one of the remaining Mormon colonists, and during the active phase of the Expedition this car would be his headquarters. He left Dublán for southern Chihuahua, followed in train by correspondents in their own Fords, Hudsons or Dodges bought or leased in El Paso. Sharing a car, Floyd Gibbons of the Chicago *Tribune* and Robert Dunn, a forty-year-old adventurer hired by the New York *Tribune,* followed Pershing to the next field headquarters at the San Geronimo Ranch, one hundred and ten miles from Dublán. Before leaving, Pershing told Gibbons and Dunn, "You can sign for gasoline, but you'll need a better car than that to keep up long, with me." Then one of Pershing's special aides, a tall, hard-looking second lieutenant named George Smith Patton, Jr., handed Gibbons and Dunn a pair of Springfields and told them the rifles were to be used in case of attack. Then Patton got in the car with the general, the chauffeur and Pershing's cook, a Negro named Booker, and started for San Geronimo.

Dunn remembered the journey "over the world's worst ruts, no road whatever, we seldom bettered fifteen miles per hour— through thousand-foot box canyons, over passes with orchids like small pineapple plants on the limbs of oaks. My job was to fill canvas waterbags at the rare water holes and quench our sizzling radiator.

"When we stalled, a small guard deployed to feel out the temper of approaching Mexicans in steeple-crowned straw hats. They drove burros, or carts with ponies—worms visibly eating withers to the bone. Women walked afoot, babies peeking from the slit of a blue *rebozo* [shawl]. As blowouts took longer to fix, Pershing paced back and forth. Once I heard his teeth crunch a lump of sugar.

"Natives hoeing their fields hailed us, but lost their tongues when the general stopped and spoke. Their fear was plainly not of us; but the canyons, they said, were full of Villistas. And though our men were at Bachíniva they would take no messages there—it was too dangerous. They flattered us and wished us well, but had dread of and loyalty for Pancho."

Pershing arrived at San Geronimo on March 29 and waited there for news of contact with the enemy by the columns he had sent out from Dublán. The *New York Times* man, Frank B. Elser, recalled: "It was 7,500 feet up in the Sierras and snowing. The wind-driven sand and snow cut like a knife. The horses stood miserable and dejected at the picket lines like cattle drifting before a blizzard. Pershing had no tent, no table, not even a folding chair. To build a fire and not have it blow away we stretched a sun-dried bull hide between two poles and squatted in its lee. All the available cavalry was afield; the general had as a headquarters guard possibly thirty men. This included scouts, guides and correspondents pecking at tabloid typewriters behind the bull hide.

"We waited, grimy and sand-pestered. The general would crouch with us behind the hide or crawl into his car and censor our despatches which we hoped to get back to the border by horse courier or airplane. As a mainstay we all ate the same thing: hardtack fried in bacon grease."

One of Pershing's civilian guides was an Arizona bronc buster named C. E. Tracy, a lank rawhide of a man who was conspicuous by the red shirt he wore. Elser was present when Tracy contributed the one piece of humor to emerge from the campaign. "Tracy was squatting on his boot heels listening while Pershing explained how the cavalry seemed to have Villa surrounded.

" 'Uh huh,' " replied Tracy. 'Completely surrounded—on one side.' "

There were visitors at San Geronimo. One evening at dusk when the wind had died and the valley was hushed, a rickety wagon approached the camp and halted. Pershing was sitting on an empty box, his chin in his hand, silent. Elser and the other correspondents guessed that Pershing must have been thinking about his lost family; he often fell into these reveries, which none dared disturb. But Pershing looked up and motioned the occupants of the wagon to approach. A Mexican woman, three small children and a quartet of country musicians drew near Pershing's campfire, hats in hand and smiling sheepishly. They had just returned, they said, from playing at a birthday celebration up the valley and wondered if the American general would mind if they played for him. When Pershing said yes, the musicians lined up: a fiddler, a guitar player, a cornetist and "a thin little fellow with a huge bass viol." The *mariachis* began with sad love songs, hearty dance music and then—with some apprehension—launched into the swinging, bouncy strains of "La cucaracha," Pancho Villa's marching song that contains five hundred stanzas of hyperbole boasting of Villa's prowess in battle, in bed and elsewhere. This offended no one, and when the sombrero was passed, headquarters staff contributed a load of silver coins.

It was at San Geronimo that news of Colonel Dodd's successful assault on Guerrero reached Pershing. While planning his next moves, Pershing received another group of visitors, but these were not carrying musical instruments. General Luis Herrera and two hundred smartly uniformed Carranza cavalrymen cautiously circled the camp, then rode boldly in. Pershing rubbed his chin and watched them come. They were well mounted and heavily armed.

Pershing, observing military protocol, sent an orderly to hold the Mexican general's horse as he dismounted. Booker swept a space clean of camp litter and wiped the tops of two empty fuel cans. Pershing indicated one to Herrera, then took a seat himself, and there, mounted on five-gallon gasoline cans in the wind-swept elevated valleys of San Geronimo, the two generals locked eyes. Herrera's troops leaned on their rifles and listened impassively as their commander opened what he thought would be an interrogation. As he talked the correspondents noted that he had "fine, white teeth."

How large a force did the Americans have afield? Herrera began. Where were they going? How far south? How long were they going to stay in Mexico?

Pershing shrugged, then shot back with questions of his own: How many troops did Herrera have, and where was he going, and how many federal troops were actively hunting Villa, and where were they?

Correspondent Elser observed: "Seeing that it was a case of

dog eat dog and that the general was not a garrulous person,
Herrera bowed with Latin courtesy, mounted a pacing roan and
rode away. Stripped of urbanity, his words were warning that the
Americans had gone far enough in Mexico."

Pershing, obdurate, calmly dictated new field orders for a drive
deeper into Chihuahua. General Funston had made good his
promise of reinforcements and sent Pershing a company of engineers, another battalion of the 4th Field Artillery, two battalions
of the 24th Infantry and the 5th Cavalry Regiment. Pershing
stationed the artillery at Dublán, the cavalry at Gibson's Ranch on
the border near Columbus, and the engineers and the infantry
were strung out along the line of communication, which was now
getting very long. Then he pressed Funston to act upon an un-
orthodox, if practical, suggestion for Villa's capture: offer a stag-
gering reward to any Mexican who would lay Villa at Pershing's
doorstep.

Hesitant at first, Funston gave in and endorsed the idea in a
telegram sent to the Adjutant General on April 4: "I am now prepared to recommend that reward of 50,000 dollars be offered for
[Villa's] delivery into the hands of American troops, also that I
be authorized to offer a reward of 5,000 dollars that will lead to
his capture. It is realized that no money is available for this purpose but it is believed that necessary funds can be obtained from
Congress upon request of War Department." But the suggestion
was never acted upon. Pershing realized that if the bandit was to
be caught, his troops would have to do the job themselves without
any help from Villa's countrymen.

Pershing regrouped the 10th, 11th and 13th Cavalry into four
columns and sent them plunging south; the columns parallel, but
miles apart. The 7th Cavalry quickly pulled itself together after
the lively fight at Guerrero and struck to the southwest through
the most rugged part of the Sierras. Pershing was certain that
Villa and his escort would not be making their way eastward—
and certainly not toward the north. Above all, Pershing wanted
speed; with Villa's band flushed and scattered at Guerrero, the
American general wanted the remnants relentlessly hounded.
Movement orders transmitted to regimental and squadron commanders almost always were prefaced by "at once" or "immedi-

ately." Officers who did not share Pershing's sense of urgency
later regretted it.

Of the columns that had originally left Dublán the one led by
Colonel Brown of the 10th Cavalry moved the slowest, although
after marching away from Babícora the terrain east of the mountains offered the fastest going. Brown lost valuable time by day-
long layovers at El Toro and El Oso on the way toward Guerrero,
and this nettled Pershing, especially when he later learned that
Brown had come closer to Villa's main force than any other American unit. Captain W. S. Valentine, one of Brown's troop commanders, commented: "Colonel Brown repeatedly led the 2nd
Squadron in person, and in advance of the advance guard which
followed him in column. I believe that these delays were not due
to personal timidity in any way, but were rather due to a kind of
mental paralysis having its cause in a fear of assuming responsibility to put the squadron into a fight." But a few days after
Dodd's adventure at Guerrero that is exactly what Brown had
to do.

Brown had stopped at the entrance to the pass leading through
the mountains to Guerrero, trying vainly to contact Pershing or
Dodd to find out in which direction they wanted him to move in
pursuit of the scattered Villistas. Bitter winds and sudden snow-
storms seemed to swallow his messengers. He decided to move
toward Guerrero. One horse simply dropped dead from fatigue
while plodding along the rocky trail.

Fifteen miles into the mountains the advance guard approached
the dreary little town of Agua Caliente, a collection of adobe
houses scattered randomly like cow droppings in the folds of the
earth. There were approximately one hundred and fifty Villistas
under General Francisco Beltrán in town, and some of them nervously opened up with rifles, shooting at the Americans from doorways and windows at the optimistic range of three hundred yards.
The men of E Troop dismounted to return the fire while a messenger galloped back to bring up the main body trailing several
hundred yards behind. Captain Albert E. Phillips, the aggressive
commander of the machine-gun troop, galloped forward with his
gunners and deployed the Benét-Merciés on the crest of a hill
overlooking the town. Overhead machine-gun fire to cover the
advance of attacking infantry and dismounted cavalry was a

tactical feature of warfare on the Western Front, and this Phillips planned to use.

Major Charles Young, one of the six Negro officers in the U. S. Army and a hearty, strapping man liked by almost everybody who knew him, came up at the head of F and H Troops preparing for a charge into Agua Caliente. The machine gunners were poised, ready to sweep the town. Then, as Phillips later remembered, "We had four guns lined up ready to fire on a party of 15 or 20 men running for the hill out of town when Colonel Brown came running towards me, waving his hat, and said, 'Don't fire. They may be Carrancistas.'

"That," said Phillips, "stopped the action on the part of the machine-gun troop."

With Brown's detachment were eight Carranza soldiers—three officers and five noncoms—who, in a rare show of co-operation, had come along from the camp at El Toro to help distinguish friend from foe. They rushed forward to observe the flight of armed men from town. Excitedly they shouted to Brown, "They're Villistas! They're Villistas!"

Now Major Young went in with the charge: pistols were drawn, the horses moved forward and yelling broke out all along the line. Young spurred his horse and the line followed. The horses clattered down a steep slope, gaining momentum. Villistas who had been firing at E Troop from behind a rock wall fled the sanctuary and melted away into the woods beyond the town. Young's troopers scrambled after them across ravines, up rocky slopes and through belts of pine trees until late in the afternoon, but without regaining solid contact. "They disappeared in the Camino Real, going in all directions, rendering the tracking of them impossible."

The chance encounter at Agua Caliente cost four Mexicans their lives—one of them a *pacífico* felled by a random round— and an American horse, gut-shot and put out of its misery by a trooper. Brown gathered his command and forged south and east through the mountains, seeking fresh spoor.

Villa continued his painful flight. The narrative of Modesto Nevares traces Villa's movements and reveals his agonies: "He used [potassium permanganate] to bathe his leg and would then wrap it in cotton; place splints on four sides over the cotton and wrap it with bandages. The legs of his pants and drawers were cut away nearly to the hip, leaving his leg bare, and after some days it turned very black for about twelve inches above and below the wound. After that he nearly lost his courage, and at times seemed to be unconscious. He would cry like a child when the wagon jolted and curse me every time I hit a rock. After we passed San Antonio [thirty-five miles southeast of Guerrero] and started south through the mountains, he got so bad that he could not stand the wagon any longer.

"They then made him a litter out of four poles. They wove this litter with a network of rope and placed his bed on it. They detailed sixteen men to carry it in turn, but did not trust it to any but his staff officers and friends. His brother-in-law [Manuel Corral] rode close by him leading Villa's horse, a beautiful roan pinto, with Villa's empty saddle, and he seemed to have personal charge of the patient. He is very strong and lifted Villa around in his arms like a child.

"They had me drive the wagon close behind them and we traveled almost day and night. When they wanted to stop Villa would not stand for it; he was the worst scared man I ever saw. His staff officers procured for him everything dainty that they could find, but he ate very little and seemed to grow gradually weaker day by day. The day after they made the litter was a very bad day. It was snowing hard and the ground was slippery. On going down a steep hill I lost control of the horses and the wagon turned over and was broken." Nevares and a guard were left behind to repair the wagon, but it was beyond fixing. They walked on to Villa's next stopping place, a small ranch called Cienégita. Here, so Nevares learned, violence had been done. Manuel Corral took a fancy to the overseer's wife, and when the man protested, Corral shoved the couple inside a house, shut the door and opened fire with a revolver. The overseer was killed, his wife wounded. The Villistas plundered the hacienda, taking twenty-five hundred silver pesos, and continued south a little ways past San Francisco de Borja to the Rancho Casa Colorado. Here, roughly halfway between Guerrero and Parral, Nevares and a boy named Benito Valdez managed to escape and walk back to El Valle, where the adventure had begun nearly three weeks previously. "When I last saw Villa," said Nevares, "his big, robust, fat face was very thin and pale."*

---

* Here end the recorded movements of Villa's flight south. He may have gone as far as the state of Durango, taking shelter with friends until his wound healed, enabling him to resurface dramatically months later.

.   .   .

Major Frank Tompkins was at Bachíniva, itching to get his provisional squadron of the 13th Cavalry into action. He had not closed with Villistas since the running fight across the border on the morning Columbus was attacked. His brother, Selah, had already distinguished himself at Guerrero; Brown's black 10th was blooded at Agua Caliente; Dodd's 7th was moving swiftly to the west, and Major Robert L. Howze was readying the 11th for a strike down the Sierras to the east. Tompkins pleaded his case in person to Pershing, who was visiting his camp: his small command, two troops, could move faster than others; it could be concealed if necessary when a larger force could find no place to hide; it could live off the country when a larger command would starve, and its very size might tempt the Villistas to engage in a showdown battle. Tompkins told Pershing that he "would head for Parral . . . The history of Villa's bandit days shows that when hard pressed he invariably holes up in the mountains in the vicinity of Parral. He has friends there."

Pershing pondered this; then, to Howze's outrage, he turned over a dozen mules, five days' rations, grain for horses of the 13th and five hundred silver pesos to Tompkins from the 11th's stores. Tompkins left Bachíniva early in the afternoon of April 2. He moved the command at a slow trot, averaging seven miles an hour, and kept this pace as long as the terrain permitted.

Within fifty hours Tompkins covered more than eighty-five miles through rugged, spectacular country. They entered the town of Cusihuiriachic, sited deep in a canyon, and Tompkins found the natives "curious, friendly and accustomed to Americans." Tompkins chatted with the Chief of Arms, Major Reyes Castañada, who told Tompkins that the bulk of the Carranza forces in the Cusi district were camped forty miles south. Castañada offered to let three of his soldiers guide Tompkins' men to General José Cavazos and his garrison troops.

Tompkins reached the outskirts of San Borja the next day. The command paused in a depression where a stream crossed the road. Tompkins dismounted a troop and deployed the riflemen along the crests, "thus retaining military control of the situation in case our Mexican friends should think of indulging in any little act of treachery." Cavazos and his staff rode up under the flying national colors. The general told Tompkins that Villa was dead, buried at Santa Ana, and that he was taking his men there to search for the body. Then Cavazos warned darkly that he could not give Tompkins permission to pass through San Borja, that there might be trouble; he could not answer for the conduct of the townspeople.

"I jollied him up a bit," said Tompkins, "when he finally pulled out a quart of brandy, took a drink, then handed it to me. I took a good long pull and handed it to Lieutenant Ord, who got his share and handed it to other of my officers, all who helped lower the line. When the bottle got back to Cavazos he took one look at it, made some explanation in Spanish that sounded like strong language, and threw the bottle in the brush."

Tompkins moved his column past Cienégita and on to Santa Rosalía de Cuevas, where he paused to shoe mules and horses and buy salmon, eggs and tortillas for his men. Colonel Brown's detachment of the 10th stopped at Santa Rosalía, on its way to Parral via a different route, and while Brown and Tompkins were bent over maps Tompkins noticed that Brown's orderly was eying the chickens that had gathered with the children and the town idlers. He watched the orderly deftly grab one of the chickens, snap its neck and stuff the bird into a saddlebag. "The colonel will have chicken for supper tonight," Tompkins thought, "and won't know where it came from."

The troopers bathed in a nearby stream and beat holes in their already shabby underwear by washing it in the Indian manner of slapping the wet cloth against rocks. "We were ragged," Tompkins observed, "rapidly losing all outward resemblance to regular troops. Our shoes were almost gone and nearly everyone had a beard. We presented a hard-boiled, savage appearance."

Based on what intelligence he had been able to gather, Tompkins calculated that besides the estimated three hundred Villistas in the vicinity, there must be two or three thousand Carranza troops either on his flanks or between him and the United States. By April 9 Tompkins was deep into Chihuahua, less than three days away from Parral, out of touch with Pershing's headquarters and with uncertain communications between his own small column and the others off somewhere to the west. On the morning of the ninth a handful of Carrancistas fired into his column. He chased them for three miles, capturing only horses and mules. The next day Tompkins' column was fording a clear, swift-running river that led out of the ancient town of Concho. There were Villistas there, about twenty-five of them, looting a small factory. They fled at the sight of the approaching cavalry, leaving loot-laden mules behind. Tompkins returned the stolen goods to the owners, and the townspeople were so grateful at having the bandits driven off that they agreed to let Tompkins' men buy such items off the shelves as canvas trousers, work boots, wing-tip shoes and cotton socks.

When the first troop eagerly marched into town to make purchases, women and children ran away screaming; they thought the Americans, like the Villistas before them, were preparing to sack the place. This was smoothed over and the troopers of the 13th returned with durable, if bizarre, additions to standard cavalry issue.

Tompkins then summoned the town chief and told him he wanted "beans cooked for the entire command for breakfast, to be delivered at daylight." The *jefe* complained that there was not a bean in the community, nor anything to cook them in. As Tompkins recalled: "I told him we would have nice hot beans for breakfast or his house would burn." The beans came at the time specified—there was enough, Tompkins said, for breakfast and for lunch as well. Probably the aspect of the visit of the 13th Cavalry most appreciated by the people of Concho was the fact that the canvas pants and the beans were paid for with some of Howze's solid-silver coins.

Late that night a Carrancista emissary, Captain Antonio Mesa, arrived in the cavalry camp on a mule. He was friendly and told Tompkins he would telephone ahead to Parral so that the Americans could be "met, pastured, fed, supplied and a campsite arranged for." The captain assured Tompkins that the people of Parral would receive the Americans with "friendship and hospitality." They could reprovision themselves with drink, food, clothing, forage and even have access to railroad transportation in order to continue the march south toward the Durango border. Tompkins understood that Parral, with a population of some twenty thousand, offered a good hotel and even a decent club— Canadian, he believed. The spirits of the saddle-weary, short-rationed Americans soared at the prospect of reaching this paradise. The next morning Captain Mesa regretfully reported that the telephone lines to Parral were down, but no matter—a courier would be sent ahead on Mesa's saddle mule to get everything ready. He gestured to the beast "so that if [Tompkins] should see this mule again he would know it."

Tompkins put the command on the road to Parral on the morning of April 11. The weather was warm but not hot, the country varied but not forbidding. They reached Santa Cruz de Villegas, thirteen miles from Parral, slept that night beside a clear running stream under a line of cottonwood trees, and moved out at seven the next morning on a good road. As they trotted along, Tompkins and Lieutenant James Ord and Captain Aubrey Lippincott enthusiastically talked about the good time they would have in Parral: the hot baths, the cold drinks, the good food—and who knew what else might be in the offing?

But the reception waiting for them at Parral was not what they had imagined.

Meanwhile, Pershing had moved south and east, to be closer to the columns driving into the heart of Chihuahua. With the correspondents in tow and 1st Aero Squadron trucks loaded with mechanics and spares for Foulois' few remaining Jennies bumping along in the rear, the strange little headquarters group spent three days covering fifty miles to reach Satevó, some sixty-five miles north of Parral. Near Satevó the convoy passed slowly through idling groups of Carranza soldiers on either side of the road. To correspondent Frank Elser, the troops appeared docile and unconcerned. The cars "plunged into a thicket of mesquite, then shots came." Elser said the Carrancistas fired about a hundred rounds in the direction of the convoy, hitting nothing. The mechanics in the trucks returned the fire with Springfields, then the firing stopped and after a few miles more Pershing halted the vehicles in a cornfield outside Satevó. The correspondents rushed up to the general's car and Elser asked, "Were they trying to get you, General?"

"What do you think?" Pershing replied, then had the four automobiles and three trucks deployed in a hollow square, the gaps filled in with bedrolls and packs, just as though they were preparing to stand off an attack by Comanches or Sioux. Pershing ordered shallow trenches dug inside the perimeter. He lined everybody up for rifle and side-arm inspection, and gave Elser hell for having left his Springfield behind at San Geronimo. Satisfied that his command—the truck drivers, mechanics, aides and correspondents—were in a reasonable defense posture, Pershing had his cot moved outside the "barricade" and sat there with one boot off, rubbing his socked foot.

They could see the campfires lighted by the Carranza troops only a quarter of a mile away, but as the evening wore on and no move came from that direction tension lessened. The moon rose, bright and full, and to Elser it seemed to touch the landscape with "luminous and breath-taking beauty." The correspondents took turns holding a smoky kerosene lamp, penciling dispatches about what they guessed had been an attempt to assassinate Pershing. Booker and some of the mechanics were down on their knees in attitudes of prayer, but they were only shooting craps. A few yards away, stretched out on a cot with his boots near at hand, slept the Punitive Expedition's commander.

The newsmen noted that his breathing was deep and regular.

A few minutes before noon on April 12 Tompkins' provisional cavalry squadron entered the town of Parral, more than four hundred miles deep into Mexico. The troopers had beaten some of the dust from their clothes, stuffed in shirttails, shoved their campaign hats forward rakishly, and the Springfields were hidden deep in the leather "bucket" holsters forward on the horses' thinned withers. They contrived to appear both as military and unmenacing as possible on this, their first entry into a major Mexican town since leaving Columbus, now nearly a month behind them. The town baked in the sun. Nobody came out to greet them. Tompkins and the advance guard trotted forward and located a guardhouse near the railroad station. The major asked to be taken to the Chief of Arms at Parral. A few minutes later, having gained permission from the Carranza guard to enter town, Tompkins was ushered into the office of General Ismael Lozano.

The interview went badly. Lozano was agitated, wanted to know what prompted Tompkins to enter Parral. Tompkins told him the invitation had been extended by Captain Mesa, one of Lozano's own officers. Lozano said that he had not heard from Mesa's courier, that he had probably been taken by Villistas. He told Tompkins that Villa was somewhere to the north, probably near

Satevó, that the Americans should never have entered the town. Riled, Tompkins said he would be glad to get out of Parral—but first he needed corn fodder for his horses and a place to camp. He looked out of the window, observing with a commander's pride that his squadron of a hundred men was ranked smartly in the square. Lozano summoned a merchant named Scott, who promised to deliver forage for Tompkins' horses, then hurried away. There was a sudden commotion outside; Tompkins looked out again and saw a mule that was shackled to a heavy cart plunge and rear, then bolt down the street. Tompkins believed that an agitator had purposely stirred the mule to action in order to create confusion in the ranked cavalry. He watched "a big Yank grab the mule by the bit and stop that little act." Tompkins slipped his .45 holster to the front "in anticipation of immediate need."

The merchant did not return, but Lozano nervously pleaded with Tompkins to get his men out of town and said he would lead them to a temporary campsite. When they went outside, Tompkins saw that an ugly crowd had gathered in the square to taunt the Americans. He calmly ordered the squadron to form into columns and move out of Parral. "As we approached the outskirts of town the rabble was pressing pretty close. I dropped back to the rear of the column to keep an eye on the situation. As our rear cleared the plaza the crowd followed us. I noticed a small, compactly built man with a Van Dyke beard who was riding a fine-looking Mexican pony. He seemed to be trying to stir the people to violence. He was well dressed in gray clothes and looked like a German. He rode into the crowd yelling *'Todos! Ahora! Viva México!'* I watched this bird very closely and made up my mind to fill him full of holes should the break come, as he evidently wanted it to." On an impulse, Tompkins wheeled his horse Kingfisher around and shouted "*Viva Villa!*" The crowd paused, then broke into laughter. But they kept coming.

Lozano led the Americans a few hundred yards north of town, then crossed the railroad tracks through a gap between two hills and into a hollow. To Tompkins it seemed as though Lozano had led them into a "perfect cul-de-sac." Now firing broke out at the edge of town: armed civilians were shooting at the American rear guard. Tompkins angrily demanded an explanation. Lozano disclaimed responsibility, said he would ride back and try to stop the shooting. Tompkins saw that Carranza troops were gathering on the crest of a hill a few hundred yards to his right. A Mexican soldier rode up to Tompkins and handed him a message from Lozano urging Tompkins to keep his men moving away from Parral; Lozano admitted that he was unable to control the civilians and could not guarantee the conduct of his own soldiers. Rifles still popped.

Tompkins and Sergeant Jay Richley of M Troop were lying prone in the cinders atop a railway embankment observing the actions of the Mexican troops on the hill. Somebody on the hill began waving a large Mexican flag. Tompkins asked Richley for his rifle, then stood up and began shouting to the Mexicans to go back. The answer was a sudden volley of shots. Tompkins raised the Springfield, hoping to get the man carrying the flag, but it disappeared. Tompkins reached behind him with the rifle and said, "Here, Richley." There was no reply. Richley had been shot through the head.

First Lieutenant Clarence Lininger and eight hand-picked rifle-men were deployed at the tail end of the column. They fired care-fully aimed rounds at the Mexicans on the hill while Tompkins took the point to lead the column out of the cul-de-sac and toward the road leading back to Santa Cruz de Villegas. One hundred-odd Mexicans detached themselves from the group on the hill and rode forward, hoping to flank the American column. Lininger and his men poured fire at them; the Mexicans slowed, then stopped. Lininger's marksmen killed twenty-five Carranza troops and wounded as many.

The column closed up and reached the Santa Cruz road. The Mexican troops came on again, firing at long range. Private Hobart Ledford was knocked out of his saddle by a rifle bullet through the lung. The 13th's medical officer, First Lieutenant Claude W. Cummings, dropped beside Ledford and started dress-ing the wound. Bullets fell all around them, but Cummings coolly finished bandaging Ledford's chest, helped him to his feet and onto a horse. Corporal Benjamin McGehee was struck in the mouth with a Mauser slug. When Cummings had stanched the flow of blood and applied a field dressing, McGehee climbed back on his horse, his face swelling grotesquely.

With the column moving briskly toward Santa Cruz the civilians of Parral fell back, but the mounted Carrancistas pursued the

VILLA RIDES

THE DEFENDERS

Lieutenant Lucas,
the barefoot gunner.

The fight at Columbus was close-in, vicious and unexpected. The famous Benét-Mercié gun seen at left helped stop Villistas advancing down Main Street in an attempt to sack the town. *Above:* 13th Cavalry troopers pose with dead Mexican bandit, killed on U.S. soil during hot pursuit that continued miles deep inside Mexico.

Colonel Herbert J. Slocum was responsible for the town's defense. Board of Inquiry later cleared him of any blame for destruction wrought at Columbus. *Opposite page (top):* The burned area of the town and *(below)* view of charred remains of the hotel. *Below:* troopers stand guard over Villista prisoners.

COLUMBUS

REVOLUTION

President Porfirio Díaz's oppressive rule of Mexico was broken by plotters and popular unrest. *Below:* Francisco Madero *(at right)* is seen in 1910 laying plans for Díaz's overthrow by violence. Guiseppe Garibaldi *(at far left)*, Italian soldier, idealist, schemer.

Revolutionists rolled to battle on top of cattle cars, fought in streets and in ditches to win back a land theirs by heritage.

Right: Swift back-to-the-wall justice was dealt to traitors to the holy cause of land and freedom to the poor, the righteous, the hungry.

CONFRONTATION

Victoriano Huerta

Venustiano Carranza

Above: When President Taft relinquished the White House to Woodrow Wilson, his smile was broadest. Wilson's Mexican headache would be of long duration. General John P. Pershing's first meeting with Villa and Obregón in 1914 *(opposite page, bottom)* gave no hint of troubles to come. *Below:* General Hugh Scott and Villa emerge from a promising conference at Juárez. At Villa's right, Rodolfo "The Butcher" Fierro, Villa's executioner.

VERA CRUZ

The salute that was not forth-
coming from a government
Wilson did not recognize
resulted in bloody fighting,
seizure of a foreign port and
long, costly American occupation. Armed bluejackets
patrolled the streets, often
stopping to search Mexican
citizens at the point of .45
automatics.

NATIONAL ARCHIVES

CHIHUAHUA

The U.S. Army entered a land hostile in every way. Distances across arid wastes were forbidding to man and horse; wind and rain lashed at puny tents; and sturdy Jeffery Quad trucks mired hub-deep in sand.

INFANTRY

Footsloggers' thankless task was guarding lines of communication. Here, tough regulars of the 6th Infantry dismount from trucks to begin wearying sweep of shifting terrain. Only occasionally was there water to cool aching feet.

Apache Scout Es-Ki-Ben-De, a
frightening sight to Villistas.

SCOUTS

Mounted Scout Estes, with friend.

First Sergeant Chicken
(at left) led his Apaches
at Ojos Azules.

AIR POWER

Above all, Pershing needed eyes for the cavalry, but the 1st Aero Squadron was pitifully equipped for its mission. *Above:* Mechanics worked overtime to keep JN-2s in repair. *Right:* Pilots like Ira Rader were eager for action, but endured endless frustrations throughout.

Airborne ! Jenny makes it off the ground for brief sortie. *Below:* Aviators Foulois *(at left)* and Carberry return to camp in wagon after Jenny let them down, hard, on May 15, 1916.

COMMAND AND SEARCH

Lieutenant George S. Patton, Jr. Captain Lewis S. Morey

Pershing's mobile headquarters, an open Dodge, helped him keep track of scattered command. *Below:* 16th Infantry on the move.

Major Charles Young

Major Robert L. Howze

Colonel George A. Dodd

Dodd drove the 7th Cavalry
harder than any other, but the
nagging question remained....

...where was Villa ?

BASE CAMP

Pershing at Colonia Dublán faced political and natural obstacles. Supply trucks bogged down in summer mud, and those left too long were cannibalized down to the frame to keep others going.

Uneasy summer passage of Carranza. Cavalry through base at El Valle; home-built adobe and canvas huts shared by troopers at Dublán; and the luxury of the weekly shower permitted each man while at Namiquipa.

SPOILS

American prisoners taken at Carrizal *(top)*, Villistas who were at Columbus taken in Mexico *(above)* and Colonel Pedro Luján, taken in bed *(below)*.

THE FOX INTACT

Villa lived to fight another day. Below: On January 31, 1917, the last column of the Punitive Expedition left Colonia Dublán and started north for home-and for another war on the distant side of the Atlantic.

Americans by taking to the fields along the road. These areas were divided by thick stone walls four feet high. The Mexican cavalry galloped madly across the fields until they came to a wall; then, instead of jumping, they would dismount and pull the wall to pieces, remount and keep going until they came to the next one. "They finally awoke to the fact that this was getting them nowhere and was wearing them out," Tompkins recalled. "Some of the bolder spirits turned and came for us." Tompkins and Lininger's sharpshooters rode off to the flank and dismounted to snipe at the Mexicans from behind one of the stone fences. Tompkins called the shots with the help of his field glasses. The roar of the Springfields spooked some of the American horses, throwing off the troopers' aim. Disgusted, one of the riflemen turned to Tompkins and ordered, "Hold my horse, Major." Another trooper sounded off, "Here, hold mine too!" Tompkins did as he was told.

A few seconds later one of the horses was shot in the head and began galloping crazily around in the open field. Tompkins jumped up on Kingfisher and started in pursuit. Just as he grabbed the runaway's reins Tompkins himself was shot through the fleshy part of the left shoulder. The wound was not incapacitating and he managed to ride back to the wall, where he told Lininger to pull his men back and rejoin the column. One of the riflemen gained his saddle, only to have his horse shot fore and aft, crashing dead to the ground. Tompkins watched in admiration as Lieutenant Lininger wheeled his horse around and dashed back for a Wild West rescue. Corporal Proffit, the horseless trooper, reached up and grabbed Lininger's elbow on the fly and swung himself up behind the saddle, still holding his rifle in one hand. They galloped back and rejoined the column under fire. Lininger later received the Distinguished Service Medal for this action.

Another D.S.M. was earned by Tompkins' adjutant, Lieutenant James B. Ord. A Mexican rifle bullet clipped off part of Ord's left ear and blood drenched his O.D. shirt. Ord clapped a hand to his head and looked around for the surgeon. He saw instead the lung-shot Private Ledford sway in the saddle, then topple to the ground. Carranza troops were still coming up the road, firing. Ord rode back to where Ledford lay in the dust, picked him up and heaved him into the saddle, then led the horse back to the column. Ledford was too far gone to keep his horse moving forward in concert with the rest of the column, so Ord kept the reins while Tompkins rode behind, urging Ledford to hang on while beating the beast with a rawhide whip. Ledford begged them to leave him behind, but Tompkins gave the trooper a pull from his canteen and told him safety was only five minutes away. Ledford was hit again, the bullet traversing his body from shoulder blade to belt buckle, and he fell, dead before hitting the ground.

The running fight lasted until late in the afternoon. A mile south of Santa Cruz the Carranza troops decided to send in one final charge. Captain Frederick G. Turner was ordered back with twenty men to meet the onslaught astride the road while the rest of the column trotted for sanctuary among the adobe houses in town. "In a minute or two they came," said Tompkins, "without formation, hell-bent-for-election, firing in the air, yelling like fiends out of hell . . . When they were two hundred yards off, Turner's men fired one volley; ponies and Mexicans rolled in the dust, some of those in the rear tripped over the fallen. The others checked their ponies and wheeled and raced for the rear. Our fellows sprang to their feet and gave the enemy a taste of rapid fire. We heard later that we had killed forty-two Mexicans."

Tompkins got his men under cover and counted his casualties. Two were dead, six wounded (including himself) and one man was missing. Seven horses had been killed and sixteen others had been hit. The command was short on rations for the men and forage for the horses. Ammunition was critical. There were no machine guns. Tompkins knew that General Lozano, by summoning the entire garrison at Parral, could muster between five and six hundred troops for an assault against his poor defenses. If Lozano brought up artillery the town could be energetically shelled to bits. The rolling country here offered no place to hide; Tompkins was in a more dangerous situation than Villa's men had been in at Guerrero. He dispatched three troopers to the north to seek help, then began sweeping the southern approaches to the town with field glasses.

Lozano had halted his men a half mile from town, trying to decide what to do next. Lying on the flat roof of one of the adobe houses was Captain Lippincott, described by Tompkins as "one of the best rifle shots in our army." Through his own glasses Lippincott watched as the Mexican troops deployed in a long skirmish line. He observed the Carranza officers mounted on horses wave their arms forward. The Mexicans were coming for Santa Cruz de Villegas. Lippincott put down his glasses and picked up a Springfield. He wet a finger and poked it into the air, estimating windage and transferring the information to the rear leaf sight with a few clicks of the windage knob. Allowing for the hot, rising air from the desert floor, he set the elevation on the sight, estimating the range at eight hundred yards. Then he settled into the classic prone firing position, with the leather sling tight against the outside of his left wrist and inside the left bicep. He sighted on one of the mounted figures, the tiny target almost covered by the front bead sight, and gently squeezed the trigger. The Springfield roared, Lippincott's ears rang, and the Mexican rider toppled from the saddle. Lippincott stood up and shouted down to Tompkins, "I got one, Major! I got one at eight hundred yards!" It was incredible shooting, and the Mexicans, to whom the pistol is a more familiar weapon, pulled back out of what they hoped was the range of the gringo's rifle.

A little later a Mexican courier entered the town under a flag of truce and handed Tompkins a message from Lozano: "I have just arrived at this camp, and I have been able to sustain my troops a little bit. I supplicate you to leave immediately and not bring on hostilities of any kind. If on the contrary, I shall be obliged to charge the greatest part of my forces. I pray you then to retire as soon as possible, and if you wish to confer, send me word. If it is that you leave, send me word by the bearer so that I can withdraw my soldiers."

Tompkins, who was eager to spar for time, sent back a reply in Spanish pointing out that the Americans had come to Mexico as friends, that it was the Mexicans who had started the shooting, that Lozano's troops had followed him for five leagues "firing at every opportunity." Tompkins concluded by saying he would continue to the north if Lozano could guarantee that the Americans would not be molested; otherwise, they would stay in Santa Cruz and await reinforcements.

Tompkins hoped there would be a whole series of notes exchanged until reinforcements arrived. Otherwise he would face the same decision William Barrett Travis had had to make almost exactly eighty years previously, and Tompkins did not want another Alamo.

The three cavalrymen sent out by Tompkins struck north across flat, deserted country, but making poor time because their mounts had been pushed hard and poorly fed in the past few days. It took them two hours to cover eight miles, and they were so anxiety-ridden at being alone in what was demonstrably hostile country that they rode by the rear guard of Colonel Brown's 10th Cavalry without seeing it. However, they were seen by Captain George Brydges Rodney, who observed that the troopers were "riding like John Gilpin." He hailed them from a distance with no response, but stopped them by firing a shot over their heads. To Rodney, the men of the 13th seemed "scared almost beyond speech." He thought they were running away, and after hearing about Tompkins at Santa Cruz he sent them forward to report to the colonel.

Brown ordered Major Charles Young to get on the road to Santa Cruz with a squadron; the rest of the 10th and the packtrain with food, forage and ammunition would follow in their wake. Young had the bugler sound Boots and Saddles and within ten minutes the relief squadron was galloping toward Santa Cruz. They pulled into town an hour later. Tompkins, nursing his wounded shoulder and favoring a leg injured when he fell into a trench, hobbled out to greet his saviors. He shouted, "I could kiss every one of you!"

Young grinned and replied, "Hello, Tompkins! You can start in on me right now."

8

Penelope's Web

Pershing was still camped in the cornfield near Satevó when the clash at Parral occurred, but it was two days before the news reached him in a roundabout way. He was cut off from direct communications with his flying columns, from the base at Columbus and from General Funston in San Antonio; he now had to depend upon Foulois and his handful of fading Jennies to track the movements of his cavalry, to deliver messages to his subordinates and to deliver telegrams to be wired to the United States via the consul in Chihuahua City, Marion Letcher. Chihuahua City is forty miles north of Satevó, but the terrain here is reasonably flat and there is an easy pass between the mountains guarding the approaches to the town from the south. All that was needed was for the Jennies to hold together, and Pershing would be able to communicate with his superiors.

The first mission was flown from Satevó on April 12, the day of Tompkins' fight. Foulois ordered Lieutenant Carleton G. Chapman to make a reconnaissance flight to Parral to bring back news of the 13th Cavalry. Chapman successfully negotiated a takeoff, but he did not reach Parral. En route the heat-warped propeller snapped a blade and the resulting uneven torque nearly tore the engine from its mountings. By strenuously applying full opposite aileron, Chapman managed to fight the airplane down to a landing without injury to himself, but it was Number 53's last flight.

Foulois and Joseph Carberry flew to Chihuahua City the next day, and this time the pilots were not threatened by a mob. It was here that Letcher told them about the fight at Parral. More ominous was his report that General Luis Gutiérrez, the Military Governor of the state of Chihuahua, was demanding that Pershing remove every American soldier from his district so that there could be no further hostile encounters between American and Mexican regulars. Foulois and Carberry hastened back to Satevó early the next morning with the news.

Pershing was furious. The correspondents had never seen him so angry. "He was mad as hell," Elser reported. "Off flew the censor lid," said Robert Dunn. " 'Nothing, now,' said Pershing, 'should be kept from the public. You can go the limit.' " Pershing even lent his own editorial hand to a dispatch Dunn was writing for the New York *Tribune*. "When I called the Parral trap 'an ambuscade,' " said Dunn, "Pershing leaned over my machine on the running board to write in the word 'treachery.' "

Pershing sent two of his staff officers, Captain William O. Reed of the 6th Cavalry and First Lieutenant James Lawton Collins,* 11th Cavalry, in automobiles to Santa Cruz de Villegas (they were accompanied by correspondents) to get full details of the fight and of Tompkins' situation. They found the camp filled with talk of war. The atmosphere was touched with poignancy because of the fresh graves nearby: the bodies of Ledford and Richley had been recovered (one wonders why they had been abandoned in the first place) and buried just near the camp. Ledford's body, stripped by the Mexicans of shoes, pants, shirt and valuables, had been found on the road where he had fallen. The corpse was guarded by a nondescript white dog which had taken up with the 13th on the march to Parral and which Ledford had befriended until his death.

Colonel Brown told Reed that he believed Pershing should come to Santa Cruz in person because the fight at Parral had "changed the entire character of the campaign." The officers discussed the advisability of establishing a subbase north of Parral so that the gathering columns could be better supplied for a thrust down to the border of Chihuahua and even into Durango. Although Villa was wounded, he was not dead; in any event, a new base farther south was vital if Carranza decided to declare war on President

* Later, "Lightning Joe" Collins, lieutenant general commanding the U. S. Army VII Corps in the European theater of operations during World War II. Collins spearheaded the First Army's drive to the Rhine in March 1945.

Wilson, or the other way around. Before Reed and Collins and the correspondents climbed into the cars for the long night ride back to Satevó, the Chicago *Tribune's* enterprising correspondent, Floyd Gibbons, traded Major Tompkins a side of bacon, brought along for the purpose, for Tompkins' account of his combat with the Carrancistas.

Pershing had not the slightest intention of withdrawing a single soldier from Chihuahua; in fact, he was already going over in his own mind a lengthy message to Funston detailing the status and future needs of the Punitive Expedition, including a request for added reinforcements. Firmly convinced that Tompkins had not been at fault, Pershing dictated a stiff note to General Gutiérrez demanding that he arrest and punish those responsible for killing and wounding Americans at Parral. He told Foulois to return to Chihuahua City and deliver his message for Gutiérrez to Consul Letcher for action. Earlier that morning Foulois had been uneasy about the hostile atmosphere in the city, and in order to avoid another overt demonstration he decided to make the journey back by car, followed by one of the squadron trucks loaded with fourteen armed men. The convoy reached the city without incident, but Foulois ordered the truck secreted on the outskirts of town while he and Corporal Arthur Westermark proceeded to the consulate by themselves in the sedan. Pershing's angry demand startled Letcher, who said he would defer action until he could get it cleared through Secretary of State Lansing.

Pershing realized that he could not control this potentially explosive new situation from the running board of his Dodge in the middle of an isolated cornfield. His "front" was now more than a hundred miles wide, from Santa Cruz de Villegas westward to the other side of the Sierra Madre Occidental, and stretched more than four hundred miles to the rear. Intelligence reports indicated that there were at least fifteen thousand Carranza regulars in the region of Monterrey, in the state of Nuevo León, and General Obregón could have them astride Pershing's line of communication within twenty-four hours. Although the hunt for Villa could be conducted from his mobile headquarters, Pershing knew that the contingency of war with Carranza would require a more protected base nearer the border, one offering better forage than the barren regions south of Satevó. On April 16 Pershing left Satevó and started back to Namiquipa.

*Times*man Frank Elser recalled: "We drove all day and all night. Pershing sat grim and silent, his big frame taking the jounces of the rocky trails. He was suffering from indigestion. At dawn, Sunday, we fetched up at Namiquipa. As we neared the place we could hear men's voices singing. Presently over a rise in the road a column of marching troops swung into view. They were the 6th and 16th Infantry. Behind them came the guns and ammunition carts of the 4th Field Artillery. As the men recognized Pershing they broke into a cheer. My throat hurt; we knew what their exultant thought was. They had hiked miles until their dogs hurt, and at last they were going to see action. It was war and the cavalry wasn't going to hog it all. Pershing's lips went into a tight smile, and he saluted."

That evening Elser drafted a story for the *Times,* which Pershing said he could send over the Signal Corps wireless. First Pershing read what Elser had to say: "The United States Punitive Expedition directed against Pancho Villa and his followers has come to a standstill. Whether the halt is to be permanent or not depends on circumstances beyond the control of General Pershing. But from a military standpoint he has for the time being come to the end of his line . . ."

Elser observed that "He stroked his chin, pencil raised. A stubborn look invaded his face."

"Is this your deduction?" Pershing asked.

Elser nodded.

"Then send it," Pershing said.

It was not Pershing's deduction, but he had sober and realistic thoughts concerning the further pursuit of Villa, wherever he was, and for Funston's benefit he presented a forecast of what lay ahead in a long memorandum. "It is very probable," he wrote, "that the real object of our mission to Mexico can only be attained after an arduous campaign of considerable length. It is possible that the truth of this statement may not be fully appreciated. But it should be realized that the country through which our cavalry is now operating is unfamiliar to every member of our command; very few white men of any class know it in the interior; it is sparsely settled by ignorant people usually unreliable and almost wholly terrorized by roving bands of robbers and bandits." Pershing pointed out that "our various forces have had to rely for their guidance upon the inaccurate knowledge of untried American employees, or else upon the uncertain information of frightened or unwilling natives. Thus have well laid plans often miscarried and the goal has moved further and further into the future." Pershing stressed the fact that Villa knew every inch of Chihuahua's terrain, took fresh horses when he needed them, was able to travel light and "thus has had the advantage since the end of the first twenty-four hours after the Columbus raid occurred."

He stipulated five points upon which the success of the expedition rested: continued occupation of as many districts in Chihuahua as possible; securing of reliable native informants; total reconnaissance of the search area; expanded and stabilized lines of supply; and the guarantee of enough men and animals to occupy territory and to keep columns moving in pursuit.

The logistical problem was becoming acute. There were more than six thousand horses to be fed and the horses alone required a minimum of sixty thousand pounds of grain and eighty-four thousand pounds of hay daily. But the horses seldom received these rations. When troop commanders managed to buy corn, each trooper had to spread a blanket on the ground and dump out the ration, scattering the kernels, then get down on his knees and painstakingly search out and throw away pebbles that were inevitably mixed in; once a horse bit into a stone he would refuse that particular nose bag and the whole ration had to be thrown away. Then, many horses began to refuse corn altogether and became so skinny that the McClellan saddle no longer fit but rubbed bloody sores along the rear part of the withers. When Carranza stopped the trains, rations for man and beast dwindled to 60 percent of what the expedition required. There were only one hundred and sixty-two White and Jeffery Quad trucks plying back and forth between Columbus and the forward base at Namiquipa. Pershing urged Funston to get him more trucks.

In Washington General Hugh Scott took direct action in order to alleviate John Pershing's pressing problem. The Chief of Staff was furious at Carranza for finally denying the use of Mexican rails. He stormed into the State Department offices and said, "If Carranza got in my way I would run over him." But State told him he could not do that, and anyway, the supply of Pershing's men was not the State Department's affair. Scott was now madder at his own diplomats than he was at Carranza. "I was so angry with such callousness about our troops four hundred miles south in

Mexico," he said, "I could hardly find my way back to my office. I was so appalled at the inevitable consequences to our men if not supplied with food and ammunition promptly that I could have burned down the State Department with everybody in it."

He picked up the phone and shouted into the receiver at General Sharpe, the Quartermaster General, "Have you got enough trucks to supply General Pershing from Columbus with food, clothing and ammunition?"

"No, General," Sharpe replied.

"How much would it cost to get them?" Scott demanded.

"Four hundred and fifty thousand dollars, General."

"Have you got the money?"

"No, General."

"Then send right out and buy these trucks, with the necessary traveling garages and mechanics. Put a chauffeur on every truck and send them by express to Columbus and start food and ammunition to Pershing at the earliest possible moment."

Then Scott confronted Secretary of War Baker: "You will have to use your good offices with the President, Mr. Secretary, to keep me out of jail. I have just expended four hundred and fifty thousand dollars of public money that has not been appropriated by Congress."

"Ho!" Baker replied. "That's nothing. If anybody goes to jail I'll be the man—I'll go to jail for everybody."

Scott's daring move raised the total of one-and-a-half-ton trucks available to supply Pershing to two hundred and seventy. They streamed back and forth along the rutted "Lincoln Junior Highway," more than one hundred and seventy-five miles long, between the border and Namiquipa at every hour day and night, seven days a week. The road was Pershing's *Voie sacrée*, as vital to him as was the Sacred Way to the French troops engaged in the titanic battle for Verdun then raging. There was never a problem in recruiting drivers; soldiers preferred to jounce their kidneys to hiking under the Mexican sun, but there were problems with repair in the desert. Truck-company commanders quickly learned that it was never safe to leave vehicles stranded for any length of time while waiting for new parts to be sent out from Columbus. Captain Francis H. Pope left a disabled truck by the side of the road at El Valle, and when he returned a week later with a new part he found that "Our truck looked like one of the gaunt skeletons of the cattle so often seen on the desert. Nothing was left but the frame and the headlight, which latter had been installed on the roof of the adobe guardhouse."

Putting additional trucks on the line would help obviate another vexing problem faced by the cavalry columns whose commanders had largely been using vouchers to buy occasional supplies from Mexican merchants who were willing to sell. Among other things, there was a critical shortage of cash in the expedition; nobody had been paid since leaving Columbus. Colonel Brown, in order to feed his 10th Cavalry troopers, often wrote out personal checks for such items as flour, coffee, bread and sugar. Once, early in April, Brown had cashed a check for $1,100 at the American-owned Cusi Mining Company to buy goods, and from what was left over he lent $10 to every officer in the regiment for pocket money. In three weeks, Brown contributed $1,453 out of his own account for the welfare of his command.

Mexicans only grudgingly accepted vouchers from the Army. One citizen of Cusihuiriachic explained, "Now, you buy a cow from a man who lives a hundred miles from any railroad. Even if that railroad were operating it would be six months before he could get his mail. You take that cow and you kill it and you give a receipt. He mails that receipt to the Quartermaster in San Antonio, Texas. It takes maybe six months for it to get there, if it gets there at all. When the Quartermaster gets it he cannot pay for it; he returns duplicate vouchers to be signed. They take another six months to reach the man, and then he cannot write nor can he read English. But if he can do all these things and signs in the proper place—even then he gets, about eighteen months later, a check he cannot cash."

In the solitude of his tent at Namiquipa, Pershing sat down and summed up his frustrations in a letter to an old friend in Washington, General H. H. Crowder. "I feel just a little bit like a man looking for a needle in a haystack with an armed guard standing over the stack forbidding you to look in the hay . . . From my own observations," Pershing added, "I do not believe these people can ever establish a government among themselves that will stand. Carranza has no more control over local commanders or of states or municipalities than if he lived in London."

Adding to Pershing's woes was the total disintegration of the 1st Aero Squadron. Foulois had recently received a new Brock automatic aerial camera, a machine that sequenced itself to make exposures at predetermined intervals. Pershing, looking ahead to when he might need accurate information about the approaches to Chihuahua City for his cavalry, infantry and artillery, ordered Foulois to put the new camera to use mapping photographically hundreds of square miles of Carranza-held terrain. On the morning of April 19 Lieutenants Herbert Dargue and Robert Willis took off and flew northward, leisurely taking photographs. An hour or so later the Jenny was over the hills twenty miles northwest of Chihuahua City. The engine faltered, then died. With only the noise of the wind whistling in the wires for solace, Dargue frantically looked around for a level place to land. There was none, and he did not have the altitude to enable him to glide to the wide valley floor on his right. He was forced to crash-land in the forested hills below and the Jenny was torn to pieces, coming to rest upside down. Dargue crawled out unhurt and began pulling away the tangle of wood, wire and fabric to get at Willis, who was pinned underneath the wreckage. He hauled Willis to his feet and helped stanch the blood flowing from an ugly scalp wound. Willis complained of a painfully bruised ankle, but said that he would be able to walk.

The new camera was smashed, the plates ruined. The aviators decided to burn what was left of the airplane so as to leave nothing of value to the Mexicans. They set fire to the highly flammable doped fabric and stepped back. The wreckage blazed hotly, flames leaped out on all sides. To the fliers' surprise the surrounding green but dry trees caught fire, and crackling sheets of flame shot into the air. Dargue and Willis stumbled down the hill to escape from what an official report later described as "one of the largest forest fires in Mexico. The mountains burned for fully forty miles."

Like Gorrell before them, the two pilots started walking home, to San Antonio de los Arenales, more than forty miles away. With the help of a commandeered mule they arrived at base, gaunt, parched and burned from the sun, two days later. They were driven to Namiquipa, but found that Pershing had sent the entire squadron back to Columbus, hopefully to refit and start all over again.

. . .

Pershing's first appraisal of the future of the Punitive Expedition had caused concern in the War Department, and in the State Department as well. The Expedition was straining at every seam. But what Pershing next proposed escalated concern to shock. "In order to prosecute our mission with any promise of success it," Pershing wired to Funston "is therefore absolutely necessary for us to assume complete possession, for time being, of country through which we must operate; and establish control of railroads as means of supplying forces required. Therefore recommend immediate capture by this command of City and State of Chihuahua, also the seizure of all railroads therein."

Pershing's drastic proposal of military takeover of one of Mexico's largest and richest states in order to lay hands on one man, the bandit Villa, would mean immediate all-out war with Carranza's de facto government. President Wilson and Secretary of War Baker reacted with alarm; mobilization and embroilment in war were the last things they wanted. They summoned Hugh Scott and told him to go down and get things straightened out with Pershing's boss, Funston. The general packed his bags and took the train for San Antonio.

In San Antonio's torpid atmosphere of late spring, far from Pershing's immediate tactical problems and Washington's political machinations, Scott and Funston calmly reviewed all that had preceded, all that could possibly arise in the future. On April 22 the Chief of Staff telegraphed his conclusions to Baker. One course open, said Scott, was to act upon Pershing's latest recommendation and drive straight through by force, taking over the railroads. But, Scott pointed out, "this will not result in the capture of Villa, who can go clear to Yucatán." An alternative suggested by Scott would be for Pershing to concentrate his forces far to the north, near Nueva Casas Grandes. Here there was water and forage, and the troops would be in a position to protect the Mormon colonists still left at Colonia Dublán. "These forces," Scott said, "can be maintained here indefinitely as an incentive to Carranza forces to kill or capture Villa." Scott's third option was to withdraw the expedition altogether. His final paragraph warned that the approach of the rainy season would render the Columbus road impassable, that it would be necessary for the Army to make use of the Mexican Northwestern Railway from Juárez to Casas Grandes. Scott recommended the second option.

Baker rushed the telegram to Wilson, who immediately seized upon Scott's compromise solution. Peremptory withdrawal would seem disgraceful; driving forward would mean war. Wilson told Baker to have Scott issue the necessary orders.

On the day that Scott's telegram was received in Washington, Dodd's four troops of the 7th Cavalry again went into action with Villistas. Dodd had marched hard to reach the far side of the Sierras after Guerrero, and by late afternoon on April 22 his command—15 officers and 175 troopers—was poised on the summit of a crenelated hill overlooking the squalid little town of Tomóchic, an ancient village containing a dozen or so adobe buildings inhabited by a mixed population of Mexicans and Tarahumara Indians. Tomóchic is located in a small pocket opening into the valley of the Tomóchic River, an insignificant stream dwarfed by the surrounding mountains clothed with pines, rugged peaks that reach more than 9,000 feet into the sky. Dodd had been at Yoquivo the previous day, where he learned that approximately two hundred Villistas under the command of Candelario Cervantes had been there and left for Tomóchic. Another grueling night march at great altitude in the cold that tired the horses and "left the men's legs numb from the knees down" (as Captain Samuel F. Dallam remembered it) and Dodd was astride the valley. Dodd's men, scarcely fed and spending prodigiously of their physical reserves, were partially hypoxic; all of them had difficulty breathing in enough of the rarefied air, many of them complained of a pounding headache and not a few suffered from nosebleeds.

At three o'clock in the afternoon Dodd started them down the winding trail that led to Tomóchic. The troop commanders made skillful use of the terrain, keeping the file of horsemen hidden in defilade by ridges until they had descended three thousand feet to the level of the town. A machine-gun squad was dropped off on the crest of the lowest ridge eight hundred yards from the center of town to provide a base of fire. The rest of the command went on another half mile to debouch into a grassy plain only a thousand yards from Tomóchic.

It was four-thirty. Dodd ordered the charge. Tired horses were urged into a gallop through the grass, then they stumbled down a steep bank and splashed into the riverbed, forced upward by shouts and spurrings onto the rocky shelf and out of the river and onto level ground again to sweep forward. Rifles cracked from the slopes surrounding the town, but the fire was inaccurate and the first troopers plunged into Tomóchic without casualty. As at Guerrero, the Villistas were fleeing into the hills in scattered groups. Some were mounted, some were on foot. Some ran north, some ran south and some ran east.

Dodd observed a large herd of horses milling around in the valley a mile north of town; they seemed to Dodd to be cavalry. He sent two troops galloping off in that direction, to the delight of Cervantes, who knew what Dodd did not: the horses were only broodmares, kicking up in fright at the unaccustomed sounds of combat.

There was firing everywhere. Dodd's troops inside the town dismounted and began killing Villistas scrambling for safety north and south of the river; these were scattered small groups which were most exposed. Cervantes saw that the American force was split in two and he managed to draw together the bulk of his men who had sought refuge on the more precipitous eastern ridges, getting them to take cover behind rocks and thick trunks of pine and oak. The Mexicans held the high ground, and with the first surge of panic gone, their fire began to tell. Saddler Ralph A. Ray was shot in the head and died instantly. Private Oliver Bonshee took a rifle bullet in the middle and lived three hours with his stomach on fire before he died. Private Thomas Henry was shot through his right ankle. A buddy of his from L Troop, Private August A. Hanna, left cover and ran crouching over to Henry, picked him up and slung him over his shoulder. He staggered six hundred yards across open ground with bullets cracking all around him to reach the shelter of an adobe hut.

A grass knoll sixty feet high just north of the town enabled Dodd's split command to regain the initiative. Major Edwin B. Winans led E Troop through fire to reach the knoll, and once there, his troopers began to return the Mexican fire with Springfields. Sergeant H. H. Rogers came forward with a machine-gun squad, took cover at the corner of an adobe house to the right of the knoll and began raking the eastern ridges with sustained fire; the Benét-Mercié was running sweetly and did not jam. Dodd and Headquarters Company rode up to the knoll to add weight to the shelling being directed from there. With a fire base established, Dodd ordered elements forward to clean out the sniper pockets scattered along the lower parts of the ridge. Private William F. Matthias was ordered to leave the knoll and carry the movement orders to troopers off on the left bank. Halfway to his destination he was shot in the side and rolled to the ground. Sergeant Charley Levi jumped up and ran across open ground and helped Matthias to his feet. Levi was handicapped by the Springfield he carried in his right hand, but a Mauser bullet slammed into the stock and knocked it loose from his grasp. He let it go and managed to get Matthias to cover before returning for the rifle. The rear sight was shot away, and he fired over the front sight into the ridge.

Sergeant P. B. Rogers thought he saw rifle flashes coming from the mouth of a cave halfway up the ridge. Alone he scrambled up the side of the hill armed only with a .45 automatic pistol. Bullets from the Villistas and from the machine gun spattered all around him, but moving low, crablike, he reached the cave unhurt. He plunged into the dark interior and emptied the clip, then ran outside again and took cover. No Mexicans came out.

Lieutenant Horace M. Hickham led a handful of dismounted men up the hill, flushing and killing Villista riflemen. With his immediate area cleared, Hickham looked around to see what he could do next. As a mounted trooper rode by, Hickham grabbed a stirrup strap and propelled himself along the ground to follow the trooper in his solitary charge up a gentler portion of the hill. Both men went forward firing.

The Mexican fire slackened, then died. The sun dropped behind the mountains and it grew dark very suddenly. Night pursuit across that steep ridge was not feasible, so Dodd reassembled his force, posted sentries, saw to his wounded and told the men of the 7th to be prepared to resume action at daybreak. Dawn came, but the ridge was empty. Cervantes and the survivors had melted away.

Taking their dead, the 7th marched out of Tomóchic and moved westward, stopping at Miñaca, below Guerrero, forty miles away. There Ray and Bonshee were buried. About thirty Villistas had been killed at Tomóchic, another twenty-five wounded. Cervantes managed to take out some of his wounded with him, but others had crawled into brush or ditches and were left behind. The troopers of the 7th later learned what happened to the wounded that Cervantes had abandoned.

When the combatants departed, the Tarahumaras emerged from hiding and poked around the dead and wounded Mexicans. These Indians live in unimaginable poverty and squalor; they took from the Villistas whatever was of value. Typhoid-ridden themselves, the Tarahumaras were in no way able to care for the Villistas lying caked with blood and moaning for water. So they simply dragged them all together, the dead and the dying, poured pitch over them and set them afire. It was Easter Sunday.

New overtures were made to Carranza by the State Department, and his malignant attitude turned benign long enough for him to agree to Wilson's proposal for a meeting between Generals Scott, Funston and Obregón, who was now Carranza's Minister of War, at a place of the Mexicans' own choosing. The future of the Punitive Expedition was in jeopardy and Wilson believed that Scott, who had enjoyed such success in years past in personal confrontations with Villa, could bend Obregón to accept Wilson's preference for neither war nor withdrawal. In San Antonio on April 26 Scott and Funston received Wilson's instructions.

The President wanted General Obregón to understand that the United States "earnestly desires to avoid anything which has the appearance of intervention in the domestic affairs of the Republic of Mexico." Wilson desired co-operation between Pershing's forces and the Constitutionalist regulars in apprehending Villa. "So long as he remains at large," Wilson pointed out, "and is able to mislead numbers of his fellow citizens into attacks like that at Columbus, the danger exists of the American public opinion being irritated to the point of requiring general intervention. For, of course, depredations on American soil and the loss of lives of American citizens cannot be tolerated." Wilson thought it might be a good move if Scott suggested to Obregón that the de facto troops launch a general offensive against Villa, driving his band to the north where Pershing would be waiting to pounce. Wilson foresaw the possibility that Obregón might rule out co-operation and insist upon immediate withdrawal of Pershing's men. In that case, said the President, Scott should stall for time by telling Obregón that such a decision would have to be handled by the diplomats. Scott and Funston left for El Paso that night.

The confrontation began on the afternoon of April 30 inside the dreary gray concrete customs building at the Mexican end of the bridge connecting El Paso and Juárez. Obregón, in deference to the feelings of the Mexican public, had insisted that the meeting be held on native ground, a point Scott made no issue of. Scott explained all that was in Wilson's letter of instructions, but Obregón politely waved aside the President's suggestions and bore down on what was to him the main issue: when was Pershing going to get out of Mexico? Villa, he said, was dead—but even if he were alive he would be "innocuous." Two hundred of his followers had been killed, the rest were dispersed and "there is no one now to seek for." Scott returned to the point of co-operation, of using the railroads to supply Pershing so that his mission could be expeditiously completed. Obregón again asked for a date to be set for withdrawal. The talk seesawed back and forth for two hours.

"We evidently came to discuss one thing, Obregón another," Scott thought. Funston blew up; leaping to his full height of five and a half feet, he waved his hands and slammed his fist on the conference table. As Scott described it, "General Funston allowed his real sentiments to be expressed so brusquely that he lost his influence in the conference. The emphatic actions that accompanied his words were seen through the window by Mexican newspapermen, whose interpretations of the matter were broadcast all over Mexico. General Funston thought it best for him not to attend any more." Scott cooled the atmosphere heated by Funston's outburst by suggesting an adjournment. The conference could be resumed, he said, when he received word from Washington on the question of troop withdrawal. Then he invited Obregón to dine that evening in the American generals' private car parked on a siding in the El Paso yards. Scott found Obregón amicable, but adamant.

The next morning Funston received a telegram from Colonel W. S. Scott, commander of the garrison at Douglas, Arizona. The contents were alarming. Somehow Scott had managed to lay hands on orders sent by Carranza to General Arnulfo Gómez. Translated the orders read: "Dispose your troops so that they shall be in a position [to] cut off American expeditionary forces now in Chihuahua. The action must be sudden and will take place after the Scott-Obregón conference. It will make no difference what else may be decided upon in conference; unless there is absolute with-drawal of American troops the above plans will be carried out. The Sonora troops will be assisted by the troops in Chihuahua." Funston immediately wired a copy of the Carranza orders to Secretary of War Baker. Hardly had the wire cleared when another message arrived for Funston, this time from Pershing, who relayed dated but significant intelligence that would have a bearing on the Juárez conference when it resumed. Reports from his field commanders cited "instances not hitherto reported and give absolute proof of deliberate and premeditated intention on part of Carranza forces from first to prevent success of this expedition."

Pershing was especially incensed at what had happened to Major Robert Howze and his detachment of 11th Cavalry during their sweep down the eastern slopes of the Sierra Madre. Near the village of San José del Sitio, only fifty miles north of Parral, Howze's advance guard of eight troopers rounded a point and came face to face with approximately two hundred mounted Carrancistas commanded by General José Cavazos, the Mexican officer whose brandy Frank Tompkins had helped drink three days earlier. Leading the American advance guard was Lieutenant S. M. Williams, who recalled: "Cavazos was in an ugly mood, and he evidently thought he had come upon a very small force of our troops, as we were strung out and only the advance guard was in sight at the time. His force took up a gallop and started for us. I put the advance guard in an arroyo and prepared for action. We would have opened fire had we not seen Major Howze dash ahead of us, waving his hat. His black sweater attracted our attention immediately, otherwise an engagement would have been inevitable."

When all four troops of the 11th Cavalry closed up on Howze, Carranza tempers cooled rapidly and after a brief parley the Americans trotted on, glared at by the Carrancistas. "We would have wiped them out," commented Williams.

General Hugh Scott wired his superiors in Washington saying that the next time he and Obregón talked he expected "a flat ultimatum to get out of Mexico at once or take the consequences," adding that if such a demand were acceded to it would mean "a complete victory for Mexicans over the United States in the eyes of the Mexican people already arrogant and encourage further aggression." What, Scott asked, did Washington wish him to do?

Wilson replied to Scott's telegram only a few hours later: "This Government cannot withdraw troops from Mexico until it is satisfied that danger to our people on the border is removed." The President went on to say that if Obregón remained stubborn and a break seemed inevitable, Scott should say to him frankly that he believed Pershing's troops would be withdrawn to a place where they could protect the border until the danger of further raids had passed. Scott should stress the fact that Pershing's men would scrupulously respect the dignity of the Mexican people and its de facto government, but if the American troops were attacked, or their operations obstructed, the responsibility for the inevitable grave consequences would rest upon Obregón. "On no account give excuse for attack," the President warned, "but if attacked, take all necessary steps to make answer decisive and speedy."

In El Paso was an American acquaintance of Scott's, a man with vested interests in the outcome of the conference. He was A. J. McQuatters, vice-president of the Alvarado Mining Company located near Parral. McQuatters, who was reported to be paying protection money to Carranza officials to keep the mine safely operating, would have preferred outright intervention and total occupation of Chihuahua by the U. S. Army, but failing that, he wanted no inconclusive war that would result in either the wrecking of the mine or its appropriation by the Constitutionalist government; he wanted things to go smoothly between Scott and Obregón.

McQuatters rented a large room at the Paso del Norte Hotel in El Paso and asked Obregón to confer there privately with Scott, man to man. Obregón agreed, and so did Scott, who pointed out that "delicate negotiations cannot be successful in a crowd." Scott was distressed at the attention the conference was drawing, especially from the press. "There were about thirty press correspondents in town watching events with a camera constantly near each end of our [railroad] car. Our departure from the car was telephoned all over town, and our every movement watched."

On the morning of Tuesday, May 2, Scott left the car and set out for the hotel, his movements resembling those of a man heading for an assignation instead of a meeting with a foreign official that would decide the fate of two nations in contention. He moved his bulk slowly, sauntering toward town in a direction away from the Paso del Norte. He dawdled in front of store windows, occasionally stepping inside to make a small purchase. When a covered laundry wagon happened by, Scott discreetly hailed the driver and got inside, asking to be put out at the service entrance of the hotel. A baggage elevator carried him to the floor where McQuatters had rented the room. Scott cautiously made his way down the hall, looking for the right number. A reporter stepped out of his room and almost collided with Scott. "I got you!" he cried out, and within a few minutes the corridor was jammed with newspapermen; twenty-seven of them, as Scott recalled.

He located Obregón's room and managed to squeeze through the crush of correspondents and slam the door. Inside sat Obregón, his empty sleeve pinned neatly to his uniform jacket, an interpreter, a stenographer and the pink, portly figure of McQuatters. In Scott's mind was the fact that Carranza had mobilized seventeen thousand troops at Pulpit Pass in Sonora, apparently poised to move against Pershing's western flank. "I had no sort of anxiety about Pershing's ability to take care of himself," Scott said later, "but a real battle would culminate in a war, which the President did not want and which I, as a loyal soldier, must prevent."

Scott's main task was to obtain Obregón's signature on a document that would allow the Punitive Expedition to remain in Mexico as long as Wilson wanted it there, without coming to battle with de facto forces. The struggle began a few minutes before noon and went on for twelve straight hours, broken only by the comings and goings of the waiters who brought their meals. The document was painfully forged, line by line, paragraph by paragraph; points were agreed to, then changed again and again. "We would agree amicably on two or three paragraphs," Scott recalled, "which I considered as put out of the discussion, only to find to my surprise that these points were brought up again into the next paragraphs, as if no previous decisions had been arrived at at all." Exasperated, he was reminded of "the web of Penelope, which was knitted in the day only to be undone at night." Scott's contest with Obregón "was not equaled by any similar struggle with the wildest and most exasperated Indian heretofore encountered."

During the breathing spells afforded by the arrival of food, Scott spoke bluntly to Obregón. "No doubt you want Pershing to leave Mexico, but if you don't change all that and stop those preparations in Tamaulipas [state on the Gulf of Mexico], instead of getting rid of Pershing here you will have another Pershing over there in addition, and who knows then if either will ever come out of Mexico?" Scott was referring to apparently reliable reports that a Carranza general named Nafarrate was encouraging the build-up of a bandit force for an attack on Brownsville, Texas.

Scott's gruff, easy manner kept Obregón at the discussion table until an agreement had been reached. It was nearly everything that Wilson wanted, and worded so that the sensibilities of the Mexican people would not be offended. The agreement pointed out that the de facto government was carrying on a "vigorous pursuit" of Villa's scattered band, that de facto forces were being augmented in the north in order to guard against future bandit incursions. On Scott's side it was agreed that the Punitive Expedition would begin a gradual withdrawal, commencing immediately.

The final draft of the agreement—one copy in Spanish and one in English, both signed by Scott and Obregón—totaled less than four hundred and fifty words; not many, considering the interminable arguments and the number of hours required to produce them. Moreover, the references concerning the Mexican government's "vigorous pursuit" of Villa's band was a lie, as was the assurance that de facto troops were moving to help safeguard the common border; Scott knew, as did Obregón, that those troops were being rushed north in case Carranza should decide to pull the trigger on Pershing. However, the final paragraph contained several sentences which safeguarded Wilson's new and firmer stance, and which would prove to be embarrassing to the de facto government only a few days later.

The conclusion of the agreement read: "The decision of the American Government to continue the gradual withdrawal of the troops of the Punitive Expedition from Mexico was inspired by the belief that the Mexican Government is now in a position and will omit no effort to prevent the recurrences of invasion of American territory, and the completion of the withdrawal of American troops will only be prevented by occurrences arising in Mexico tending to prove that such belief was wrongly founded . . ."

When Scott and Obregón emerged from the hotel room in El Paso it was after midnight and both men were drained. The newspaper reporters, who were "lying about in every attitude on the floor," got to their feet and began bombarding Scott with questions. Wearily Scott waved them away, saying only that an agreement had been reached but the details would have to be obtained from the politicians in Washington. Before parting, Scott and Obregón agreed that it might be wise to remain in the vicinity pending the reactions of their respective governments to the document they had struggled so hard to create.

Wilson received the text of the agreement between Scott and Obregón early on the morning of May 3. After a hurried reading he called in Newton Baker, and both men expressed their delight at what Scott had accomplished. Wilson and Baker were eager to inform the public about this significant breakthrough in Mexican-American relations; the situation had festered for so many years that Scott's clean surgery would be welcome news indeed.

Baker went to work on a draft of a statement to be released to the press. When he had finished, Wilson reworked the draft to his satisfaction. The final version contained the essence of the Scott-Obregón document, to which Wilson added: "The ratification of this agreement removes all controversy from [Mexican-American] relations and I have decided officially to receive Mr. Elisco Arredondo, Ambassador-designate of Mexico, and shall direct Mr. Henry P. Fletcher presently to proceed to Mexico City as the representative of the United States to that Republic." Wilson was sure that Carranza would approve of the El Paso document—after all, Obregón had signed it—and that as soon as word was flashed from Mexico City of the First Chief's approval, the statement would be given to the press. It was now May 5.

9

The Charge at Ojos Azules

The southward thrust to hunt down Villa ended with the clash at Parral. But Pershing, with the singleness of purpose that so irritated French and British military hierarchy in 1918, chose to deploy his forces not in a defensive posture against Carranza's divisions that threatened him on every side, but as offensive instruments against what remained of Villa's band. In a general order dated April 29, Pershing broke up the provisional squadrons and reassembled the troops under their own regimental guidons, assigning each regiment a district in Chihuahua from which strikes against Villistas could be made if opportunities presented themselves.

The 7th Cavalry would be sent to Guerrero; the 10th assigned to headquarters at Namiquipa; the 13th moved to Lake Bustillos; the 5th sent to Satevó; and the 11th marched to San Francisco de Borja. The area to be occupied by the Punitive Expedition comprised a rough parallelogram a hundred miles long and thirty miles wide, all of it to be sustained by the road stretching back to Columbus.

Major Robert Howze, fifty-one, received the order from Pershing to retire the 11th Cavalry to San Francisco de Borja with mixed emotions: he was relieved because his command badly needed a rest, but frustrated because it seemed that the chase would end with Howze denied the opportunity to lead a classic cavalry charge against an armed enemy. To Howze, a rugged

Texan and a career officer who had been with the 11th Cavalry since 1911, this would have been unthinkable.

Howze had started the campaign with horses that needed long rest in lush pastures even before setting foot inside Mexico. Many of the mounts destined for Pershing's flying columns making up at Columbus had traveled for five days and nights packed tightly in cattle cars all the way from Fort Oglethorpe, Georgia. They had lost weight and most of them were feverish. Lieutenant Colonel Henry T. Allen's provisional squadron had taken first choice of the animals, leaving Howze with the worst of a poor lot. In forty-two days of hard campaigning Howze drove his squadron almost seven hundred miles, always farther south, convinced that Villa would be found across the next mountain, over the next hill. In two sharp clashes with Villistas, one trooper, four horses and a pair of mules were killed in action, but thirty horses had died of exhaustion.

Howze may have come closer to Villa than any other squadron commander after the battle at Guerrero. Before dawn on April 11 Howze attacked the small town of Santa Cruz de Herrera, above Parral, driving out a number of Villistas after a flurry of shooting. The Villistas escaped into the darkness. Howze's column had been on the move almost constantly for seventy-two hours and was in no shape for further combat, having fought its way out of a canyon only the afternoon before. Howze ordered a halt. The troopers flopped down beside the Balleza River, rolled themselves in blankets and slept.

At daylight Howze ordered a search of the town, but the inhabitants were nervous and uncommunicative; they claimed not to know any of the Villistas but did surrender a small arms cache uncovered by one of the troopers. Howze gave up as useless further questioning and bivouacked his squadron south of town to let the horses graze, the men rest. What happened next was described by Lieutenant S. M. Williams:

"I was sent during the afternoon with the packtrain into town to requisition corn and such other supplies as could be obtained. While in the town I saw coming from a ranch house about a mile distant fourteen Yaqui Indians in full war paint, but unarmed. When they came into the town the natives were tense with excitement. I returned rapidly to camp and reported this to Major Howze, and several of us urged him to send a troop to this ranch house and search it, but he would not do so. No one of us could get him to listen to the possibility of Villa and a small band hiding in this house. He prohibited any of us from going to this ranch house, and the following morning we marched south.

"I fully believe that this is where Major Howze and his column lost Villa and also lost our great opportunity."

Howze's attitude is difficult to understand. He had energetically pursued the elusive bandits across some of the most hostile terrain in Mexico, taking long risks and sustaining casualties, pushing his command to the point of exhaustion—yet he refused to allow a handful of men to ride an extra mile in broad daylight to investigate a house to determine if the object of the entire expedition might not be lurking there.*

Howze, who during the grueling past weeks had often wished for Apache scouts, was surprised to find twenty of them apparently idling their time away in the camp at San Antonio de los Arenales, where he would let his squadron rest before moving on to San Francisco de Borja. The Indians had been brought to the camp at San Antonio, fifteen miles north of Cusihuiriachic, by one of Howze's own officers, Lieutenant James A. Shannon, who had been selected as liaison officer with the Apache scouts for the length of the campaign. Shannon had journeyed to Columbus early in April to escort the Indians back to the interior of Mexico, but had arrived too late to parcel them out among the flying columns.

During the long truck-train trip to Columbus, Shannon had tried to imagine what the Apache scouts would be like. "I expected to find tall, lean, eagle-eyed, eagle-beaked redskins with little or nothing on except moccasins and a rifle belt, with probably a knife or tomahawk fastened somewhere." Shannon, who had never seen an Apache, imagined "*Leatherstocking* heroes, silent and fierce." He wondered how he would manage to equip them all with regu-

---

* On October 3, 1916, Major Frank Tompkins' former adjutant, Lieutenant James B. Ord, wrote Tompkins from El Valle: "Had a talk with a Villista who was with Villa when he went south. Villa was in the Santa Ana mountains within sight of us that day, April 5, while we were talking to old General Cavazos at San Borja, and Major Howze's outfit passed him by near San Borja." San Borja is less than fifty miles from Santa Cruz de Herrera; thus it is possible for Villa to have been in the ranch house there. But no proof exists.

lation uniforms and equipment for the campaign that lay ahead. When Shannon arrived at Columbus to meet his charges, he was surprised and a little disappointed to find "twenty short, stocky, pleasant-mannered individuals fully equipped from leggins to campaign hats." The Indians averaged five feet six inches in height, many were fat, and it didn't seem to Shannon that any of them could run full speed over the tops of the Sierra Madre as he had imagined.

Although the Apaches had received the standard government issue, Shannon made the mistake of asking the warriors if they needed anything else before crossing the border. They clustered around him asking for dust goggles, sweaters, flashlights and other scarce items. Once on the trucks, the Indians complained of various ailments and badgered Shannon for boric acid for their eyes, vaseline to rub on chapped lips and Big Sharley pleaded for mustard plasters to stick on his sore back. Shannon was disgusted and began to wonder if the Apache scouts weren't too soft for the rigors of campaigning against the tough Mexican bandits.

At the camp Shannon soon discovered that the Indians tolerated enforced idleness even worse than did white soldiers. He observed: "The Apaches are as easy to control as a lot of children—except when they get drunk." Although liquor was nominally forbidden to Pershing's troops in Mexico, there was no effective way to stop the flow of bottles smuggled aboard truck trains by enterprising drivers. Americans also availed themselves of the potent home-brews peddled by starving *pacíficos* in the towns through which the troop columns passed.

One of the veteran scouts, Hell Yet Suey (hereditary chief of the White Mountain Apaches), and Loco Jim (whose body was covered with scars from earlier encounters with white men, Mexicans and other Indians) got roaring drunk on the first day in San Antonio de los Arenales. Another sat under the hot sun and drank a bottle of mescal, a potent liquor fermented from the juice of cactus fibers, and went for one of his friends with a loaded Springfield. He was disarmed and thrown into the guardhouse. After this incident Shannon gathered up all of the Apache rifle bolts and pistol clips and locked them safely away in his tent. Six Indians went on a two-day binge and Shannon confined them under guard for two weeks. "This was a terrible jolt to them," he remembered, "and after that we had no further trouble."

One of Shannon's duties was writing letters home for the Apaches, none of whom were literate. Correspondence between the field and the scouts' permanent base at Fort Apache was a public affair. With Shannon sitting at his field desk, First Sergeant Chicken, B-25, Skitty Joe Pitt, Corporal Nonotolth, Sergeant Chow Big, Nakay, Big Sharley and the others listened as Shannon took dictation, and gathered again when replies were received. The Indians did not cherish keeping secrets from one another. One scout admonished his wife: "Some scouts got letter saying you crying all the time since I left home. Stop that crying. Don't let anybody borrow my wagon or steal my horse. Get some of your family to cut my corn and brand my calves. See that my children get plenty to eat. I be home pretty soon. That's all. Goodbye."

News from Fort Apache was often gossipy, always to the point. "Everything just the same here at Apache," informed a friend. "Everybody well. Your wife made some toodlepie [a form of mescal] and got arrested the other day. B-25's two wives are fighting over the money he sends home. His wife B-17 spent too much money and his wife B-23 got mad. Y-2 has a baby. It looks just like Y-2. Send me a silk shirt from Mexico. Goodbye."

The white soldiers were fascinated with the novel method of bathing preferred by the red men. They built a frame of branches four feet high and four feet in diameter by the side of a stream, then covered the structure with blankets until it was virtually airtight. Large stones were heated and placed inside the hut, followed by naked Indians who set up a howling chant they called their "bath song." In ten or fifteen minutes they burst from the wickiup drenched with sweat and plunged into the icy waters of the stream. To troops who had never heard of a Finnish sauna, the Apache bath was a thing of wonder.

In order to relieve the tedium of camp life and to bring back the scouts' sharp elemental edge, Shannon organized two- and three-day safaris into the rolling hills around San Antonio. He returned enthusiastic from the first of these hunts. "To get off twenty or thirty miles away from the command with a rifle and one or two Indians who speak only a few words of English has strong appeal to the wild man that is near the surface of each of us. Hunting was perfect drill for the Apaches. The trailing of the game, the alert watching for its appearance, the quick dismount and going into action when the game appears, the firing

at a moving target sharpened every phase of the scouts' business."
The Apaches were phenomenal trackers, effortlessly locating and
killing seven deer the first day out, game an American with them
had not even seen until pointed out to him by one of the scouts.

The Apaches wasted very little of these hundred-pound white-
tail deer, which they brought back to camp slung behind their
saddles. They showed the others how to tan hides. The hide was
cut away with a skinning knife and soaked in water for twenty-
four hours, then scraped clean of hair and stretched out to dry.
The deer head was put into an open fire to cook the brain, which
was then scooped out and put into a bucket of water to soften
for use in kneading the hide. Soaked again, the hide was stretched
to dry to a final white, beautifully supple condition and easily
sold to officers as souvenirs of the campaign. As prepared by the
Apaches, venison tenderloin "totally lacked any strong gamy
flavor and could be cut with a fork like sausage."

Howze stayed at San Antonio de los Arenales for eight days,
then was presented with another chance to engage a force of
Villistas in combat before moving the 11th Cavalry to San Borja
under Pershing's new redistricting scheme. On the afternoon of
May 4 Pershing received in his tent two men from Cusihuiriachic,
the small mining town fifteen miles south of San Antonio. They
told Pershing that the Villistas had attacked a smaller force of
Carranza soldiers at the Ojos Azules Ranch, twenty miles southwest of Cusi, had killed many, captured others and boasted how
they were going to move on San Antonio and wipe out Pershing's
command. The Villistas were led by Cruz Domínguez, Julio Acosta
and Antonio Ángel—three of Villa's veterans. They claimed to
have a thousand men at their command, but the two citizens of
Cusihuiriachic said they believed there were less than two hundred Villistas between Cusi and Ojos Azules. The people of Cusi
were mostly *pacíficos*, the representatives said, and feared for
their lives and what little property they had left. They indicated to
Pershing that the Carrancistas, after being driven out of the ranch
known as Blue Eyes, would offer no resistance should Villa's men
decide to sack Cusihuiriachic.

At six o'clock in the evening Major Howze received orders from
Pershing: "Move on Cusi and disperse the Villistas, if found."
Within two hours Howze assembled six troops of cavalry, the
machine-gun troop and a packtrain loaded with three days' ra-

tions. To Lieutenant Shannon's delight, Howze ordered the Apache scouts to take the point. Shannon ran to his tent, unlocked the rifle bolts and pistol clips and reissued them to the Indians. By eight-fifteen the 11th Cavalry, fourteen officers and three hundred and nineteen men, were on the road to Cusi.

The country here, east of the hills guarding the ramparts of the Sierra Madre, is level, and although the night was velvet-black with no moon in the sky, the column made good time, reaching the outskirts of Cusihuiriachic shortly before midnight. Shannon and the Apaches silently entered the town and found it empty of Villistas, but filled with remnants of the Carranza garrison that had been ousted from Ojos Azules. They seemed a rabble to Shannon. Sergeant Chicken fingered his rifle nervously and growled, "Heap much Mexican. Shoot 'em all." Shannon sent him back to Howze to inform him that it was safe to enter the town.

The adjutant, Lieutenant Williams, later remembered that the Carrancistas smelled strongly of liquor and were eager to tell of the battle that day with the Villistas. "It appears that they fought desperately all day, with an hour for luncheon, and had both retired in good order at nightfall. Casualties zero for both sides." Since none of the Carrancistas would guide the Americans to Ojos Azules, Major Howze was in a dilemma. If he gambled on finding Ojos over unknown terrain he might easily miss the place in the dark or blunder into it. If he wasted time trying to find guides he might not reach the ranch before sunrise in time to deploy the command properly; the surprise element would be lost, the game would be flushed. Now that the opportunity was at hand, Howze wanted nothing to jeopardize his set-piece cavalry charge, catching the enemy unaware. There was not time for the Apaches to find Ojos and return to lead the way. Howze dismounted the soldiers, and three precious hours of darkness were lost before guides could be found. Both were physicians, one of them an American. At three o'clock in the morning the troopers mounted and set off at an easy trot through the night, now windless and cold.

Howze's plan of attack was simple, based on information about the layout of the ranch given him by the two volunteer guides. The hacienda was a *cuartel*, a walled-in square in the center of an open plain. Three smaller adobe buildings and a well were in an arc to the right and to the rear of the *cuartel*. The complex of buildings was, in essence, a potential fortress contained within a circle three hundred yards in diameter. Behind the ranch buildings rose a series of steep hills leading into ancillary ranges of the main Sierra Madre massif. Howze based the assault plan on "the well-established fact that the Mexicans will not stand where their line of retreat is endangered." A Troop would ride straight for the ranch buildings, given covering fire by Machine-Gun Troop. The other five mounted troops would split, left and right, executing a pincer-type movement to get to the rear of the buildings and cut off the Mexicans as they fled for the hills beyond. The Apache scouts were to pass to the left of the buildings, without stopping to fight, and get onto the high ground behind the ranch, dismount and keep up steady fire on the buildings and to discourage any Villistas from trying to flee in their direction.

Howze urged the column on, racing the sunrise. Despite the predawn cold, the horses began to lather and blow. Machine-Gun Troop fell behind; the mules, only fourteen hands high and weighing less than eight hundred pounds, could not keep up with the cavalry. The ammunition mules were burdened with 312 pounds of cartridges, and the gun mules carried 292 pounds each —too much for the undersized beasts, which had been driven too hard for too many hours. Howze, frantic to reach Ojos before dawn, let the mules lag. There would be no halts. At the point, Shannon had to keep pressing the Indians, whose scouting instincts induced caution rather than rashness.

At five forty-five the point of the column slowed down and stopped. One mile distant lay the buildings of Ojos Azules. A red rim split the horizon, the sky grayed. Howze had lost the race.

Without pause Shannon waved the Apaches forward at a gallop. They veered to the left and beat across the level ground. A rifle cracked from somewhere in the ranch and blew dirt in front of the Indians. More shots rang out. The Apaches instantly reined in, dismounted, pulled the rifles from their leather boots and lay prone to return the fire. The idea of being under fire and not returning it "was foreign to every fiber in their being," Shannon realized. "They were being true to a thousand years of training and to natural instincts." But he was furious. He milled around the prostrate Indians, alternately cursing and pleading with them to remount and ride on. The Apaches paid no attention to his exhortations, but stonily continued to work the bolts of their Springfields, sending rounds into the buildings nine hundred yards away. Shannon wheeled his horse around and rode back to join the charge, leaving the Indians where they were.

Waiting for Howze to issue the ultimate command, the troopers settled their heels a little more firmly in the stirrups and fastened the chin straps to keep their campaign hats from blowing off when the charge came. Those of G Troop, last in column, anxiously looked back for signs of Machine-Gun Troop, but all they could see was a thin cloud of dust far, far down the road.

The one hundred and twenty men of the troops who were to deploy to the right gazed with dismay at the two thousand yards of barbed-wire fence strung between them and the cultivated field through which they were supposed to sweep in order to get behind the ranch and cut off the Mexicans' retreat. A Troop's commander, Lieutenant A. M. Graham, looked straight ahead down the dirt road leading into the *cuartel* at Ojos Azules.

The order was given to draw pistols. The troopers pulled their Colt .45 automatics from the holsters, pulled the slide back and let it snap forward, thumbing up the safety. The bugler wet the mouthpiece of his short brass bugle hung with the cavalry's red silk rope and tassels. Rifles popped off to the left: the Apaches were dueling at long range with the Villistas. Mexicans were seen running from the buildings trying to make for the horses grazing in the hills beyond Ojos.

Everything was wrong, but Howze could not delay setting the charge in motion. The bugle shrilled in the warming air.

Graham spurred his horse, leading A Troop straight down the road. He and his men were forced to swerve sharply to his left by the packed mass of horses of C and F Troops, which could not deploy to the right because of the barbed wire, and thundered ahead at extended gallop. They came under heavy but inaccurate rifle fire from the *cuartel*. Thirty or forty Villistas had determined to make a stand on the roofs of that building.

D and E Troops, on open ground, managed to deploy to Graham's right and plunged ahead until they came under fire from Villistas hidden behind a stone wall on a hill flanking the ranch buildings. E Troop diverted to wipe out this resistance while Lieutenant John A. Pearson got D Troop extended for the dash behind Ojos.

Graham's men swept through the ranch buildings, pistoling Villistas who were running through the yard half dressed, pulling at boots and belts. A few had managed to get mounts and were fleeing to the safety of the hills. Graham watched as one superb horseman cleared a gate connecting a barbed-wire fence that ran at a sharp angle behind the ranch buildings. Graham followed the Villista in a spectacular leap over the gate that brought him down almost beside the other horse. Graham gigged his mount and got so close that he was able to shove his pistol under the Villista's armpit and pull the trigger. The Mexican was blown out of the saddle.

D Troop was stopped by the fence, but wire cutters snipped a hole wide enough to allow the horses to pass through in column. They were again stopped a hundred yards past the fence by fire coming from Villistas who had elected to stand among the pines on the slope of a hill. The troopers dismounted to return the fire, joined by the Apache Scouts, who had, after all, decided to follow orders. Several Mexicans were killed, the others fled up the hill.

The fighting at Ojos Azules was over twenty minutes after it began. Machine-Gun Troop had gotten into action after the battle opened, firing into the buildings at a range of fifteen hundred yards and doing no damage. But pistols and rifles killed forty-two Villistas in and near the ranch, and another nineteen were accounted for by A Troop, which pursued the retreating enemy into the hills south of Ojos. Miraculously, no American was hit in the close-in combat, although several men fingered holes in their uniform or equipment after the battle.

Ojos Azules was fought on the fifty-fourth anniversary of the Battle of Puebla, when soldiers of the army of Mexico under Benito Juárez defeated Napoleon III's French Dragoons and infantry on May 5, 1862. Puebla was almost the only instance when a Mexican army was able to defeat a foreign force invading the land. For this reason "Cinco de Mayo" has been celebrated in Mexico with the same ardor as Bastille Day in France and with the same gusto formerly shown on the Fourth of July in the United States. The drunkenness exhibited by the Carranza soldiers at Cusihuiriachic was probably brought on by pre–Cinco de Mayo fever.

None of the Villistas at Ojos felt like celebrating this day, but after the battle American troopers discovered four men who did: they were a Carrancista lieutenant and three of his men who had been captured in the fighting the day before. Only the unexpected arrival of the 11th Cavalry had saved them from a firing squad.

10

Cadillac Pursuit

Pershing's private conviction that Carranza had no more control over what happened along the border "than if he lived in London" was borne out on May 5, the day Wilson put the finishing touches on a press release promising the end of Mexican-American controversy, based partly on the belief that "the Mexican Government is now in a position to prevent the recurrence of invasion of American territory . . ."

It was on that day that Mexican bandits struck across the Rio Grande in the first incursion inside American territory since the raid on Columbus, nearly two months previously. The targets were the tiny settlements of Glenn Springs and Boquillas, Texas, only miles apart in the 708,000-acre wilderness of Big Bend country, whose limits are traced in the south by the Rio Grande where it swoops deep into Coahuila, and northward by chains of volcanic mountains, thickets, hostile desert, lava flows, dried riverbeds dead eons ago; inhospitable country filled with wild javelina pig, cougar, bobcat, antelope and giant tarantula, where high summer offers noonday temperatures of 120 degrees and midnight readings close to freezing. At Boquillas the river is almost out of sight down a vertical rock canyon wall nearly 1,500 feet high. Glenn Springs sits in the foothills of the Chisos Mountains, the highest a sugarloaf almost 8,000 feet high.

Glenn Springs was settled in 1914 by a retired U. S. Army captain named C. D. Wood, a veteran of the Cuban and Philippine campaigns. Wood and a partner, W. K. Ellis, built a wax factory there employing fifty Mexicans who produced about a thousand pounds of crude wax daily. Wood and Ellis also set up a small general store catering to the needs of the workers and their families. There were, besides the frame houses in which Wood and Ellis lived, an adobe house, a corral, a home that belonged to a family named Compton, the few tin sheds of the wax factory, and across the dry creek bed, a scattering of adobe dwellings housing the labor force. That was all there was to Glenn Springs, except for four pyramidal tents recently erected by the town's small guard detachment, Sergeant Smythe and eight men of A Troop, 14th Cavalry.

On the night of May 5, 1916, a force of about a hundred armed and mounted Mexicans crossed the river near San Vicente, upriver from Glenn Springs, and there split into two raiding parties. The larger force made for Glenn Springs, the other for Boquillas. The first band galloped into Glenn Springs a few minutes past eleven o'clock, firing into every dwelling. Six troopers and Sergeant Smythe grabbed their weapons and barricaded themselves inside the adobe shack only a few yards away from the tents. They kept up a lively fire with Springfields and Colts that beat back several rushes, then one of the raiders threw a kerosene-soaked torch on the dry grass roof over the soldiers' heads. Within moments the adobe fortress became a fiery oven. Sergeant Smythe shouted "Outside, boys!" and the door was flung open. Trooper Cohen was first out the door and was immediately killed, his face blown off. Trooper Coloe was killed ten feet past the door, and Trooper Rogers, his uniform pants and shirt on fire, made a blazing target in the night as he ran screaming out of the shack, to be felled a hundred yards away. The others somehow made it through the gauntlet of rifle fire into the safety of darkness, but two of them were wounded and all were badly burned "with blisters as large as hen eggs" on their bodies. The other two cavalrymen, firing into the confusion outside, remained in their tent and escaped death or capture.

One of the bandits broke open the door of the house owned by Mr. Compton and shouted for the occupants to come outside. There was no reply. The bandit fired into the house, killing seven-year-old Tommy, who was alone. Compton had taken his youngest child, a girl, to the safety of one of the Mexican worker's huts when the fighting started, and failed to make it back to his house in time. Compton's other son, nine-year-old Robert, wandered terrified and unharmed through the settlement; a deaf-mute, Robert was safe from the superstitious Mexican raiders, who believed it was bad luck to harm "the crazy."

The general store was looted of everything that could be packed on a horse except the canned sauerkraut, which the raiders flung in disgust on the floor in the belief that it was some kind of food that had gone bad. The only things left were the heavier bags of corn and flour, which could always be retrieved later.

When the firing began, C. D. Wood was asleep in his house, two miles north of town in the hills. Wood hurriedly dressed and aroused his neighbor Oscar de Montel, who, like Wood, was a veteran of the Philippine campaign. Armed with rifles, the two old soldiers set out for town. "High flames broke into the dark night," Wood later recalled, "and we stumbled through whipping brush and annoying cactus for a half-hour, when the firing and the blaze died down. We pushed on in the darkness. About two hours later we reached the Mexican quarter of the settlement southwest of town and passed unnoticed through the commotion. When we were within a hundred feet of the store, only a heavy silence filled the air and a lone lantern moved about in the field near the burned adobe shack. A Mexican shouted out, '*Quién vive?*' [Who goes there?] Oscar shouted back, '*Quién es?*' This was the wrong thing to do; raiding bandits had one or two passwords, depending upon the crowd: *Viva Villa!* or *Viva Carranza!* The sentinel immediately began emptying his gun at us as we ran through the darkness, dodging the whizzing bullets."

Wood and De Montel hid out in the hills until dawn, when the raiders slowly packed up and rode toward the river, taking with them their wounded, the loot and the nine horses belonging to A Troop. Seven pools of blood were found near the corral and the burned-out adobe shack, but only one body was ever found, left behind by the bandits, that of a Carrancista captain named Rodríguez Ramírez, hastily buried under a pile of shrub some distance from town. Whether he died from wounds received at Glenn Springs or was shot by his own men was never determined.

At daybreak the second group of raiders struck Boquillas, twelve miles downriver from Glenn Springs. They quickly seized Deemer's general store, making Jesse Deemer captive as well as his Negro clerk, Monroe Payne. Deemer and Payne wisely offered no resistance as the Mexicans methodically stripped the shelves and loaded the pack mules. A few hours later, shortly after ten o'clock, the Glenn Springs raiders rode into Boquillas; then the reunited band started back for Mexico, taking Deemer and his helper with them as hostages.

Across the river was a ramshackle adobe village also named Boquillas, where lived workers of an American-managed silver mine three miles distant. The horsemen passed through the village and stopped at the mine, where they looted the small company store and robbed the mine payroll. Here they captured four more Americans, including the miners' physician, Dr. Homer Powers. The mules were so burdened with loot taken in Texas that the bandit leader, Lieutenant Colonel Natividad Álvarez, confiscated a truck belonging to the mining company and heaped in the supplies taken from the store. He ordered Powers and the three mining officials into the truck, then got in himself along with two guards. Álvarez sent the others ahead, saying that the truck would bring up the rear of the column.

The heat and the condition of the road progressively worsened as the afternoon wore on. The truck slowed to a crawl, then the American driver stopped it in the middle of a dry creek bed. "It's got to cool off," he told Álvarez. Everybody got down to have a smoke, and while resting, the Americans racked their brains for a way out of the dangerous situation; to remain with the bandits meant at best uncertain months of hard captivity, but more likely execution once their usefulness was at an end. By now the column of horsemen was miles ahead down the road. There were four of them to only three Mexicans, although the others had guns. The Americans decided what to do.

When the cigarettes had been dropped to the ground, Dr. Powers suggested to Álvarez that the quickest way to get the truck started was for everybody except the driver to help push the vehicle to firmer ground. Álvarez agreed, so he and his men put their shoulders against the truck and started straining. The driver switched on the ignition, let in the clutch and slipped the gear into reverse. "Now!" he shouted. The Americans on the ground stepped smartly back as the driver slipped the clutch, throwing the Mexicans backward into the creek bed. The Americans fell on them, took their guns and bound their hands behind their backs. Then, with the Mexicans walking ahead, the truck started the painful thirty-mile drive back to Boquillas.

. . .

On the morning of May 6 in Mexico City, while the frightened townspeople of Glenn Springs and Boquillas were cleaning up the bloody debris of the raids, Carranza was in audience with the State Department's Special Representative James L. Rodgers. Carranza showed Rodgers a copy of a press release he intended to hand out that day. It was lacking in detail, but did inform the Mexican public that the Scott-Obregón conferences in El Paso had resulted in an "amicable agreement." Rodgers was elated, until Carranza turned and added that certain changes in detail would, however, be necessary before the document could be ratified as a whole. Disappointed, Rodgers asked what changes the First Chief had in mind, and was told that the Americans must fix an early date, in writing, for the withdrawal *in toto* of the Punitive Expedition—the very condition General Scott had worked so hard to exclude. Rodgers left Carranza to send the news to President Wilson. Thus, even before word of the raids into Texas reached either the White House or the National Palace, the relationship between the two nations was the same as it had been after Parral. With the intent of the El Paso "agreement" negated by Carranza's attitude, all of Scott's Machiavellian maneuvering was rendered void.

Details of the depredations in Big Bend reached Washington, Mexico City and El Paso at about the same time: early in the morning on May 7. Carranza immediately issued a statement claiming that the raids had been carried out by lawless elements from the American side of the river; not even Mexicans would believe this, but Carranza did not want to admit that a new Columbus had to be faced up to. General Funston asked Secretary of War Baker for permission to beef up the border patrols with an additional four thousand regulars and to send cavalry across the Rio Grande in hot pursuit. Wilson concurred, and Baker told Funston to go ahead.

In El Paso, Obregón received a telegram from Carranza ordering him to meet again with Scott and inform the American general that the original draft agreement was not acceptable, nor would any such document be blessed by Carranza until it fixed the time for departure of Pershing, adding that if more American troops crossed into Mexico after the Boquillas raiders, they would be considered invaders and dealt with accordingly.

Scott received the threat calmly, then wired Secretary Baker: "We feel that the whole proposition is redolent with bad faith, that Mexicans are convinced that they are not able to carry out agreement even if ratified and they desire to keep United States troops quiet until Mexican troops are in position to drive them out of Mexico by force.

"We expect many attacks along the whole border similar to latest attack in Big Bend. Our line is thin and weak everywhere and inadequate to protect border anywhere if attacked in force.

"There are no adequate reserves. There are many calls for help on border which cannot be given, and we think the border should at once be supplied by at least 150,000 additional troops.

"We have struggled for a different result with all our intelligence, patience and courtesy, hoping against hope for a peaceful solution but are now convinced that such solution can no longer be hoped for.

"In order to give additional protection to border points exposed to raids it is recommended that militia of Texas, New Mexico and Arizona be called out at once, final action as to that of other states to be deferred until receipt by us of Obregón's [final] proposal."

Baker acted immediately upon part of Scott's recommendations. On May 9 he called out the National Guard units of the three states in question and ordered them distributed along the border. The call-out resulted in a pitiful showing. Arizona could muster only 990 men; New Mexico, 1,128; and Texas, 3,003—in all a mixed bag of little more than 5,000 men, mostly infantry, two batteries of field artillery and only one squadron of cavalry.

The renewed conferences between Scott and Obregón lasted for another three days. Obregón suggested that a gentlemen's agreement might be reached whereby Pershing would withdraw, assured that de facto troops would be sent northward in great numbers to guarantee protection of the Texas border. Scott was not at all convinced that such Carranza troop movements would guarantee anything other than a distinct danger to Pershing. He counterproposed gradual withdrawal, with total withdrawal when the Americans were sure there would be no more bloody incidents in small Texas border towns. But neither side would budge; there were no compromises. On the final day of the meetings, May 11, the atmosphere grew heated when Scott warned Obregón that unless the final American offer were accepted by Carranza he, Scott, could promise not only to keep Pershing where he was but to keep sending troops to the Mexican border until bandits would not dare cross. Obregón flared, then subsided. Both men realized that they had reached a deadlock, that any further meetings would be pointless. Resigned, they shook hands for the last time and departed. The wearying conferences had accomplished nothing, after all.

The pursuit of the Glenn Springs raiders was an expedition within the main Expedition, and the officers and men of the 8th Cavalry chosen for the job were at first enthusiastic; they had been greatly disappointed when Pershing left them behind at Fort Bliss on routine garrison duty while the rest of the cavalry plunged into Chihuahua seeking glory. First Lieutenant Stuart W. Cramer, Jr., remembered that "great was the rejoicing in the fortunate organizations" when word came to Fort Bliss that two troops of the veteran 8th were to spearhead the drive to capture the Big Bend raiders. This enthusiasm was soon dulled, even before the penetration of Mexico began.

A and B Troops left El Paso by train at six in the evening on May 7, and arrived at Marathon, forty miles north of Big Bend country, early the following morning. There the four trucks, mule-drawn wagons and troops got off and began the eighty-mile trek to Boquillas. The first half of the journey went without incident, but when the column struck the Dantesque interior of the lava and mountain wilderness past Henderson's Well, nature turned on them. The heat was stifling in the canyons, no water was to be found and mules began to balk in the traces. Horses and men breathed heavily. The civilian guide could not find Bone Spring until noon of the second day of march, then a corporal of A Troop developed appendicitis. "We left him there," said Lieutenant Cramer, "telling him we would notify the first automobile we should pass on the road to go by Bone Spring and pick him up." Past the spring the road became all but impassable and the march slowed to a walk over deep ruts and chuckholes. By late that afternoon three of the hardy army mules gave up and died, leaving one of the forage wagons stranded miles from Boquillas.

The weary column plodded into Boquillas, Texas, late in the

morning of the tenth, and the troops fell out to bathe in a huge outdoor tub hollowed out of rock, fed by a natural hot-water spring. Three of the wagons creaked their way into camp a few hours later, and a dying mule was taken out of harness. At five o'clock that afternoon a detachment led by Captain James C. Rhea crossed the river at several points and surrounded the Mexican town of Boquillas, driving all of the male citizens into the plaza. While they stood milling around, the American mining officials who had endured the brief captivity at the hands of Álvarez picked out a dozen Mexicans whom they said they recognized, and these were taken back across the river for interrogation. The following day was spent waiting for reinforcements from the 14th Cavalry, stationed at Fort Clark, Brackettville, Texas, two hundred and fifty miles away, but word came that the 14th had gotten lost in the wilderness and would be delayed another twenty-four hours. The 8th's commander, Major George T. Langhorne, decided to cross the Rio Grande in force without further delay; the 14th could catch up later.

The crossing began at twenty minutes before midnight on May 11. Darkness, coupled with the plunging cliffs on both sides of the river, made progress difficult. Mule teams were hitched to the expedition's passenger cars and towed across the river. One of the Fords broke down and had to be dragged back to the other side. Mules and men manhandled the remaining vehicles to more level ground and up to the plateau overlooking the river. It wasn't until dawn that everything was across and assembled for the thrust into the interior of Mexico.

As finally assembled, the task force was made up of a hundred mounted men, one of the forage trucks brought along from El Paso, two of the Ford sedans rented by a pair of newspaper correspondents and two motion picture cameramen, and the prize of the expedition, an eight-cylinder Cadillac touring car belonging to Major Langhorne, a dapper, well-to-do career officer who believed in taking the amenities into the field with him. The Cadillac was chauffeur-driven, and like the Fords, was fully loaded with grain for the horses where luggage was ordinarily carried.

The going was tough, with the horses far outdistancing the motor vehicles, which crawled over the ruts and deep arroyos, the drivers fearful of shearing axles or puncturing oil pans. A half-hour past noon, nearly five hours after the march began, the column had covered only twenty miles; the cars were three hours behind. Twice the truck had to be unloaded, pushed up the side of an arroyo, then reloaded by cursing soldiers put aboard the truck for solely that purpose. Once a passing string of Mexican burros was pressed into service to extricate the truck from an especially deep fissure where it was mired to the hubs.

The truck and the cars caught up with the resting cavalry at Agua Salada late in the afternoon, then were sent ahead of the mounted force with a thirty-minute lead time. Five miles down the road Lieutenant Cramer, in charge of the wheeled transport, was halted by a small boy and handed a message addressed to the commander of the American troops at Boquillas. The note was from Jesse Deemer, who said he and Monroe Payne were still held captive by the Glenn Springs bandits, at Santa Fe del Piño, about thirty miles south. Deemer said that the bandit chieftain was willing to exchange them for Álvarez and the other Mexicans taken prisoner by the American mining officials several days earlier. (The bandits did not yet know that the cavalry had crossed the river in force.) The boy told Cramer that there were about sixty armed men at Santa Fe del Piño, then he drew a map in the sand showing the layout of the town and indicated the house where Deemer and Payne were held prisoner.

Langhorne knew that it was imperative to move on the town before the raiders could be warned, but the horses were weary and he doubted that they could make it to Santa Fe del Piño before morning. The boy told him that after the next five miles there was a first-class road leading straight into town. Langhorne decided to strike at Del Piño, using the cars and the truck as motorized cavalry. A dozen of the best rifle shots were selected from each troop to form the assault force. Lieutenant Cramer and twenty men were put aboard the truck, Cramer riding precariously on top of a gasoline drum. Langhorne's big Cadillac, with the major and five others, led the point, leaving one of the Fords manned by Lieutenant Victor S. Foster, two troopers and a guide to bring up the rear. The small strike force set off at midnight, leaving the horses to rest and graze in the hills and to follow the cars as soon as possible in case Langhorne's small command got into serious trouble at Santa Fe del Piño.

The moon was bright, but the road was bad. It is a characteristic of Mexican youth never to offer strangers discouraging information, as Pershing's men had learned soon after leaving Columbus, and as Langhorne now discovered. The cars crept along over the ruts and holes with headlights extinguished. A soldier stood facing the rear, signaling the others *Slow, Stop, Proceed* with Langhorne's flashlight. On a good road Langhorne estimated that the convoy might have averaged 10 mph, enabling them to reach the vicinity of the town by three-thirty in the morning, when the moon would set to give the attackers the cover of darkness. But two hours of jouncing across the lunar roadscape earned them only nine miles of travel. Langhorne abandoned the motorized attack and halted the cars. He sent Cramer back down the road on foot to advise the approaching cavalry of the change in plan. Cramer met up with the horsemen at four o'clock near a grassy field by the side of the road. "Every man dropped in his tracks," Cramer reported, "halter shank in hand, not seeming to care whether he slept on a clump of grass or a cactus plant."

A grass fire broke out early in the morning, spreading throughout Langhorne's camp. Two hours of beating at the flames with blankets finally extinguished it, but Langhorne feared that the clouds of smoke might have been seen at Del Piño, flushing the quarry. He delayed movement until late that night, putting the column two miles north of Del Piño when the moon was down. The troopers dismounted and made their way to the lee side of a hill only four hundred yards from town, where they deployed in a skirmish line and waited silently in the cold for the sunrise.

At dawn Langhorne stood up, pistol in hand, and yelled "Charge!" The troopers scrambled to their feet shouting war cries and dashed over the crest of the hill and down the other side, expecting to close with the enemy. But not a sound greeted them. They swept into town, rifles at the ready; then they stopped, feeling foolish. The bandits had cleared out several hours earlier, leaving behind Deemer and Payne, who were filthy and hungry but otherwise unharmed after their eight days in captivity.

The expedition had now been inside Mexico for three days and nights and seemed no nearer to coming to grips with the bandits than when it left Boquillas. Langhorne wondered what to do next. Just then three cars bounced into Del Piño, bringing news that twenty of the bandits were camped at Rosita, fifteen miles down the road. Grabbing rifles and extra bandoleers, a dozen officers and men climbed back into their cars and started for

Rosita. As the motorcade, blowing orange dust in its wake, approached an abandoned house five miles south of Del Piño, a handful of Mexicans issued from the door and scattered across the desert. The cars lurched to a stop, and the Americans got out and began chasing the bandits on foot. One of the Mexicans suddenly appeared from behind the house on horseback and galloped southward. Langhorne jumped back into the Cadillac and ordered hot pursuit. The car "bounded over ditches and bushes like a steeplechaser," Springfields roaring in the hands of the excited soldiers seated front and back. The dismounted cavalrymen lost the other Mexicans after a futile chase that lasted for nearly a mile, and the Cadillac returned without having done damage to anything except its own suspension.

After one more fruitless foray eight miles down the road, Langhorne decided to return to Del Piño and set up an advanced headquarters. There, Langhorne told Cramer, he would wait for the arrival of the 14th Cavalry and more provisions so that the search for the Glenn Springs raiders could begin all over again. Langhorne and his staff left Cramer, eight men and a guide with orders to probe deeper into Mexico before returning to Del Piño, where the fresh water and the food and the good grass were.

Cramer protested that the region offered almost nothing in the way of forage for horses or men, and that if Langhorne and the others were going back to Del Piño, they might at least leave their food behind for Cramer's party. Langhorne turned him down flat "on the ground that to make a march of three days through the desert without supplies and with worn and hungry horses and men would, in Langhorne's words, 'be a valuable experience and would require the exercise of great ingenuity.' " Cramer watched the major climb into his Cadillac and drive away; then he sent the sergeant off to buy whatever food he could find from the soldiers who were leaving and from Mexicans. The sergeant returned with a pitiful amount of coffee and jerked beef, "purchased at five to twenty times its value," barely enough to feed Cramer's men for a day.

Cramer's mission was to investigate a vague report that a dozen bandits were holed up at the Castillón Ranch, fifteen miles farther south. The drooping horses were saddled and Cramer's small band started out for Castillón at five-thirty that afternoon. Cramer set a slow pace, and at eight o'clock, under a rising moon, the detachment was still far from Castillón, but had reached the vicinity of the Santa Anita well. Cramer had been told that the well was abandoned, but when he swept the area around the windmill with his field glasses, a dozen figures leaped at him through the lenses. They were all armed and seemed ready to move out; the mules in front of a loaded wagon were still in the traces. Cramer guessed, correctly, that he had come upon a part of the Glenn Springs raiders and that the wagon was filled with loot taken from the stores. He decided to attack.

Cramer deployed his men abreast on top of the hill overlooking the windmill. Then he stood up and fired, signaling a volley from the Springfields. The surprised bandits scattered in all directions. A Mexican, hit at the first fusillade, jumped into a bush on the American flank as the cavalrymen rushed whooping and firing down the hill. He was hit six times by troopers who sent rounds crashing into the bush as they ran by. An old man holding up a shattered forearm stopped Cramer at the foot of the hill, crying loudly that he was a *pacífico* taken by the bandits two days earlier to drive the wagon. Cramer sent him back to the horse holders and continued the pursuit up an arroyo. Two Mexicans were hit by American rifle fire but were dragged away by their companions. Darkness made further pursuit impossible, so Cramer returned to the windmill to count the spoils.

The bandits had abandoned, besides the wagon, seventeen horses and mules, nine rifles, two swords and a number of saddles. Cramer asked one of the horse holders where the old man was. The trooper showed him: at the bottom of the well, put there for safekeeping while the soldier was busy rounding up loot. Cramer was furious. "It was a safe enough provision, but the water was entirely spoiled, as the old man was bleeding like a pig. This prevented us from staying until morning, as we had very little water in our canteens." Incredibly, the Mexican who had been shot so many times was still alive; he was hauled from the bush and placed on the wagon with the old man for the long ride back to Del Piño.

The bone-tired, achingly hungry troopers passed through the small town of Cerro Blanco, which was deserted, then continued to Del Piño. From Cerro Blanco to Del Piño the ground rises very rapidly, and as dawn approached, the detachment had climbed two thousand feet. It was bitterly cold, and the soldiers regretted having left their heavy wool sweaters behind when the expedition began. They pulled out Mexican blankets from the captured saddle bags and draped them over their shoulders, too cold to care about the lice. They longed to halt and build a fire and brew coffee, but Cramer drove them on, remarking that they looked like bandits themselves. One of the men wore a tattered straw sombrero, and all needed shaves.

At dawn the miserable column was still climbing. Cramer and the guide were at the point, a quarter of a mile ahead, when a trooper galloped toward them waving his hat and shouting that a great cloud of dust was coming up fast from behind. "My heart sank," Cramer recalled. "I was in no shape to fight, with my men dead with fatigue and with all the plunder to hamper us. I saw visions of being attacked by a big bunch of bandits or Carranza troops, the spoiling of my success and the losing of my loot just as I was about to get into camp with it." Cramer wheeled his horse around and shouted to the trooper to turn back and order the men to deploy into the brush and lay an ambush. But the messenger shot past Cramer and thundered down the road, yelling over his shoulder, "They can't. They're right on top of us!"

Cramer swore and spurred his horse down the road, followed by the guide, who cried out, "Jesus Christ! Why'd they done us this way?" Cramer braked his horse, then jumped to the ground to find his men already deployed in the brush, Springfields ready. He looked anxiously down the road and made out about fifteen men advancing toward them only fifty yards away. But before any firing broke out, one of Cramer's men shouted that the menacing line of skirmishers were Americans. And they were. The riflemen, who were part of A Troop, believed that they had caught up with straggling Mexican raiders, so disreputable-looking were Cramer's men. Only the growing light had averted tragedy.

The arduous, if somewhat farcical, chase after the Glenn Springs raiders was called off by Funston two weeks after it began. By then the troopers had chased the raiders nearly two hundred miles into the interior, killing some and capturing five. Funston noted that during the pursuit not one Carrancista soldier had been seen; Carranza's boast of protecting the border where it most needed guarding was a lie: the only Carrancistas in evidence were the two de facto officers who had taken part in the raid.

11

To the Brink at Carrizal

Reports of Carranza troop movements in Chihuahua arrived on Funston's desk almost daily. After Parral, Funston told a correspondent that "John could take care of himself," but now he was not so sure. The striking elements of the Expedition were deployed for offensive operations against guerrilla bands; widely scattered, the isolated cavalry regiments could be overwhelmed one by one, the supply line was thinly guarded and could be cut anywhere by superior forces. The specter of five separate Little Big Horns occurring at San Francisco de Borja, Satevó, Lake Bustillos, Guerrero and Namiquipa grew alarmingly. On May 9 Funston wired Pershing at Namiquipa to pull the entire Expedition back to Colonia Dublán. Pershing protested; although the active hunt for Villa himself was necessarily at an end because of Carranza's obstructionist attitude, such a pullback would put his troops forever out of reach of those remnants of Villa's bands still at large in southern Chihuahua. Many of Villa's chieftains were still active, and in the minds of many, the score at Columbus was not yet settled. Pershing could not persuade Funston to leave the command deployed as it was, but he did manage to allay Funston's fears and get him to agree to a compromise: Pershing could keep his headquarters at Namiquipa, holding the bulk of his forces in the vicinity.

Pershing put a broad interpretation on Funston's word "vicinity": he did pull back the engineers, sanitary troops, field artillery, wagon companies and forward infantry elements to Namiquipa, but he stationed the best of his cavalry twenty-five miles south of there, at Providencia and at the San Geronimo Ranch, where they could strike down the valley toward Guerrero. This done, he ordered active patrolling and scouting parties sent out daily, as before.

One of Pershing's most assertive subordinates was his special aide, Second Lieutenant George S. Patton, Jr., thirty, a reedy-voiced West Pointer who had been in the cavalry for nearly seven years waiting for action and subsequent promotion. At the time of the Columbus raid Patton was attached to the 8th Cavalry at Fort Bliss. When immediate movement orders were not forth-coming, Patton jumped channels and went directly to Pershing's headquarters and asked to be taken along into the field, in any capacity. Pershing, occupied with the myriad details of organiz-ing the Expedition, curtly brushed the brash lieutenant aside. Undaunted by Black Jack's stern reputation, Patton camped out-side Pershing's door for two days, piping his request for active duty to the brigadier at every opportunity. Pershing finally gave in and told Patton to report as headquarters commandant and aide, backing up the regular aide-de-camp, First Lieutenant James Lawton Collins.

Patton, who had been serving along the border since October 1915, was fascinated by characters with whom he came in con-tact; these lean, hardened Texans wearing cowboy boots and spurs and armed with six-guns during every waking moment were a world away from his own aristocratic riding-to-the-hounds Virginia background. Although Patton's pay as a second lieutenant amounted to only $157.50 per month, independent means allowed him to buy handcrafted boots and tailored uniforms far better than anybody else wore—including Pershing—and he once earned a colonel's wrath by bringing into Fort Bliss his own blooded mare and a string of six privately owned polo ponies. His wife, the New England heiress Beatrice Ayer, was as rich as any Texan, but like her husband, ingratiated herself with the fifty-odd citizens of Sierra Blanca, where they were stationed, because of her knowl-edge of horses and her down-to-earth manner. Patton, one of the best pistol shots in the Army, was respected by the locals for his deadly aim, use of profanity and a willingness to buy beer for hired guns and Texas Rangers alike in Sierra Blanca's only saloon. Patton's favorite was the town marshal, white-haired Dave Allison, who earned Patton's undying admiration when Patton learned that the old man had shot five Mexican bandits in the head with a Colt .44 at a range of sixty yards.

The Pattons shared a house for a short time with Major George Langhorne and a Chinese servant. Patton admired Langhorne's eight-cylinder Cadillac, which was kept in the adobe garage at the rear of the house, and as far as Patton could determine, Langhorne was the only officer in that baking wilderness along the Rio Grande whose aristocratic family connections and income matched his own. Had not Patton wangled his way on Pershing's staff, there is little doubt that he and Langhorne would have shared the Cadillac in the pursuit of the Glenn Springs raiders.

Although Villa himself was still in hiding somewhere south of Parral, General Julio Cárdenas, sometime leader of his Dorados, was at large near Namiquipa. Pershing ordered small cavalry units to scour the area around Guerrero to see if Cárdenas could not be captured or killed. Sensing that time was running out for the active phase of the campaign, Patton begged Pershing to be allowed to accompany one of the troops in search of Cárdenas. To Patton's delight, Pershing assigned him to Captain Eben Swift's H Troop of the 11th Cavalry, and on a warm morning early in May, Patton joyfully mounted his horse and rode out with the others in quest for adventure.

The troop was bound for the San Miguelito Ranch, where, rumor had it, Cárdenas' wife and mother were living. The ranch was north of the small town of Rubio, in the elevated valley running south from Namiquipa, and the troop made good time across the dry, flat ground. At Rubio they turned north and ran into a column of the 16th Infantry that had just left San Miguelito. The infantry commander told Eban Swift, Patton and the other officers of H Troop that his foot soldiers had surrounded the ranch shortly after sunrise, only to see several armed Mexicans gallop out of the small hacienda and escape into the hills west of town. The infantryman assured Swift that the quarry had been flushed. Swift decided to march on to the ranch anyhow.

They reached San Miguelito a short time later and deployed for action, but found the place deserted. A search of the hills to the west proved fruitless. However, Patton, who somehow divined that he would once again pay a visit to the ranch, carefully studied the buildings and the surrounding terrain, noting that the hacienda had only one door, facing east, large enough to allow egress to mounted horsemen.

The troop returned to camp empty-handed, but a week later Patton headed back for San Miguelito. The mission this time was corn, not bandits. Patton, a corporal, six privates of the 16th Infantry and a civilian interpreter named Lunt were sent out by Pershing in the three headquarters Dodge touring cars to purchase feed from outlying ranches. At a place called Las Ciénegas, Patton managed not only to purchase a few bags of corn but to interview, through Lunt, one of Julio Cárdenas' uncles. The old Mexican seemed uneasy when questioned about the Dorado leader's whereabouts. Acting on a hunch, Patton ordered everybody into the cars and drove to San Miguelito, eight miles to the north.

Patton waved the cars to a halt along a sunken road in back of the ranch, then got out and described his plan of attack. The cars would be parked at the rear corners of the big house, allowing the riflemen to watch for Mexicans jumping out of the windows to reach the horses in the corrals, while Patton, Lunt and the corporal dashed around to the front to cut off anybody trying to ride out through the main door. Patton got to the front of the house first, pistol raised. He saw only an old man and a boy skinning a steer in the courtyard. They stared at one another; Patton holding his .45 aloft, the Mexicans holding the long skinning knives dripping with blood.

Then the hacienda door burst open and three heavily armed Mexican riders dashed into the courtyard brandishing pistols and rifles. Patton hesitated; no firing could be initiated by Americans until positive, hostile identification was made. This came seconds later when the Mexicans opened fire on Patton and on Lunt, who had just rounded the corner of the building. Patton lowered his pistol and began squeezing the trigger. One of the riders fell and started crawling along the ground.

The soldiers in the back now ran from the cars to the front of the house and started firing at the two Mexicans on horseback. Patton and Lunt were in the line of fire. They crouched and ran for safety to the northern wall, followed by the two Mexicans galloping past them less than ten paces away. Both riders shot at the Americans, but missed. Patton squeezed off another round, killing one of the horses. He waited until the rider scrambled to his feet, then killed him with a shot under the left arm. The remaining horseman started for the main gate leading out of the courtyard, but was dropped by a fusillade of rifle and pistol bullets.

The Mexican first hit by Patton was cornered by the infantrymen behind a wall on the south side of the house. A few shots were exchanged, then the man behind the wall dropped from sight and remained silent. Patton's first shot had been fatal, but the Mexican kept firing until he died.

His blood up, Patton decided to mount to the roof of the hacienda so as to command the situation in case more Villistas were lurking inside. He ordered a dead tree lying in the courtyard placed against the side of the house, then scrambled up the bark on all fours and jumped onto the roof. The dirt gave way and he plunged through the roof to his armpits, where he dangled and kicked his legs in the air. A Villista in the room below could easily have hacked his legs to ribbons with a machete. Patton quickly heaved himself back through the hole. Two riflemen got onto the roof to command the courtyard, while Patton eased himself back to the ground. He and Lunt, now armed with a rifle, summoned the steer skinners—who had calmly kept working during the heated fire fight—and ordered them to open the gate leading to the main courtyard. To their relief they were greeted only by the solemn stares of women and children.

Since nobody in the hacienda could, or would, tell who the dead Mexicans were, Patton decided to take the bodies to Rubio and have them identified. The corpses, like deer after a hunt, were lashed to the fenders of the cars and driven in a macabre motorcade through Rubio, where one (the man Patton first shot), was identified as Julio Cárdenas, another as Private Juan Garza, the third as a Villista captain whose name nobody could remember. Identification made, Patton drove back to camp in triumph to show the trophies. Pershing, who called Patton "the Bandit," was pleased, and promoted him to first lieutenant.

To his wife, Bea, Patton wrote: "You are probably wondering if my conscience hurts me for killing a man. It does not. I feel about it just as I did when I got my swordfish: surprised at my luck."

.   .   .

Pershing could not forget the embarrassment and frustration caused by beginning a campaign with virtually no maps of a country where every mountain, hill, valley, river, canyon and fold of ground was of tactical importance; an accurate map in the hands of Colonel Dodd would have saved hours of stumbling blindly toward Guerrero in March; he would have had an easier time at Tomóchic, and Howze could have made a clean sweep during the charge at Cusihuiriachic. The debacle of the 1st Aero Squadron, including the loss of the Expedition's only Brock automatic aerial camera, placed the responsibility for mapping the wilds of Chihuahua in the hands of the 2nd Engineer Battalion using as tools transits, compasses, sketchbooks and small folding Kodaks. A mapping detail was considered good duty by those assigned: usually, pesky West Point shavetails were not included; there was the chance to hunt fresh meat; and any trooper relished the opportunity to be away from the irksomeness and tedium of routine camp life. Since mid-May a certain zest had been added to mapping details with the news that Candelario Cervantes and his band of Villistas—routed by the 7th Cavalry at Tomóchic in April—were loose in the hills near Namiquipa, boldly looting the countryside. The stricken farmers and small ranchers had nowhere else to turn for help, so they humbly pled with Pershing to put an end to the pillaging. Cavalry patrols swept in all directions, but so far Cervantes had not been seen by the Americans.

At seven o'clock in the morning on May 25 a small detachment of mappers and riflemen from the 2nd Engineers and the 17th Infantry trundled out of the camp at Las Cruces, twelve miles north of Namiquipa, on a day-long terrain study of that part of the Santa María Valley. In charge was Sergeant James M. Mayson, who commanded seven others of the 17th, a pair of Engineer privates who had brought their horses, and a Quartermaster private who drove the open mule-drawn wagon, which also carried tools and rations. It was a fine spring morning, and while the engineers went about their business of mapping, Mayson looked forward to hunting wild javelinas, small bristly pigs sometimes known as peccaries, which are easy to kill and provide tough but quite edible pork. Mayson led the party to the designated mapping area, six miles south of Las Cruces, where the wagon was parked. The engineers, Chester Stewart and George Swartout, picked up their sketchbooks and other tools and started walking toward nearby Alamía Canyon. Two others stayed by the wagon, and the rest of the riflemen drifted up the canyon to look for pigs. Mayson took off on his own in the opposite direction, and soon the eleven-man detachment was scattered hundreds of yards apart.

Farthest up the canyon were Lance Corporal Davis Marksbury and Private George G. Hulett. They were beating the brush looking for pigs, when they noticed movement up ahead. At first they thought it was a packtrain approaching, but as the animals and men came closer they realized that a force of about thirty armed Mexicans was bearing down on them. Before either of them could take cover the Mexicans opened fire, hitting both Americans with the first volley. Marksbury, shot through the lungs, dropped heavily to the ground and lay still. Hulett was hit a few inches above the fleshy part of the left knee, but he pulled his .45 from the holster and emptied the whole clip at the advancing Mexicans.

Forty yards behind Hulett was Private George F. Nicholson, who, like the others, had been unable to find any javelinas. At the start of the attack Nicholson was in the open, and when he saw Marksbury and Hulett fall he stood up instead of taking cover, and began working the bolt of his Springfield and squeezing the trigger. Then he was hit, and hit again; one slug tore into his arm, another into his left thigh. He dropped and began crawling for cover.

The engineers, Stewart and Swartout, were behind Hulett and Nicholson in the canyon. When the firing broke out, Stewart was peering through the viewfinder of his Kodak, aiming at the canyon heights. A Mexican rifle bullet killed his horse. He hurriedly dropped the camera, pulled his Springfield out of the boot and started firing. Stewart, as did two of the others, took note of the flashily dressed leader of the Mexican band, mounted on a large black horse. He was tall, and wore a fancy sombrero turned up at the brim. Those who saw him were impressed with the "fancy coat that looked like velvet or plush, with white braid in front." To Stewart, the massive rider "looked like a bullfighter."

The shooting had attracted Sergeant Mayson's attention, but at first he just thought that some of his men were bagging pigs. Then, realizing that a fire fight was in progress, he ran toward the wagon, several hundred yards away, where he found Corporal Earl Phillips and Private Willie Harrison rummaging in the jockey box for more ammunition to take back to the canyon. He ordered Harrison to leave his rifle, take the lead mule and hurry back to Las Cruces for help. Then Mayson and Phillips, the only noncoms still unhurt, ran for a hill nearby and took up what Mayson later described as "supporting positions."

Nicholson, bleeding from his wounds, lay behind some rocks and watched as Hulett continued the fight only forty yards away. Hulett, his pistol empty, picked up Marksbury's rifle and calmly selected his targets among the Mexican riders milling around in the canyon. He fired once and knocked the fancily dressed Mexican leader from his horse. Squeezing off another round, he killed the man who seemed to ride up to take his place. Then he put down the Springfield and crawled over to Marksbury. Hulett saw that the corporal's eyes were closed and that pink froth had formed on his lips. He believed that Marksbury was dead, but he struggled to pull the squad leader to cover behind a large boulder. Hulett started crawling back down the canyon floor to seek shelter for himself. Bullets sang through the air and spattered against the earth. Nicholson watched Hulett inch his way forward, then was perplexed to see the wounded man turn around and start back for the place where Marksbury was lying. Nicholson saw Hulett unbuckle Marksbury's pistol belt, sling it over his shoulder and retrieve the Springfield. Then Nicholson understood: Hulett wanted to make sure that the American weapons did not fall into Mexican hands. Nicholson thought it was a very brave thing to do.

Quartermaster Private Charles Brooks was sitting in the shade beneath the wagon when the battle opened. Not seeing Sergeant Mayson anywhere, he grabbed a rifle and three bandoleers of ammunition from the wagon and ran toward the sound of the guns. He came across two soldiers dashing back for ammo, gave them a bandoleer each, then led them into the canyon. Having learned that Nicholson was wounded, Brooks took cover and called out to Nicholson. His first two shouts were answered by a Mexican who called back in unaccented English, "I'm over here!" Finally Nicholson's voice came through and Brooks sent two men out to bring him in. Hulett was located too, and he made his own way back to the others.

Brooks looked up the canyon wall and saw a line of Mexicans appear on the ridge. The range was five hundred yards, but he managed to pick off one of the Mexican horses, unsaddling the rider, and after a brief flurry of firing, the bandits disappeared. Fearing that they would be flanked, Brooks ordered everybody to fall back toward the wagon. He picked up Nicholson and started carrying him to safety. Hulett hobbled along behind, still carrying Marksbury's rifle and pistol. The Mexicans sniped at them all the way back to the wagon.

At this point only Swartout was mounted, and since he had dropped his rifle in the retreat down the canyon, he decided to ride back for help. Galloping into the Las Cruces camp thirty minutes later, he gave the alarm. Two detachments from the 11th and 13th Cavalry managed to get saddled and mounted within twenty-five minutes, and started riding flat out to relieve the beleaguered mapping party in Alamía Canyon. Forty minutes after the cavalry had left, Private Willie Harrison sauntered into Las Cruces aboard the sluggish mule, booting the protesting animal in the ribs with every step. His trip had been wasted.

The cavalry reached the mouth of the canyon at eleven o'clock to find the Mexicans retiring northward. The soldiers plunged into the canyon after the bandits, but almost immediately three horses and a mule were killed by fire coming from palisaded bluffs a thousand feet above the trail. The troopers kept going for another three miles, but as at the battle of Agua Caliente, the bandits scattered in every direction and no contact was made.

Six mounted infantrymen of the 17th arrived on the scene shortly after the cavalry had swept in, and they found that Marksbury had only a few minutes more to live; Hulett and Nicholson, however, would probably recover. Lieutenant Roderick Dew ordered Marksbury and the others placed in the wagon, then rode up the canyon to look for the bodies of the Mexicans killed by Hulett. He rifled the pockets of both, discovering inside the plush jacket of the leader a personal letter addressed to Candelario Cervantes. The other man's papers identified him as Captain José Vencomo. Dew stuffed the documents in his own pockets and rode back to the wagon, ordering the party to return to camp.

Respect for the dead was not a strong feature of the Punitive Expedition. Sergeant Alexander P. Withers, a hospital corpsman brought along by Lieutenant Dew, later recalled that a second escort wagon had been brought out from Las Cruces in case it was needed for transporting wounded. Withers, Dew and the wagon driver, known as Barney Oldfield, were at the extreme rear of the troops marching slowly back to camp after the fight. "The three of us were alone," Withers said, "and had barely got under way when Lieutenant Dew signaled for us to stop. He had been busily studying the papers taken from the dead Mexicans, and when he halted us I sensed what was to follow."

Dew rode up to Withers and said, "We must have the bodies of those dead Mexicans for identification—one of them is Cervantes—you go get them." Withers saluted, then apprehensively started riding back to the canyon. One lone American, he thought to himself, in a mountain defile encumbered with a pair of dead bodies, would make easy pickings for concealed riflemen. He finally reached the spot where the corpses lay sprawled among the rocks, and nervously dismounted. There was no sound except the sighing of the wind and the creak of saddle leather as his horse dropped his head to nibble at short tufts of dry grass.

Withers hurriedly grabbed one of the bandits by a leg and dragged him beside the other. He took a buckskin thong from one of the Mexican saddles and lashed one of Cervantes' legs to one of Vencomo's, "as if for a three-legged race," Withers observed. Then he took a braided lariat from Cervantes' horse and tied it securely to the bandits' bound legs, running the other end to his own saddle. "I mounted and started dragging the bodies down the rough trail toward the place where I had left Lieutenant Dew and Barney Oldfield. I could easily imagine a hidden Mexican behind every bush and rock. At any moment I expected to hear a shot. My progress was slow in spite of my hurry. At one point the descent was so steep that my two dead companions rolled ahead of me down the slope."

The bodies were bruised and battered almost beyond recognition by the time they were hauled into Las Cruces, and Lieutenant Dew decided to bury them then and there after he was certain that the corpses were indeed those of Cervantes and Vencomo. But a telegram from Pershing ordered the bodies to be sent by truck to headquarters for final inspection. When they arrived the Expedition's intelligence officer, Major James A. Ryan of the 13th Cavalry, raised hell, wondering how men killed in a fire fight could look so horrible.

Pershing, however, was pleased with the whole affair, mentioning Hulett in a special dispatch and saying that "the killing of Candelario Cervantes was particularly fortunate as, next to Villa, he was the most able and the most desperate of Villa's band." Hulett's commanding officer, Captain Edward S. Walton, put him in for the Congressional Medal of Honor for his actions at Alamía Canyon, but the request was denied. Congress was not yet ready for heroes.

On the last day of May, Pershing took two members of his staff and started the rugged eighty-mile drive north from Namiquipa to Colonia Dublán to meet with Carrancista General Gabriel Gavira, commander of the de facto forces stationed at Juárez. Pershing had requested the meeting to see if there was some way in which field differences between the two military forces occupying Chihuahua could be ironed out so as to avoid further clashes that would inevitably lead to war.

Gavira came down in a special railway car that was parked between the camps of the American and Mexican troops stationed near Dublán. Gavira opened the conversation by proposing that his troops occupy every town between Dublán and Namiquipa. Pershing set his jaw and replied that any large movements of de facto troops along the railroad and his left flank would be considered by his government as a hostile indication. The arguments seesawed for two hours, when Gavira suddenly became more tractable and professed to see things Pershing's way. When the conference ended the two men shook hands, and before returning to Namiquipa, Pershing sent a wire to General Funston in San Antonio.

"Final conclusion," he wrote, "as follows: Carranza troops occupy four stations on Central Railroad north of [El] Sauz with fifty men each, also four stations Carmen Valley fifty men each. Total number on my left flank north of Sauz not to exceed at any time more than 400 men. Same number now occupying garrisons along Northwestern Railroad not to be increased. This number now stated to be 400. In return it was agreed on my part that I should advise General Gavira of our retirement if made from any town along my line of communication so that his forces could occupy it. Also that I should investigate and settle any complaints against American troops made by local *presidentes* in towns within our lines now occupied by Carranza troops.

"Regard conference as very satisfactory," Pershing concluded, "inasmuch as we are committed to nothing we should not otherwise do and no restrictions are placed on our movement . . . [but] Gavira is committed to limited number troops on our flanks."

Gavira told Pershing that Villa was dead, but Pershing didn't believe it.

On that same day Secretary of State Lansing was handed a lengthy, vituperative note dictated by Carranza but signed by his new Foreign Minister, Cándido Aguilar, which angered Lansing and totally negated any agreements reached by Pershing with de facto commanders in the field. The note, more than six thousand words long, began with a heated protest against the pursuit by the 8th Cavalry of the Boquillas–Glenn Springs raiders, then continued with a dreary résumé of events in Mexico beginning with the raid on Columbus the previous March, events with which Lansing, Wilson and the rest of the world were only too familiar. One flight of fancy led Aguilar to state that "The Mexican Government has made every effort on its part to protect the frontier . . . ," then added that "if from time to time these lamentable incursions into American territory are perpetuated by bandit groups, this fact is rather a matter of pecuniary reparation and a reason for combined defense, but never the cause for the American forces to invade Mexican soil." Lansing could recall no instance when Carranza troops had in any way aided in the pursuit of Villa or "made every effort" to protect the frontier.

Aguilar stated that "the time has come to insist that the American Government withdraw the new expedition from Boquillas [which] the Mexican Government considers as an act of invasion of its territory and, in consequence, will be obliged to defend itself against any body of American troops on its soil." He also demanded the withdrawal of Pershing's men in Chihuahua. If the withdrawal was not carried out, Aguilar warned, "there is no further recourse than to defend our territory by appeal to arms."

Aguilar claimed that "failure to advise and co-operate with the Mexican authorities was the cause of the encounter which took place between the American forces and Mexican citizens." This was a gross distortion of fact; Tompkins had, indeed, advised the military commander at Parral of his intentions. Then Aguilar once again raised the matter of Pershing's including infantry and artillery in the Expedition, calling it an "insult" that could be explained in no other way "than as a precaution against a probable attack by the Mexican forces." This was military nonsense; infantry, like cavalry, was a scouting arm, and pack artillery pieces were weapons of offense useful in reduction of strongpoints and certain counterbattery missions. Aguilar had howitzers confused with machine guns, which he thought were perfectly all right for Pershing to bring along.

Aguilar, still echoing Carranza, accused the United States of committing "a large number of acts [that] seem to show that the influence of the American Government is directed against the consolidation of the present Mexican Government." He pointed out that "the decided aid lent at one time to Villa by General Scott and the Department of State was itself the principal cause of the prolonged civil war in Mexico. Later the continuous aid extended by the American Catholic clergy to that of Mexico, which labored unceasingly against the Constitutionalist Government, and the constant activity of the American press favoring intervention and the interests of the businessmen of the United States, are still further indications that the present American Government cannot or will not prevent the work of conspiracy which is being effected in the United States against the Constitutionalist Government."

To Lansing, the charge of conspiracy was as ridiculous as it was irrelevant. Wilson was the first to admit that he regretted recognition of Carranza, once saying that "I have never met a man more impossible to deal with," but ever since he had come to realize that he could not guide the Mexican Revolution along his own lines, all that he sought was protection for heavy American capital investment, as well as protection of the thirty-six hundred U. S. citizens still living in Mexico.

Of the thirty-four paragraphs contained in the note it was the thirtieth that incensed Lansing more than any other:

"30. The American Government incessantly demands from the Mexican Government an effective protection of its frontier, and yet the greater part of the bands which take the name of rebels against this Government are cared for and armed, if they are not also organized, on the American side under the tolerance of the authorities of the State of Texas and, it may even be said, that of the Federal authorities of the United States. The leniency of the American authorities respecting these bands is such that in a majority of the cases the conspirators, who are well known, when they have been discovered and taken to prison, obtain their liberty by insignificant promises which allows them to continue in their efforts."

The note ended with a complaint about the arms embargo that had been reinstated by Wilson months previously, then demanded "the immediate withdrawal of the American troops which are today on Mexican soil."

Lansing was so outraged at the tone of the Carranza-Aguilar note and at the fantastic allegations it contained that he contemptuously put it aside. It would be nearly three weeks before Mexico City got its answer.

That Lansing was incensed is understandable; the accusations made in paragraph 30 applied to Carranza and not to Wilson. For months, reports from U. S. agents in Mexico had been coming to the State and War departments concerning the Plan of San Diego, a fantastic scheme for wholesale takeover of large amounts of U. S. territory by renegades on both sides of the border. Receipt of the inflammatory note from Mexico City prompted Lansing to ask for an updated history of the plan from Vice-Consul Randolph Robertson in Monterrey. On June 9 Robertson's concise résumé arrived on Lansing's desk.

"On or about January 8, 1915," it began, "several Mexicans of the Huerta, or Federal, faction, who were military prisoners charged with political offenses, while confined at Monterrey [in the state of Nuevo León] signed what they called the Plan of San Diego. This plan was a scheme for the promulgation of a revolution in the states of Texas, Oklahoma, New Mexico, Arizona, Colorado, Nevada and California with the object of establishing an independent republic and was to have been participated in by the Mexicans, Negroes and Indians. After the success of the movement, the new republic was to either remain or become a part of Mexico. After securing the establishment of this republic, the originators and followers of the movement were to assist the Negroes to take six more of the States belonging to the American Union and from these form a Negro republic."

Robertson named the leaders of the movement as Basilio Ramos, Jr., of Nuevo Laredo, Mexico, and Agustín Garza. Ramos was arrested by American immigration authorities in mid-January, and was indicted by the U. S. District Court for the Southern District of Texas in May 1915. However, when the case for conspiracy came to trial, there was not sufficient evidence and Ramos was dismissed. Among papers taken from Ramos upon his arrest was a letter from co-conspirator Agustín Garza alluding to General Nafarrate, commanding the Carranza troops at Tampico. "At the time of Ramos' apprehension," reported Robertson, "he was an exile from Mexico, but some months later amnesty was granted him and he was banqueted and fêted by Carranza officials at Nuevo Laredo, Monterrey and Tampico and proclaimed a great hero. For months he has been actively engaged in furthering this Plan of San Diego.

"In the summer of 1915," Robertson continued, "another movement along the lines of the Plan of San Diego was started by Luis de la Rosa and Aniceto Pizano, former residents of Cameron County, Texas, where the former had been a deputy sheriff at Rio Hondo, a farming community near San Benito, and the latter was related to a number of the leading Mexican residents of South west Texas. Newspapers printed at Matamoros, Monterrey and Tampico all printed the manifesto of this new movement, and the press of northern Mexico continued thereafter for days to give glowing accounts of the victories won by the Texas revolutionists, the capture of towns, looting of banks, killing of American soldiers, hasty retreat of those of the inhabitants of Texas who had not been killed, the abandonment of Washington by President Wilson and the American Senate, et cetera. Anyone at all familiar with the way newspapers are published in Mexico is aware of the fact that no paper can keep on day after day printing articles of the nature of these articles without the consent and approval of the authorities, hence the deduction that the publication met with the approval of the Carranza authorities."

Robertson pointed out that "no one in Mexico carries arms without the knowledge and consent of the authorities," and that De la Rosa and his men were always seen walking the streets armed with—as many Mexicans claimed—guns provided by General Nafarrate, now commanding at Matamoros and a personal friend of both De la Rosa and Pizano.

"The followers of the original Plan of San Diego," said Robertson, "and Luis de la Rosa and his adherents have formed a revised plan of which De la Rosa is president and Ramos is secretary.

They have organized a number of juntas, or lodges, in Texas and Mexico. To enlist the Negroes in this movement, these people sent a Negro doctor, a fugitive from justice in the States, through Texas and Oklahoma, but my information is that this man met with no success among his colored brethren. Among the numerous officers of the Carranza Army who are in accord and working for the furtherance of the Plan of San Diego is Colonel Maurilio Rodríguez of the Osuna Brigade. This man is the party with whom I am informed Mr. Pablo Burchard, the German Consul at Monterrey, has been in conference . . . at the Hotel Aurora, which is just across the street from the capitol of Nuevo León." Robertson reported that soon after Wilson had recognized the Carranza regime, Colonel Rodríguez was given $50,000 by Carranza in person and told to "cease his activities, as the object of the raids had been accomplished."

Secretary Lansing could only assume that the $50,000 Carranza gave Rodríguez was routed via Berlin, and the mention of the German, Burchard, came as no surprise. Germans were everywhere in Mexico; German investment properties alone were spared the pillaging which other foreign oil and mining interests suffered. The Justice Department had carefully been following German agents in New York and Texas since early in 1915 when one of them, a German naval intelligence officer, Captain Franz von Rintelen, arrived in the United States with nearly $40 million to back the Huerta counterrevolution. But Huerta was arrested and Von Rintelen was recalled; however, it was all the same to the Germans as long as the United States could be kept entangled in Mexico while Germany fought the war to a successful conclusion on the Western Front, unhindered by the specter of massive American participation. There was little doubt that money earmarked originally for Huerta was now being spent to buttress Carranza's determination to oust American troops from Mexico, although Lansing could not yet make a direct connection between Berlin and the Plan of San Diego.

Robertson's report to Lansing concluded with the following observation: "Shortly after a conference at Nuevo Laredo, Mexico, between Governor James E. Ferguson of Texas and Don Venustiano Carranza, Aniceto Pizano was apprehended and detained at Matamoros, but notwithstanding the promise made to Governor Ferguson by the First Chief, Pizano was never delivered to the Texas authorities."

On June 7 General Funston sent the Secretary of War his own unsolicited comments concerning De la Rosa and Pizano. "Both men," he said, "have been active recently recruiting for new raids and have done so absolutely openly. The above facts are notorious and are familiar to practically all informed persons on the lower border and in [the Mexican state of] Tamaulipas. They show conclusively and in most glaring manner either the bad faith of Carranza or his unwillingness to oppose one of his subordinate generals, Nafarrate.

"The necessary force having been recruited, organized and armed are now approaching our border about four hundred strong, but we cannot tell where, in a distance of a hundred and fifty miles, they may attempt to cross river. I feel I should state frankly that a resumption of these raids marked with all the savage cruelties and barbarities of the lower border raids of last fall will rouse the people of that region to fury and cause them to cross the river in large numbers regardless of the wishes of the Government and take drastic action. They came perilously close to doing it last fall.

"I have contented myself with stating facts," Funston concluded, "and do not believe it to be in my province to suggest remedy further than to say that Carranza personally is to blame for the whole situation for reasons above stated."

Funston had barely sent his message to Baker when his orderly arrived with a telegram from General George Bell, Jr., commanding at El Paso: "Following just received from most reliable source. A colonel under General Cavazos named Carlos Nuñez was doing special secret service duty in Chihuahua until last Friday when General Cavazos called him and ordered him to join his command immediately with the explanation that it was a matter of four or five days only before hostilities would probably begin between the two governments . . . if our troops are not withdrawn. Feeling against Americans is stronger now than it has ever been since the revolutions first started."

The wires were humming all over Mexico. Pershing received a telegram from General Jacinto B. Treviño, commander of the Carranza forces at Chihuahua City, who told Pershing he had orders "to prevent the American forces now in this state from moving south, east, or west of the places they now occupy." Treviño warned that Pershing's forces would be attacked if they moved in any direction except north.

Pershing fired back a brief answer to Treviño the same day, telling him that he would use his "own judgment as to when and in what direction I shall move my forces in pursuit of bandits or in seeking information regarding bandits." He added that if the Americans were attacked by Mexican forces the responsibility for the consequences would lie with the Mexican government.

In Washington, Baker could only await developments. He had ordered the remaining regiments of the Regular Army to the border to back up the National Guard units sent down earlier, and now there were 35,828 men of infantry, cavalry, field artillery and even coast artillery regiments stationed in sixty-six towns along the border, almost all of them in Texas. Detachment strengths ranged from 4,660 officers and men stationed at Douglas, Arizona, to 50 men and 1 officer at Dryden, Texas. Would it be full-scale war, more border raids, or was it all a big bluff?*

On the night of June 10 part of the De la Rosa gang struck across the border in desolate country forty-five miles above Laredo, Texas, and made off with eighty horses from an isolated ranch. The following night a small party of armed Mexicans slipped across the river near Laredo and proceeded inland until they reached a railroad bridge near the small town of Webb. The bridge was sloshed with kerosene, but before it could be put to the torch a patrol of 9th Infantry arrived on the scene and opened fire, driving the raiders back across the river in a running battle. Three of the raiders were killed and six were captured, including one Japanese. One of the slain was dressed in full Carranza uniform, and papers discovered on the body identified the victim as Lieutenant Colonel Villareal of the Constitutionalist army.**

The new commander of the de facto forces at Nuevo Laredo,

---

* On June 20, 1916, the *New York Times* published a list of U. S. Army and National Guard units deployed along the border, showing how many men of which regiment were stationed where. This list was a boon to De la Rosa and other bandits planning future raids.
** The captured Mexicans were placed on trial in the district court at Laredo on July 7, 1916. Among those tried was Captain Norberto Pessot, who made the following statement to a representative of the Mexican consul and to the court: "I am a member of the Constitutionalist army. I am not a bandit. I came here obeying superior orders. I was under the command of a superior officer. I want the government that furnished me arms to protect me. If the government of my country for which I did this will not protect me, my conscience will be clear and I will abide by the laws of this state."

General Alfredo Ricaut, actually pursued the raiders and managed to capture forty members of the De la Rosa gang. But De la Rosa escaped and boarded a freight train to Monterrey. There he was taken into custody upon orders of the governor of the state, but repeated requests to have De la Rosa, a U. S. citizen, turned over to the American consulate were of no avail.

The imprisonment of the prime mover of the Plan of San Diego failed to dampen the fiery spirits of the rest of his followers. At two o'clock in the morning on June 15, under a bright moon, approximately one hundred raiders splashed across the Rio Grande and attacked the small town of San Ygnacio, thirty-three miles below Laredo. The Mexicans expected the town to be lightly defended, but they met stiff resistance from 146 troopers of the 14th Cavalry. Rifles blazed in the night for thirty minutes, leaving 8 Mexican and 3 American dead. At first light the commander at San Ygnacio, Major Alonzo Grey, led his two troops across the river to find the raiders' trail. Downriver, at Brownsville, 360 men of the 3rd Cavalry crossed the border and fanned out to help the 14th, but the raiders had scattered into the desert.

In Laredo thirty outraged citizens descended upon the offices of *El Progreso*, a Spanish-language newspaper whose editorials had lately been given over to violent attacks on the U. S. government. The vigilantes, most of them armed, seized the managing editor, a Mexican who called himself Leo D. Walker, and roughly escorted him to the international bridge at pistol point. They shoved him across the line, shouting never to set foot again in Texas on pain of death. In Chihuahua City an angry mob stormed the American consulate, throwing stones. The consular shield was ripped from the wall and dragged through the streets. The familiar cry "Death to the gringos!" was heard again.

Lansing received a telegram from the American consul, Alonzo Garrett, datelined Laredo. Garrett had fled his post in Nuevo Laredo on June 14 when he was tipped off that Mexicans planned to kidnap him. Garrett wired that among the raiders killed by the 9th Infantry at San Ygnacio were two Carrancista officers, identified by passports and other documents, including an order signed by General Rodríguez to Major Cruz instructing him to "pass himself as a Villista and seize horses, arms, equipment and supplies." Neither Lansing nor Wilson could figure out whether Carranza was directing these attacks, or whether—as Pershing suspected—Carranza had little control of his officers in northern Mexico, many of whom obviously were in sympathy with De la Rosa's grandiose scheme and behaved any way that suited them. Whatever Carranza's actual feelings were, the effect was the same: the Tex-Mex border was on fire, people were being killed and ordinary citizens went about armed with as much ordnance as they could carry.

By Friday afternoon, June 16, Lansing had completed his reply to the Carranza-Aguilar note and laid it on the President's desk for approval. Wilson, however, declined for the moment to send it or to make its contents known to the public. He explained that the reply would be withheld until after adjournment of the Democratic National Convention, then in session at St. Louis, because he did not wish to be accused of playing politics with foreign policy in such a serious situation. The note, Lansing told the press, would probably be released early the following week.

On Sunday, June 18, Wilson startled the nation by announcing that the entire National Guard, more than one hundred thousand men, would be mustered for duty along the Mexican border. The guard was totally unprepared for instant mobilization, as were the nation's railroads, and it wasn't until twelve days later that the first contingent, an understrength regiment of Illinois infantry, arrived in San Antonio. Troops were stuffed into unlighted day coaches, often without rations, and sent rattling to the Southwest from every part of the nation. Many of the guardsmen were appalled at the region's barren, inhospitable terrain, made worse by the baking 110- to 120-degree temperature that prevails along the Rio Grande in high summer. Those who suffered worst were men from the lush New England and Northwestern states. When First Lieutenant E. M. Zell arrived at base camp from his native Maryland he alighted from the train and gazed with dismay at the forbidding scenery and cried out, "Great God! Is *this* Columbus, New Mexico?" Brother officers paid no attention to Zell's remark, but a few minutes later Zell shot himself in the head.

At Mazatlán, in the state of Sinaloa, on the western coast of Mexico opposite the lower tip of Baja California, the American vice-consul, A. Gordon Brown, hurried toward the office of the local military commander, for he had just received disturbing news: the governor of Sinaloa had issued a proclamation, under orders from the de facto government, stating that war would be declared on the United States. The citizens and soldiers at Mazatlán interpreted this to mean that war had already started and the streets began to fill with singing, shouting people. Cathedral bells tolling for late mass added to the clamor on this Sunday morning, June 18.

Brown made his way through the crowds and reached the office of the military commander, General Metza. Brown opened the interview by asking about the alleged declaration of war, adding that the United States had no hostile intentions toward Mexico, but if war was declared Americans in the district would look to Mexican authorities for protection until they could be safely evacuated. In fact, the gunboat *Annapolis* was at that moment lying offshore, ready to receive refugees. Metza started to reply with the assurances Brown sought, but was interrupted by the sounds of gunfire coming from the direction of the wharf. A Mexican soldier rushed into the office and excitedly reported that American sailors had landed at Mazatlán and were preparing to take over the city. Brown hurried from Metza's office to his own.

Brown's arrival at the consulate coincided with that of Metza's chief of staff, Colonel Guillermo Nelson, whose American father was a long-time resident of the country. Nelson was as puzzled about the gunfire as Brown, and together they drove in the colonel's staff car to the wharf, which was swarming with an angry mob. Stretcher-bearers were picking up three wounded Mexicans, but no American sailors could be seen. Confusion was great, and neither Brown nor Nelson could get a clear idea of what had happened. They got back in the car and drove to Metza's office. There Brown discovered that two American sailors, Ensign O. W. Kessing and Assistant Paymaster Andrew Mowatt, had been put in jail. Brown was escorted to their cell, where he learned what had happened.

Kessing told Brown that he and another officer had been sent ashore earlier that morning by the skipper of the *Annapolis*, Commander Arthur Kavanagh, with instructions to report to Brown that the gunboat was ready to take aboard Americans who wished to leave the city. As the boat neared land it was waved off by Mexican officers, who told Kessing that no American boat was allowed to be in contact with the city. Kessing returned with this news to Kavanagh, who immediately ordered the boat manned with three armed bluejackets and returned to the wharf in an attempt to parley with the Mexicans. Kessing said that this time they were invited ashore by a Carrancista officer, but the minute the boat heaved to and he and Mowatt stepped onto the wharf they were "immediately arrested and attacked by an infuriated mob of soldiers and civilians." Protection from beating or worse was afforded the surprised Americans by some Carranza officers, who escorted them to jail for confinement.

When the two officers were taken away, Mexicans onshore had shouted for the seamen to lay down their rifles and get out of the boat. Instead, the sailors pushed away from the wharf and started back for the ship. At this point a squad of soldiers began shooting at them. Bosun's Mate Second Class I. M. Laughter was hit and died shortly afterward. The other seamen returned the fire, hitting three of the Mexican soldiers. The crowd scattered and the boat made it safely back to the *Annapolis*.

General Metza told another story: he said that the first shot came from "a drunken Japanese" and that the Americans panicked and opened an indiscriminate fire into the crowd.

Brown faced Metza and demanded the release of the American officers. Metza seemed indifferent to the gravity of the situation and was "as hostile as if war had really been declared." Brown was afraid that if Kessing and Mowatt were kept in jail overnight they would be mobbed and killed by the people of Mazatlán, most of whom were armed. Brown bore down on Metza with the threat that if the Americans were not released immediately, the affair would assume an international significance far beyond its worth, and that if war were declared on account of the outrage, not only would Mexico suffer but he, Metza, "would suffer from angry Americans." Nelson suggested to his superior that the wisest course would be to release the naval officers forthwith.

Metza, recalled Brown, "turned rather pale and in a very few moments signed the release." Kessing and Mowatt were quickly returned to the *Annapolis*.

The next day several hundred Mexican students gathered in the great courtyard of the National Palace in Mexico City and called upon Carranza to offer their services in the war that was apparently imminent. Carranza, stiff and autocratic, appeared before the excited youths and told them, "It is impossible for me to forecast what will be the outcome, for that depends upon the

United States, not upon us. We have no desire to precipitate war, but if unfortunately we are obliged to enter into an unequal contest I have faith that we all know how to comply with our duty and we will perish before we see our national territory conquered."

On Tuesday morning, June 20, Lansing at last delivered his reply to the Carranza-Aguilar note that had so angered him. He rejected Aguilar's every contention, virtually calling Carranza a liar. Lansing's attitude was stiff and his choice of words harsh. His reply was a broadside, lacking in the usual diplomatic mollification or niceties. Lansing expressed "surprise and regret" at the "discourteous tone and temper" of Aguilar's note, then he launched into a direct attack upon the attitudes and actions of Carranza and the Constitutionalist government. "It would be tedious," he said, "to recount instance after instance, outrage after outrage, atrocity after atrocity, to illustrate the true nature and extent of the widespread conditions of lawlessness and violence which have prevailed . . . Carranza adherents and even Carrancista troops took part in the looting, burning and killing."

Lansing brought up the futility of the Scott-Obregón conferences at El Paso and in Juárez, then turned to the question of Carranza's assurances that his troops could handle bandit raiders without help from Pershing's forces. "Notwithstanding the assurances of [your] memorandum, it is well known that the forces of the de facto Government have not carried on a vigorous pursuit of the remaining bandits and that no proper distribution to prevent the invasion of American territory has been made." Lansing said that he was forced to conclude that Carranza "did not and does not now intend or desire that these outlaws should be captured, destroyed or dispersed by American troops or, at the request of this Government, by Mexican troops."

Lansing referred to the "conditions of anarchy" that prevailed in the Mexican states bordering Texas and lambasted Carranza again for the "inactivity" of his forces and their failure to cooperate with Pershing. He pointed to the "constant threat of invasion" by Mexican raiders, adding that "it is unreasonable to expect the United States to withdraw its forces from Mexican territory or to prevent their entry again when their presence is the only check upon further bandit outrages and the only efficient means of protecting American lives and homes—safeguards

which General Carranza, though internationally obligated to supply, is manifestly unable or unwilling to give."

Lansing accused the de facto government of "attempts to ab-
solve itself from the first duty of any government, namely, the
protection of life and property. This is the paramount obligation
for which governments are instituted, and governments neglect-
ing or failing to perform it are not worthy of the name."

Referring to Carranza's demand that Pershing's troops be immediately pulled back across the border, Lansing concluded his
tart riposte by stating: "For the reasons I have herein fully set
forth, this request of the de facto Government cannot now be
entertained."

Thus, a dangerous stalemate. Only a spark, it seemed, was
needed to explode the volatile atmosphere into a useless and
bloody clash of arms. In Washington, General Scott ordered his
staff to get busy with planning the logistics and movements required for a full-scale invasion of that chaotic nation below the
Rio Grande. He would move his troops along three railroad lines
leading into Chihuahua and Coahuila.

Pershing shifted his headquarters north, to Nueva Casas
Grandes, where communications were better than at Namiquipa.
He sent patrols in every direction. At the Tepehuanes Ranch, east
of Namiquipa, N Troop of the 13th Cavalry surrounded the buildings at dawn and captured another Villa lieutenant, Pedro Luján,
one of the Columbus raiders. Luján was in bed at the time the
cavalrymen seized him, and not a shot was fired.

Pershing's main concern was for his line of communication.
Of the fifteen thousand Carrancista troops that had moved in his
direction from Saltillo in May, ten thousand were said to be near
Villa Ahumada, only seventy-five miles east of Casas Grandes.
When this report reached Pershing he summoned Captain Charles
T. Boyd of the 10th Cavalry. In view of what was to happen
shortly, Pershing's exact wording of the orders given Boyd as-
sumes great significance: "Take your troops and reconnoiter in
the direction of Ahumada and obtain as much information as you
can regarding the forces there." Pershing cautioned Boyd, "This
is a reconnaissance only and you will not be expected to fight. In
fact, I want you to avoid a fight if possible. Do not allow yourself
to be surprised by superior numbers. But, if wantonly attacked,

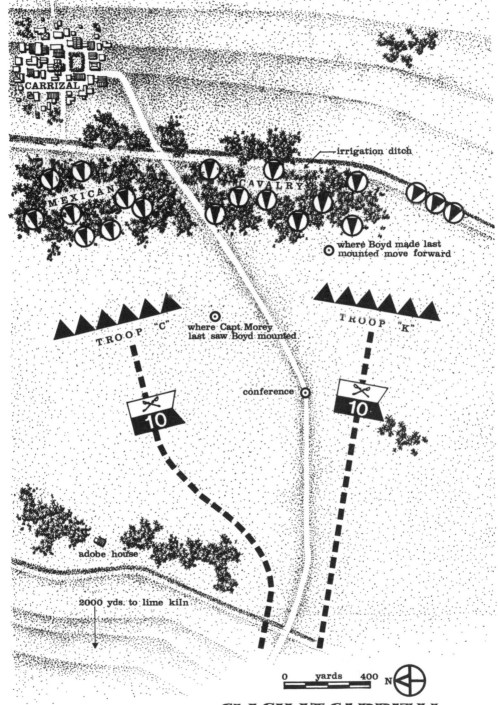

CARRIZAL

irrigation ditch

MEXICAN CAVALRY

where Boyd made last
mounted move forward

TROOP "C"

where Capt. Morey
last saw Boyd mounted

TROOP "K"

conference

10

10

adobe house

2000 yds. to lime kiln

0   yards   400   N

CLASH AT CARRIZAL
21 JUNE 1916

use your judgment as to what you should do, having due regard for the safety of your command."

Boyd, aggressive and ambitious, eagerly assembled his forty-three seasoned black troopers and set off for Ahumada on the morning of June 18. At the same time Captain Lewis S. Morey, a lean, tight-lipped, bookish-looking officer with eyeglasses, led forty-six men of K Troop, 10th Cavalry, away from the little camp at Ojo Federico, north of Casas Grandes, and started riding east. His orders were the same as Boyd's: reconnoiter, but avoid a fight. Morey observed that "The march promised to be an interesting one, [and] it appeared that some lessons might be learned." As, indeed, they were.

The cavalry men moved across a parched, thinly settled plain. Grazing was sparse, and when K Troop reached the Santa María River they found it dry. The mules, poorly fed, strained against the ration wagon loaded with a ton of supplies. Ahead lay fifty miles of barren country. Morey decided he could make better time if he stripped down his patrol, and ordered the wagon, ten men and the led horses to return to the line of communication. Rations were taken from the wagon and cached on the prairie for the return march. Thus lightened—and weakened—Morey's troop proceeded swiftly and reached the Santo Domingo Ranch, less than a day's march from Ahumada. There Morey found Boyd and his troop already encamped, resting for the final push on Ahumada. They decided to join the two troops and Boyd, who was the senior officer, assumed command.

That evening the two troop commanders, the Mormon scout Lemuel Spillsbury, and Boyd's second-in-command, dashing First Lieutenant Henry R. Adair, conferred about the best approach to Ahumada. Included in the conversation was the ranch foreman, an American named W. P. McCabe, who reported to Boyd that Carranza cavalry, four hundred strong, had recently occupied the ranch but had moved nine miles eastward and was stationed at the town of Carrizal, which lay between the ranch and Villa Ahumada.

McCabe, who knew the country, advised Boyd against moving through Carrizal to get at Ahumada because "the main part of Carrizal was a nasty trap to go through." Lem Spillsbury advised Boyd to move his command around the town, pointing out that there were three roads leading out of Carrizal to Ahumada. Morey and Adair concurred, but Boyd remained obstinate, saying that his orders directed him to pass through Carrizal—which they did not. Morey disagreed with Boyd's interpretation of Pershing's order, and McCabe overheard Morey say that "it was his judgment not to try to force his way through the town but would go into the town first, or go in alone, if Captain Boyd ordered him to." Then McCabe overheard Boyd say something to Morey about "making history." Morey took out his wallet and pocket watch and handed the valuables to McCabe with instructions as to their disposition; he was not at all sure he would be coming back from Carrizal.

At four o'clock in the morning on June 21, the troopers mounted and set out for Carrizal. They reached an irrigation ditch a mile southwest of town at six-thirty and watered the horses while the officers swept the terrain with field glasses. The town was on a gentle rise, the buildings and church tower partially obscured by cottonwood groves and an orchard fronting a deep irrigation ditch running in front of Carrizal. Between the Americans and the town stretched about six hundred yards of flat grassy plain devoid of cover. Morey could see Carrancista soldiers withdrawing from outpost positions and station themselves among the trees. Other troops emerged from the town and took cover in the irrigation ditch.

Boyd sent a messenger forward with a note requesting permission to go through town on their way to Villa Ahumada. A dozen Mexican officers rode on the plain under a flag of truce and conferred with Boyd through Spillsbury, who acted as interpreter. The parley was lengthy, but the upshot was that Boyd was refused permission to pass through Carrizal. Boyd rode back, and against Pershing's express orders to avoid combat, told the troopers to advance. They moved forward a few hundred yards, then Boyd halted them at the sign of an approaching messenger. The commander at Carrizal, General Félix Gómez, had issued a written invitation for Boyd to enter Carrizal for another conference. Suspicious, Boyd refused, and once again ordered the seventy-nine men of C and K Troops forward, this time in skirmish formation. General Gómez and some others rode out to confer with Boyd, and once again the troops halted. Gómez told Boyd that orders from General Treviño forbade movement of any American troops except toward the north, and that if Boyd insisted on moving through Carrizal "he would have to walk over the dead bodies of

Mexican soldiers." Then Gómez rode back to deploy his troops.

Spillsbury and Adair told Boyd that it might be advisable to send word back to Pershing for further orders, or to ask Gómez to wire Treviño requesting specific permission for the 10th Cavalry to move through Carrizal, but Boyd brushed them aside, ordering the command to advance on the Mexican positions. Morey didn't like it; he estimated that there were at least a hundred and twenty Mexican troops entrenched before the town, and they probably had machine guns. Boyd ordered a dismounted advance across three hundred yards of open plain.

Boyd so deployed his own small force that more than two hundred yards separated C and K Troops. The Mexicans, both mounted and on foot, had already flanked K Troop off on the right before the first shot was fired.

Boyd, still on his horse, ordered his men to charge. They rushed toward the cottonwood trees and were met with a blast of machine-gun fire. Now the line of Carrancistas, using the irrigation ditch as a trench, opened up with heavy and accurate rifle fire, and Boyd's men began to fall. Boyd was hit in the shoulder, but led his men into the trees and silenced the machine gun, but not before nearly all of the C Troop riflemen had become casualties.

Lieutenant Adair and a handful of men reached the irrigation ditch, and bloody fighting followed. The Americans drove out the Mexicans, but Mexican cavalry issued from the trees and swept toward Adair. He rose from the ditch with a pistol in his hand, but was shot dead through the heart. Boyd spurred his horse toward the ditch, but he too was shot and instantly killed.

Morey and his men were being raked from the front and flank. Morey was hit once in the arm, then moments later was knocked down by a bullet that tore through his shoulder. Mexican cavalry rode behind the Americans and scattered the led horses and their guards. Morey's men of K Troop, pinned down, could not advance. They took what cover was offered by a slight depression in the ground and, like the veterans they were, began to pour carefully aimed shots with their Springfields. Mexicans were being killed and wounded, but they would not yield. They pressed in closer on Morey's men and inflicted more casualties. A first sergeant named Winrow, hit in arm, thigh and leg, staggered toward a loose Mexican pony wandering in the confusion of battle, and managed to gain the saddle and ride away from the carnage. Morey never saw him again.

With two of the officers dead and the other wounded, with many noncoms hit and with the horses scattered, morale cracked and the survivors began drifting back, away from the deadly Mexican rifles. The Carrancistas did not press their advantage—they could have used their cavalry to kill or capture every American trooper on the field—but were content to round up the wounded and those who surrendered. General Gómez had been killed during the first furious minutes of combat and this had taken some of the aggressiveness out of the others.

Four troopers, one of them wounded, helped Morey off the battlefield and to the safety of a lime kiln two thousand yards west of Carrizal. Morey wrote out a terse account of what had happened and gave it to one of the troopers for delivery to the first American officer they came across. When darkness fell, Morey ordered the three unwounded soldiers to leave him and the other man where they were and to make their escape. Morey's wounds had stopped bleeding, and after resting as long as they dared, he and the trooper crept out of the kiln and struck off on foot across the empty prairie.

The rout at Carrizal was the worst disaster to befall any unit of the Expedition since crossing the border. Twelve men had been killed and ten wounded, and twenty-four, including Spillsbury, were taken prisoner. The Carrancista troops had sustained far worse casualties. The Mexicans admitted to thirty killed and forty wounded. The captured Americans were relieved of their arms, ammunition, cash and valuables and marched to Villa Ahumada, where they were put on a train to Chihuahua City. They were lodged in cells in the state penitentiary, there to await an uncertain fate. The prison food was not to their liking, but the guards treated them humanely.

Foreman McCabe watched the survivors of Carrizal stream into the Santo Domingo Ranch after the battle. At first he chastised them, saying they were doing "a mighty poor thing to run off and leave their comrades." But the troopers paused only long enough to cache the ammunition from the packtrain inside McCabe's barn and ride off to the west. Others came in on foot, and these McCabe fed and doctored. A few mounted troops came in and breathlessly reported that more than a thousand Mexicans were riding toward the ranch. Soon McCabe was left alone, except for two Chinese workmen. They hid all that day in some brush, but nobody came. The next day McCabe and the Chinese fled the ranch at the approach of twenty Mexican riders. Twelve miles away, at the Suterano Windmill, McCabe came upon Captain Morey and four troopers of the 10th Cavalry. They were loaded into a wagon and taken back to Casas Grandes.

Sergeant Mack Emerson, then of the 4th Field Artillery, recalled: "Captain Morey, Lieutenant Seth Cook and some other officers got together after Morey got back from Carrizal. They had several pint bottles of whiskey and Captain Morey got pretty drunk. I listened in on most of the conversation, but Morey didn't want to talk about Carrizal. When Lieutenant Cook said it looked like Boyd had bungled very badly, Morey just nodded his head.

"Colonel Young [the 10th's strapping Negro executive officer] was in a rage. He went to Pershing and said he wanted to take the regiment to Carrizal and get his men back, but Pershing wouldn't let him. We were all excited, believing that soon we would be fighting the Carrancistas. Our battery had been in Mexico for nearly four months and had never fired a shot."

At Carrizal, Morey had "learned something," as he had hoped he would before starting out on the reconnaissance mission: Treviño's orders enjoining American troop movements in any direction except north should be taken seriously; Carrancista troops would stubbornly hold ground in defense of their towns despite heavy casualties. And Boyd, as he had prophesied, had indeed "made history"—if not precipitated war as well.*

* In commenting on Boyd's incredible decision at Carrizal, Pershing praised Boyd's personal courage but added: "After my conversation with him I felt confident that Captain Boyd fully understood the importance and delicacy of his mission. No one could have been more surprised and chagrined than I was to learn that he had become so seriously involved."

CHAPTER

12

No Bugles, No Glory

Late Wednesday afternoon, June 21, Woodrow Wilson was in his White House office going over correspondence from Secretary Lansing. Aware of acutely sensitive feelings in Latin America concerning "Yankee imperialism," Lansing had sent copies of his reply to Aguilar to the diplomatic representatives of eighteen Latin American nations, adding: "Should this situation eventuate into hostilities, I take this opportunity to inform you that this Government would have for its object not intervention in Mexican affairs, but the defense of American territory from further invasion by bands of armed Mexicans, protection of American citizens and property along the boundary from outrages committed by such bandits, and the prevention of future depredations, by force of arms against the marauders infesting this region and against a Government which is encouraging and aiding in their activities. Hostilities," Lansing concluded, "would be simply a state of international war without purpose on the part of the United States, other than to end the conditions which menace our national peace and the safety of our citizens."

Wilson's attention was jerked away from the correspondence by the shouts of a newsboy crying "Extra! Extra!" along Pennsylvania Avenue. Through a window opened against Washington's sultry heat the President could make out but few of the excited words, but it seemed to him—as he reported to Lansing—that hostilities had already begun. Wilson sent a member of the White House staff into the streets to buy a newspaper. Thus, nearly eight hours after it occurred, the President learned of the fight at Carrizal.

Pershing didn't receive word of the clash at Carrizal until late in the afternoon. The meager details reached the Expedition's commander in a telegram sent by General Bell from El Paso; Bell had learned of the encounter from the Mexican consul there, who in turn had received his information from Mexico City. Pershing assumed that war had broken out, that his command was under general attack by de facto forces. Assuming that Funston knew all the details, Pershing wired the general that evening requesting approval to seize the Mexican Central Railroad, move south and take Chihuahua City; in addition, he wanted General Bell's troops from Fort Bliss to assist in the drive.

Funston was bewildered by Pershing's telegram. Why was Pershing planning a major offensive? What had happened at Carrizal? Who was to blame? Funston knew only what had been relayed to him from the Adjutant General's office, and that information had originated in Mexico City. The report stated that forty Americans had been killed. The next day Funston sent a telegram to Pershing at Casas Grandes: "Why in the name of God do I hear nothing from you? The whole country has known for ten hours that a considerable force of your command was apparently defeated yesterday with heavy losses at Carrizal. Under existing orders why were they so far from your line? Being at such a distance I assume that now, nearly twenty-four hours after the affair, news has not reached you who was responsible for what on its face seems to have been a terrible blunder."

As stragglers, some on foot and some on horse, drifted into Casas Grandes, Pershing was able to piece together the details of Carrizal. He was able to answer Funston's frantic message a few hours after it arrived, adding concrete details as they became available during the next three days. Morey's letter, written on the battlefield, was not placed in Pershing's hands until Sunday, June 25. Pershing sent a detachment of the 11th Cavalry under Howze toward Ahumada to round up survivors, and then the true casualties became known. Pershing was mortified at Boyd's "inexplicable" behavior, but he still considered the attack by the de facto troops an act of war, saying that Boyd had been led into a trap. Pershing reported to Funston that he had sent cavalry patrols as far as sixty miles to the west, but there were no indications that Carranza troops were moving against him from Sonora. Funston ordered Pershing to sit tight and await the outcome of diplomatic exchanges then in progress.

On Saturday, June 24, Secretary of State Lansing and President Wilson had gone over a note delivered to Lansing by Eliseo Arredondo, the Carranza representative in Washington. The note merely restated orders given to General Treviño by Carranza regarding the direction the Mexicans would allow Pershing's troops to move, ending with the information now known to the world that "several men on both sides were killed." Wilson and Lansing read into the note the assumption that the incident at Carrizal might well be repeated; there was no indication that Treviño's orders would be revoked in order to lessen the chance of further bloodshed, no mention of the Americans still in jail at Chihuahua City.

The move was Wilson's. On Sunday morning he replied, through Lansing: "The Government of the United States can put no other construction upon the communication . . . than that it is intended as a formal avowal of deliberately hostile action against the forces of the United States now in Mexico, and of the purpose to attack them without provocation whenever they move from their present position in pursuance of the objects for which they were sent." Then Wilson demanded the immediate release of the American prisoners taken at Carrizal and the return of U.S. government property seized after the battle. With Pershing leashed—but with his command still on alert—Wilson impatiently awaited reply from Carranza.

On Wednesday, June 28, Lansing ripped open an envelope from Arredondo and was astonished to read not a reply to the U. S. government's demands, but a ridiculous charge sheet leveled against Pershing's command, charges that had no bearing on the serious situation at hand. Pershing's men were on the rampage in Chihuahua; some three thousand American troops had descended upon the peaceful town of La Cruz, arresting three hundred harmless citizens and "subjecting them to uncalled-for maltreatment . . . a column of the same forces is committing all kinds of outrages in places along its way, those distinguishing themselves by their excesses being the Apaches . . ." Lansing bucked the offensive letter to Secretary of War Baker for refutation by Pershing, which quickly came.

Wilson, who did not believe that Carranza would yield, asked

Baker to draft a message for Congress. In its essence, Wilson's declaration was to prepare the nation for plunging into Mexico with the balance of the United States Army in order to protect the border and, if necessary, to clear all of Chihuahua of military forces of the de facto government until yet another Mexican government could be formed to relieve the Americans of the burden. Wilson was ready to write off Carranza and his Constitutionalists as representing the will of the Mexican people.

In Mexico City, Minister of War Álvaro Obregón was bragging that should war break out he would lead forces to drive the Americans from Chihuahua and march through Texas to seize San Antonio. But Carranza was forced to eschew bombast in favor of a sober appraisal of his chances in a war with the United States. Although the Constitutionalist army greatly outnumbered Pershing's command, this fact alone had little bearing; Pershing's forces were concentrated, while the de facto troops were scattered the length and breadth of Mexico. In the state of Morelos, south of Mexico City, thirty thousand of Carranza's men were tied down fighting twenty thousand die-hard irregulars led by Zapata, who refused to abandon the bloody crusade against the Constitutionalists in spite of the savage reprisals inflicted upon his people.*

Carranza's German advisers pointed out, correctly, that the U. S. Army was understrength, lacking in equipment and without even the vestige of air power. The Germans boasted of how they had managed to buy up abandoned American mines and get them working again. But Carranza needed more than encouragement and trickles of silver and copper to engage the Colossus of the North, and he knew it. The national economy was in ruin, and as a spy sent to Chihuahua by General Bell had reported, most of the Carranza cavalry "horses were skeletons and the men very ragged." Carranza could read newspapers and he learned that Secretary Baker was expediting deployment of national guardsmen along the border, promising the numbers would swell to more than one hundred and ten thousand by the end of July.

---

* When Cuautla fell, the Carrancistas hanged the parish priest as a spy for Zapata. At Jiutepec more than two hundred Zapatista prisoners were rounded up and shot to death. At Tlaltizapán the Carrancista conqueror, General Pablo González, ruthlessly executed 286 villagers, nearly half of them women and including 42 young boys and girls.

The situation was now at ignition point, but Carranza was powerless to stop the fanatical De la Rosa remnants from raiding into Texas when they dared.* As long as Carranza was unable to guarantee the integrity of the border and the safety of the Americans living immediately across the river, the chances of withdrawal of the Punitive Expedition were as remote as the stars. Risking a war he could not win would cost him not only his title as First Chief but, in the manner of revolutionary politics, his life as well.

Carranza ordered General Treviño to release the American prisoners, and see that they were put on a train and returned safely to the border. The twenty-three black troopers and Lemuel Spillsbury reached Juárez on the afternoon of June 29. Thousands on both sides of the river crowded around the train station and the International Bridge to watch the arrival of the men who were as famous in the Americas as Captain Dreyfus had been in France a few years earlier. The prisoners, who had been stripped of their uniforms and shoes, presented a ludicrous sight as they stepped from the train and were marched to the delousing station at El Paso. One trooper wore only a blanket, most were without shirts, a few were barefoot and many shuffled across the bridge in open-weave sandals. Gaunt Spillsbury marched across the bridge wearing a white yachting cap and white duck pants described as "several sizes too large."

The decision against war had been made. There was now no need for postures of arrogance. Lansing received a note from Aguilar dated July 4 that for straightforwardness exceeded any yet received from Mexico City. "The American Government," said Aguilar, "with reason believes that the insecurity of its frontier is the cause of the difficulty, and the Mexican Government considers that the continuance of American troops on Mexican territory is the immediate cause of the controversy." Having succinctly stated the problem without corollary threats or recriminations, Aguilar proposed that the open sores could be cleansed by direct negotiation between the two governments. He suggested that three com-

---

* On July 4, raiders struck across the Rio Grande near Fort Hancock, Texas, forty miles below El Paso, killing a U. S. customs inspector and an American trooper. Three of the De la Rosa gang were killed, another three captured.

missioners from each country be named, to sit face to face before an agenda until an agreement was reached that would satisfy both Carranza and Wilson.

Wilson was relieved and Lansing was delighted. Since the release of the Carrizal prisoners and publication of Captain Morey's letter, which put the blame where it belonged, i.e., on Captain Boyd, the White House had been deluged with telegrams from organizations and private citizens pleading for the United States to keep out of war with Mexico; for every wire that advocated further military intervention there were ten strongly against. Furthermore, Carranza had not made the expected demand for withdrawal of the Expedition as a requisite for opening the Joint High Commission meetings; thus, Pershing could be left where he was in Chihuahua. To pull American troops from Mexico now would be to lose votes in the coming election, only four months away.

Increasingly cordial notes flowed back and forth between Mexico City and Washington. Carranza named Luis Cabrera, Ignacio Bonillas and Alberto Pani to represent the de facto viewpoint, and a few days later Wilson selected the U. S. commissioners: Secretary of the Interior Franklin K. Lane; John R. Mott, well-known leader of the Y.M.C.A.; and a Delaware judge named George Gray. Carranza even agreed that the Joint High Commission should meet on American soil. The first meeting would be held in a hotel in New London, Connecticut, on September 6.

Pershing concentrated his command at Colonia Dublán, where the regiments of cavalry and infantry and support troops dug in for the balance of the summer and, as many believed, for the fall and winter as well. The rains started in July, bringing some relief from the heat, but turning the earth into a clayey morass that sucked at men's shoes. Large tents were not available to protect the troops from the rains, from the vicious dust storms that began later, from the sun that was always malevolent when the clouds parted. The men learned to make adobe from the wet earth, reinforcing it with straw, and erected walled huts roofed with shelter halves. They lived no better than the poorest Indian. For a stretch of sixty-two days the men of the 4th Field Artillery were fed beans three times a day, buttressed with hardtack. The engineers worked overtime to turn the muddy track leading out from Columbus into a usable military road, and by the end of the summer trucks were plying back and forth with mail, meat, flour, salt, coffee and new field shoes.

When the rains stopped the country resembled Switzerland more than it did the Sahara, but boredom was the big enemy. The camp was four miles from Dublán, behind wire which was patrolled by armed infantry to keep the troops away from the Mormons, who had suffered cruelly from bandit depredations for four years before the coming of the Americans. In a move that would have shocked the mothers of America had they known, Pershing wisely allowed the creation of a military brothel inside the compound. The girls were Mexican, the "madam" an American expatriate, the health inspector an officer of the U. S. Army Medical Corps and the fee was two dollars American. The venereal rate among members of the Expedition was far lower than among American troops serving along the border, in the Philippines, Haiti or Panama.

Pershing, as every military commander since Hannibal has known, realized that the solution to troop ennui is hard work. Strict garrison rules prevailed at Dublán, including strenuous field exercises by all arms which left the men too tired to be quarrelsome at the end of the day. Lieutenant George Patton kept busy planning daily and weekly schedules for the fighting troops, but was grieved because early in the campaign the heavy cavalry sabers had been declared useless and sent back to Columbus. Looking ahead to future campaigns Patton wrote an impassioned essay for the *Cavalry Journal:* "It is certainly well beyond the range of things probable that our nation shall not for all time confine its endeavors to the pursuit of small bands of disorganized brigands. Assuredly, we shall yet have to oppose modern armies fully on a par with our own. Armies imbued with the spirit of vigorous aggression, trained to quick and powerful blows and eager for quick results. If with fire action alone we attempt to meet the cavalry which will precede such an army, we will be made helpless and immobile and will not fulfill the duties of screening and of reconnaissance for which we have been primarily created. Truly," Patton warned, "a saberless cavalry in the face of such foes would be like a body without a soul. Can mounted infantry, or troops used as such, produce such men as Murat, Seidlitz, Sheridan or Stuart? No! Even though their sabers may not have drunk deep in every fight, it was the glorious traditions so nobly inscribed by the saber which gave these cavalry leaders their immortal place in the Hall of Fame!"*

Reviewing the campaign, Pershing cast his cold professional eye on the performances of the regimental commanders during the five months they had been in the field. Pershing had high praise for Dodd of the 7th and Howze of the 11th Cavalry, but careers of certain other field-grade subordinates were withered in a private letter he wrote to Funston on August 31.

Speaking of one full colonel, Pershing said: "He is a very agreeable man socially and one for whom I have high regard. He does many very creditable things in helping the officers and men of his regiment and has many traits that are admirable. I spoke favorable of him in the Columbus investigation as I do not think him to blame for what happened there. But he is about the limit from a military standpoint. He has done nothing of value since being with the Expedition. He knows little of service in the field, or else cares nothing. He depends upon his staff to drag him through, and he happens to have had a pretty poor staff during this time. His regiment has been reported for more delinquencies than all the others put together. Such a man should be shelved before anything real active comes along."

Referring to another full colonel, an officer liked personally by those who served under him, Pershing called him "another utter failure down here. He has not the least practical ability in the world. He is weak, vacillating and dilatory. Any other man in his place with his chance would have stood a good chance to strike Villa's band while it was in the vicinity of Namiquipa. But he delayed until it was too late. Men of this kind should make way for those who are efficient."

A lieutenant colonel of cavalry seemed to Pershing "simply asleep. He takes no interest in anything, lacks initiative and is, upon the whole, hopeless as a regimental commander. The sooner the Army gets rid of men like these three mentioned the better it will be off."

Pershing's syntax was not always faultless, but his judgment

---

* Neither bullets nor cold steel put Patton out of the campaign. He was working at his desk one night in October and attempted to adjust a kerosene lantern hanging from a tent pole. The lamp exploded and Patton was badly burned on the face and hands. He was sent to the base hospital at Columbus for treatment, then given recuperative leave with his wife and young daughter in California.

in men was unerring; none of the three victims made brigadier, none served with his command again. Pershing, however, shortly afterward received his second star.

Returning to Columbus en route home on leave or to the hospital, troopers who had been with the Expedition since March barely recognized the once-drowsy town. Tents and workshops stretched in every direction and a great din, as if from a forge, prevailed throughout. In addition to nearly two thousand troops of the Massachusetts 2nd Infantry, the New Mexico 1st Infantry, a troop of the 13th Cavalry and various truck and sanitation soldiers, there were more than a thousand civilian workers engaged in erecting buildings, repairing rails and digging ditches. These, recalled Lieutenant Vernon G. Olsmith of the Quartermaster Corps, were "a rough-looking bunch of thugs." Saloons proliferated and the natural antagonism between soldiers and civilians occasionally erupted into bloody brawls. Armed military policemen were furnished by the 24th Infantry, an all-Negro outfit, and a modicum of control over the civilian workers was maintained by twenty tough cowboys packing six-guns.

Adding to the general clamor was the day-long faltering roar of unmuffled Curtiss aircraft engines installed on test stands where the 1st Aero Squadron vainly tried to reorganize itself into an effective reconnaissance arm should the nation go to war with Mexico. The original Jennies had been scrapped late in April, replaced with the more promising Curtiss R-2s with 160-hp engines. By June 1, Foulois—now a major—had received a dozen of the new R-2s, but found them all but unflyable. They arrived from the factory lacking vital parts and revealing hasty, if not criminally negligent, assembly. The gripe sheets on each R-2 were long and bitter. One plane arrived missing compass, propeller locking ring and bracing wires for the landing gear. Some had no air-speed indicators, propeller hubs or tool kits. Soldering around fuel tanks and fuel lines was execrable, and electrical connections were often so poorly made that when a switch was thrown, fuses blew and light bulbs burned out as fast as they could be replaced. The airplanes were virtually rebuilt in the workshops at Columbus, but when Foulois and the other pilots went aloft for test hops they discovered that the laminated propellers had a propensity for coming unglued; the dry heat of New Mexican summer simply sucked the juice out of the wood. Metal propellers were fashioned, but they were too heavy to develop the necessary rpm's; props were carved out of single blocks of wood, but these warped so badly that engines vibrated dangerously in flight. One neophyte engineer finally licked the problem when he secured wood native to Mexico and crafted laminated propellers that were preseasoned and therefore would not warp. To keep the glue from drying out, this engineer constructed special humidors in which the propellers were stored when not actually being used for flight. Thus each sortie required bolting and unbolting the propellers, a laborious job the mechanics detested.

Foulois received an influx of new pilots during the summer, including Lieutenants Ralph Royce and Carl "Toohey" Spaatz, but the R-2s were never considered reliable enough to be sent very far into Mexico. Between March 15 and August 15 the 1st Aero Squadron managed to log a total of only 345 hours and 43 minutes aloft. But the government remained indifferent.

Along twelve hundred miles of border, from Brownsville, Texas, to Yuma, Arizona, more than one hundred and ten thousand national guardsmen were forced to adopt Wilson's old policy of "watchful waiting." They had settled in permanent tent cities whose streets were often awash with summer and fall rains. They amused themselves by shooting craps, tossing each other in blankets, building sandbagged fortifications at strategic points along the Rio Grande. The troopers were learning to endure, learning to soldier, and their officers were learning that logistics was more important than parade-ground pomp and ceremony; a Lister bag filled with chlorinated water was worth more to a company commander than a year's supply of boot wax.

Infantry patrols slogged through the mud and mesquite, keeping an eye out for bandits seeking to cross the river. Occasionally these men who wore stifling wool O.D. pants and shirts would spot Mexicans on the other side, and a flurry of firing would erupt, usually without result. At night, listening posts would be manned along the river, and from the other side, unknown Mexicans would call out, asking for some great richness. First Sergeant Herbert M. Mason of the 2nd Texas Infantry, then based at Pharr, Texas, remarked, "We used to throw them tobacco—the poor sonsabitches."

. . .

On September 6 the Joint High Commission met in New London to seek a final solution to the Mexican-American problem. The meeting opened in an atmosphere of high hopes and Latin cordiality, but as the days dragged by it became apparent that as at Juárez and El Paso, the Americans had come to discuss one thing and the Mexicans another. The Mexicans wanted the Punitive Expedition withdrawn, the Americans wanted to discuss Mexican internal affairs, especially the protection of lives and investment property threatened by what they referred to as conditions of anarchy prevailing in much of the Mexican nation. Wilson, then nearing the climax of his campaign for the Presidency against Republican Charles Evans Hughes, told Lane and the other two commissioners to hold fast; there could be no question of withdrawing American troops from Mexico, certainly not before the elections were over. Wilson needed to convince the nation that he was firm, but not rash; withdrawal or war could cost him the White House.

Then came shocking news out of Mexico. Pancho Villa, the cunning wolf from Durango, had licked his wounds clean and was again rampaging. The resurgent Villa, at the head of five hundred men, attacked Satevó, killing two hundred Carrancistas and driving them north. He whipped them again at Santa Isabel, where he seized a military train and rolled for San Andrés. As impudent as ever, Villa wrote a letter to General Treviño at Chihuahua City on September 14 saying that he would be in the city "to shake hands with you on the 16th." Dismissing Villa's letter as a bluff, Treviño planned a banquet for his staff instead of looking to the defenses of the city. The party did not break up until two o'clock in the morning on the sixteenth; thus when Villa and his men stormed into Chihuahua City at two-thirty, the garrison was abed and the officers blissfully wrapped in slumber.

Villa first seized the penitentiary, releasing more than two hundred prisoners to add to his ranks, then swept through the dark streets to take the Governor's Palace and the federal buildings. Treviño, at the first sounds of firing, groggily reached the street, but when his personal guard learned that Villa was in town they deserted Treviño to join with the Centaur. There was sporadic fighting throughout the town for several hours. Villa gained the balcony of the Governor's Palace and shouted *"Viva Mexico!"* Then he cried that the people of Chihuahua did not yet have their liberty, but that he, their brother, would give it to them.

Villa and his band left Chihuahua City seven hours after their dramatic entrance, taking with them sixteen automobiles loaded with captured rifles and ammunition, an estimated thousand civilians and deserters from Treviño's garrison, plus some artillery hitched up and dragged out of the city by Treviño's gunners. Casualties were approximately three hundred killed on both sides.

Pancho Villa's explosive reappearance stunned Carranza, whose long suit in his confrontation with Wilson for months had been the claim that Villa was dead, or at the very least rendered militarily impotent; therefore there was no further justification for American troops to remain on Mexican territory. A resurgent Villa would remove Carranza's trump card in the dealings then before the Joint High Commission.

On September 26 Mexico City sent its official version of what had happened at Chihuahua City to Lansing. The de facto government claimed that the attacking forces were not Villa's but remnants of various parties that opposed Carranza, including former supporters of Díaz and Huerta. The note denied that the attackers had carried away any guns or ammunition, denied that any of Treviño's troops had gone over to the enemy, denied that Villa had been seen in or near Chihuahua City. Carranza claimed that Treviño had organized his forces brilliantly for an enveloping movement "which was of a disastrous effect to the raiders, two-thirds of whom were killed, wounded or captured." The note assured Lansing that "everything in the region is quiet and that there is no fear that Chihuahua City may again be attacked."

In El Paso, however, General Bell had a long talk with an American rancher who had been in the city at the time of the attack and later talked to Treviño and General Cavazos, both of whom admitted that the situation was "very serious" and that they expected Villa to attack again.

It was the American rancher's version that Bell, Funston and Pershing chose to believe. Neither Carranza nor Obregón would admit that Villa was a dangerous phoenix, and when the Joint High Commission reconvened on October 2, this time at Atlantic City, the Mexicans could only report that Carranza's attitude was as before: there could be no discussion of Mexico's internal problems as related to the United States before a date was set for Pershing's removal and a plan agreed upon for border protection. The American commissioners threw up their hands and adjourned the meeting until Wilson and Lansing decided how to react.

On October 24 Lansing read three separate telegrams that only buttressed his belief that Villa and other revolutionaries were again threatening to remove the props from under the de facto government in Mexico. The American consul in Tampico wired that revolutionists were active south and west of the port, having defeated Carranza troops near the Grandier English oil fields at Potrero, and that "the country is passing into the worst state of anarchy yet known, with Government more impotent than ever to prevent it." Secretary Baker showed Lansing a telegram from General Bell advising that Villa was near the suburbs of Chihuahua City with thirty-five hundred men, two thousand of whom were armed and all mounted, "even those without arms, some on horses, others on mules and yet others on burros." Pershing wired that Villa was in control of three thousand square miles of Chihuahua, from south of the state capital northward to Namiquipa. Villista deserters told Pershing that Villa planned to attack the Americans as soon as he had recruited more men and captured more arms and ammunition.

On November 2 Pershing sent a message to Funston saying that the time was ideal to seize Chihuahua City with the larger part of his command, as it would bring him much nearer to the theater of operations. Pershing believed that there were probably not more than three thousand Carranza troops in the state, and these were poorly equipped and would not remain loyal to Carranza. Pershing summed up by saying: "It would probably not be difficult now to seize Chihuahua City, as there would be little opposition on the part of the de facto troops, while the populace would doubtless welcome us."

Funston concurred with Pershing—it would be militarily sound to strike again at Villa, to end the job, before he grew stronger—but Wilson was not yet ready for drastic action. He ordered his commissioners back to the conference table, while staying Pershing's hand.

. . .

Villa's drive gained momentum. He captured Parral, Torreón and Camargo, then swung his force north and moved on Chihuahua City. The battle began at nine o'clock in the morning of November 23—Thanksgiving Day to the idle troops at Colonia Dublán—and lasted until nightfall, at which time Villa broke off the attack after breaching the outer defenses. The assault resumed at dawn the next day and bloody street fighting flamed continuously until Monday, when the city fell. General Treviño and his officers ran for the depot, where a train already packed with his cavalry was preparing to leave the city under a full head of steam.

Leaderless, some two thousand de facto troops lay down their arms and delivered themselves over to Villa, who gave them two choices: join with him or join their dead and dying comrades in the streets of the city. Thus Villa gained a regiment of "volunteers." Villa now turned his wrath upon the harmless Chinese who lived in the city, most of whom ran small restaurants near the depot and classic laundries throughout the town. Many of them had fled the city when the fighting began, others squeezed themselves aboard the train headed north, but Villa's men relentlessly ferreted out those who were trapped and shot to death more than a hundred of them.

When the bloodbath was over, Villa began systematically looting the city. A Carrancista general named Francisco J. Múgica set out with sizable de facto forces to wrest Chihuahua City away from Villa, arriving there on December 2. There were inconclusive skirmishes, but before Múgica could draw the main enemy force into battle, Villa was able to evacuate the city, taking with him one hundred railroad cars filled with loot and provisions. A Carrancista officer, freed after Villa learned that the officer's brother was a Villista, reported that Villa got away with thirty pieces of artillery loaded aboard eighteen flatcars and that he was offering $200 gold to experienced artillerymen as a bonus, with the promise of another $100 gold per month as salary.

On December 9 Pershing again wired Funston with a précis of the newly developed dangerous situation, requesting permission to move his forces, now rested and replenished, against Villa. He pointed out that Villa dominated the Santa Clara Valley, east of

Namiquipa, and that small parties of Villistas were in control of the district as far north as Carrizal. Pershing believed that Villa had six thousand men in his command, and that "A swift blow should be made at once against this pretender. Our own prestige in Mexico should receive consideration at this time. In the light of Villa's operations during the past two weeks, further inactivity of this command does not seem desirable." Pershing again stressed his conviction that the Carrancistas would not, or could not, offer effective resistance and that the "civilian element would welcome us as they now wonder at our inactivity."

Funston endorsed Pershing's request, which was forwarded to the Secretary of War with Funston's own observations to the effect that if Villa's rampage was to continue unchecked he would soon control all of northern Mexico, but if Pershing were allowed to "deliver a quick, decisive blow" the rising would be crushed, Villa captured and the whole movement ended. Funston reminded Baker that this turn of events would benefit Carranza as much as it would the United States, but pointed out that no success could be guaranteed unless Pershing pursued Villa all the length of Chihuahua and into the state of Durango, which was where Major Tompkins of the 13th had been heading when the Carrancistas blocked him at Parral in April.

If any doubts concerning Villa's intentions still lingered in Mexico City or in Washington they were removed by the release of a manifesto signed by Villa, a translation of which Lansing received on the heels of Pershing's request for a strike at "the pretender." *General Villa's Manifesto to the Nation* was lengthy, passionate, dramatic, metaphorical and probably not dictated by Villa in its final, embellished version, but its meaning was clear and his intentions explicit. Certain passages revealed Villa's unmistakable hostility toward foreigners in general and toward "the abhorred Yankee" in particular.

Referring to the Punitive Expedition, Villa called for renewed sacrifices "to oppose the unjustified invasion by our eternal enemies, the barbarians of the North." Villa accused Carranza of aiding and abetting Pershing. He called for help in overthrowing Carranza and "the most corrupt Government we have ever had." Villa warned that the task of ousting the Americans and of driving the ignominious, sordid office holders from the seat of government would be arduous.

But: "Victory will crown our efforts, do not doubt it, for just causes always triumph; but if destiny is adverse to us we shall fall in the arena with our faces to the sky, similarly to the ancient gladiators; we shall fall with the crash of a volcano in eruption; we shall collapse as do the masses of granite under the impulse of seismic trepidations; we shall disappear proudly and haughtily, shouting in a chorus: 'Beloved Country, thy sons swear they will expire on thy altars.'

"And upon the traitors let fall the curse of history and the humiliating contempt of Mexicans, for on the morrow they will hurl at them the anathema of spurious sons of the race of Hidalgo and Morelos."

Villa enumerated sixteen articles upon which his new government would be based, once the Yankees and the Constitutionalists had been dealt with. Among them: no foreigner could acquire real estate unless naturalized for twenty-five years; North Americans, who "are in large part responsible for the national disaster," were excluded under any circumstances from owning or leasing any part of Mexico, as would be the Chinese; all railroads and mining properties would be confiscated to become the property of the Mexican nation; telegraph and railroad communications would be shut off to within eighteen leagues (fifty-four miles) of the American border and garrisoned by a new corps of *rurales*; nations which granted asylum to Carranza officials and refused extradition upon Villa's demand could not expect their own nationals still living in Mexico to be protected by law.

The manifesto was signed by Villa at San Andrés in Chihuahua, during October.

Now Wilson, Lansing, Carranza and the Joint High Commission knew precisely what to expect should Francisco Villa succeed in his ambitions. Pershing's force, experienced in the ways of guerrilla fighting, thoroughly toughened, now familiar with the country and mounted on full-fleshed horses, could indeed have stood a better than even chance of finding Villa and destroying him for good. Wilson believed this, and having eked out a victory over Charles Evans Hughes, could have sent Pershing's columns flying in hot pursuit with little to lose politically and with minimal risk of serious opposition from Carranza's fluid forces. But Wilson hesitated; even minimal risk of military involvement deep inside

Mexico was more than he cared to chance. Relations between the United States and Germany were deteriorating daily and Wilson was girding himself for a break that seemed inevitable. He abhorred the thought of war with Germany, but war with Mexico would be even more distasteful. If America opened hostilities against Germany on the Western Front, then chewing up lives at the rate of two thousand per day, the nation would need every member of the Punitive Expedition not only to fight but to serve as a cadre of field-experienced soldiers to train the millions Wilson would call upon to bear arms. Moreover, there was the drama of the Joint High Commission yet to be played out. By November 24 the American commissioners had finally beaten concessions from their Mexican counterparts, and a protocol was signed allowing pursuit of bandits on either side of the border for a hundred miles. The agreement further stipulated that Pershing's men would be withdrawn from Mexico forty days after ratification of the protocol, provided northern Mexico was considered free of the Villista menace at the time. The agreement was in the hands of Carranza for ultimate approval, and Wilson now awaited Carranza's reaction.

At Dublán the soldiers of the Expedition were preparing for Christmas in Mexico. Enormous pits were dug and spits erected to receive the carcasses of cattle bought and slaughtered for a mammoth barbecue promised by the experienced Negro cooks of the 10th Cavalry Regiment. Eggs, milk and cream were purchased from the Mormons which would, along with hoarded whiskey, provide the traditional Yuletide eggnog. Truck convoys delivered letters, cards and packages daily from the Army post office at Columbus, furnishing a Christmasy link for those with home and family. Even a few makeshift Christmas trees were erected in company streets, and the grim camp began to assume a festive air.

Major General John J. Pershing, however, was vexed with Black, Starr and Frost on Fifth Avenue in New York. As early as November 20 he had sent them an order for three hundred Christmas cards, "Style A, with spinning wheel and fireplace," with his name and rank engraved at the bottom. He had specified a delivery date: no later than December 15. Black, Starr and Frost, eager to please so distinguished a customer, made delivery a day early, but when Pershing opened the package he was furious; his name was spelled correctly, but New York had downgraded him to brigadier. He dispatched a curt telegram pointing out this error and demanding new cards. They arrived at Columbus on December 20 and Pershing instructed the base commander, a Colonel Farnsworth, to put the four-pound box in one of Foulois' airplanes ready to leave for Dublán. The order was headed RUSH RUSH RUSH RUSH. But a perverse high wind sprang up that very day, and it wasn't until late in the morning of the twenty-first that the Curtiss R-2 flew into Dublán with the priority cargo. Pershing kept the pilot waiting while he addressed the envelopes, then sent him back to Columbus with the package, mortified that his greetings would doubtless reach their destinations long after Christmas.

Christmas Day dawned cold and clear at Dublán. The cooks were up early, basting the glistening red carcasses of beef, filling the air with the pungent aroma of savory sweet-sour barbecue sauce. Suddenly the camp was struck by one of Mexico's infamous "blue northers." Biting cold winds howled through the streets blowing down tents, scattering Christmas trees and choking the air with thick clouds of dust. Troopers were driven inside their adobe huts, where they wrapped themselves to the eyes with blankets. The storm lashed Dublán all through the day, abating only at nightfall. The soldiers crawled outside to discover that the spitted steers were covered with sheets of gritty dust imbedded in the fibers. The meat was inedible.

On December 28 Wilson received Carranza's reply, and it was negative. The protocol signed on November 24 was rejected and the Mexican delegates were ordered by the First Chief not to engage in further parleys with the Americans until Pershing and his men were ordered out of Mexico. Nearly four months of work had gone for nothing. Like all of the other conferences that had preceded it, the final attempt at reconciliation failed because from the beginning Carranza had been obsessed with one idea, Pershing's withdrawal, and the Americans insisted upon conditions Carranza was powerless to meet, even had he wanted to meet them. Wilson and Carranza were as far apart as ever in reaching a modus vivendi that would satisfy Carranza's idea of national dignity and Wilson's ideal of a peaceful revolution that would carry with it guarantees of safety for the common border.

The first week of the new year brought a graceful means of

withdrawing the Punitive Expedition when the able Carrancista General Múgica drew the resurgent Villa army to battle north of Torreón and thrashed it so badly that Villa as a threat to American territory was obviated; there was no longer, it seemed, even the vestige of pretext for keeping four fifths of the Regular Army tied down uselessly in Chihuahua.

On January 12 Wilson told Secretary Baker that he wanted the Expedition withdrawn, and a week later Pershing received orders to ready the command for return to the United States. Baker had four questions for Pershing: Would the withdrawal be made by rail or by marching? What was the earliest date the withdrawal could begin? Should the Mormon colonies be notified in advance that the Americans were leaving? Would the operations be embarrassed if public announcement was made of the pull-out?

Pershing replied that his men would be coming out on foot and on horse, that the Mormons already anticipated the withdrawal, that the first elements could be on the road within a week, and that public announcement should be withheld until the troops were headed home.

The men cheered when the word came to strike the camp at Colonia Dublán; no soldier among them was sorry to be leaving Mexico, and they would be coming out with pride. Years later some historians would refer to the Punitive Expedition as a "wild-goose chase," as a "prolonged, famous fumble" and even as a "dirty little war." But the Expedition's trooper, officer and commander knew then, and afterward, that the mission had been accomplished within the limits imposed by the de facto government of Mexico and their own politicians' restrictions. Villa's band had been beaten and scattered, his veteran generals and colonels run to earth and killed or captured. Villa had been broken, and only Carranza's obduracy, beginning with the clash at Parral, kept them from finishing the job and going home six months sooner. Misfits in higher echelons had been exposed, and junior officers were given invaluable field experience with troops, which would benefit them in two world wars.

On January 27 the vanguard of the returning forces, the 24th Infantry and Field Hospital 3, started up the road. Coming out were 10,690 men, 9,307 horses, 2,030 Mexican, 197 American and 533 Chinese refugees; these latter were allowed to immigrate to the United States by special permission of the State Department to keep them from being slaughtered by Villistas.

By February 4 the entire expedition was assembled at Palomas, and on the morning of February 5 they began crossing the border gate, headed back for Columbus.

Epilogue

Woodrow Wilson's total political defeat at the hands of Venustiano Carranza was followed shortly afterward by a long-overdue awakening as to Germany's true intentions in Mexico. Throughout December and January, Wilson worked overtime seeking a way to end the war in Europe, naïvely hoping to mediate personally between the belligerents to persuade them to accept "peace without victory."

Germany did not discourage Wilson's efforts, but they seemed doomed over the issue of the stepped-up U-boat warfare in the Atlantic; merchantmen were being sunk at a rate that alarmed the British, who were fed, clothed and armed by sea, and American lives were being lost aboard some of these torpedoed ships. On January 31, 1917, the German ambassador to the United States, Count Johann-Heinrich von Bernstorff, handed Secretary of State Robert Lansing an official announcement declaring that the Imperial German Government would begin unrestricted submarine warfare the following morning; all neutral shipping, American included, were now considered legitimate prey for U-boats prowling the high seas. Lansing recalled that the dapper Von Bernstorff's eyes filled with tears when he said his final goodbye.

Three days later Wilson severed diplomatic relations with Germany, but he still was not ready to accept the fact that Germany meant America any real harm. On the afternoon of February 3,

Wilson addressed both houses of Congress: "We are the sincere friends of the German people and earnestly desire to remain at peace with the government which speaks for them. We shall not believe," continued Wilson, "that they are hostile to us unless and until we are obliged to believe it . . ."

Wilson was obliged to believe it on the evening of February 25, when Acting Secretary of State Frank L. Polk handed him a copy of a German telegram that had been intercepted by British naval intelligence in London. The telegram was addressed to the German minister in Mexico City, Heinrich von Eckhardt, and was signed by the Minister of Foreign Affairs in Berlin, Arthur Zimmermann. The message was dated January 16, a time when Wilson had earnestly been trying to reach amicable agreement with the Germans and a week after he had decided to withdraw the Punitive Expedition from Mexico and thus keep the peace there. The telegram read:

> IT IS OUR PURPOSE ON FEBRUARY FIRST TO BEGIN UNRE-
> STRICTED SUBMARINE WARFARE. THE ATTEMPT WILL BE MADE
> TO KEEP AMERICA NEUTRAL IN SPITE OF ALL.
>
> IN CASE WE ARE NOT SUCCESSFUL IN THIS, WE PROPOSE
> MEXICO AN ALLIANCE UPON THE FOLLOWING TERMS: JOINT
> CONDUCT OF THE WAR. JOINT CONCLUSION OF PEACE. AMPLE
> FINANCIAL SUPPORT AND AN AGREEMENT ON OUR PART THAT
> MEXICO SHALL GAIN BACK BY CONQUEST THE TERRITORY LOST
> BY HER AT A PRIOR TIME IN TEXAS, NEW MEXICO AND ARIZONA.
> THE SETTLEMENT IN DETAIL IS LEFT TO YOU.
>
> YOU WILL INFORM THE PRESIDENT [OF MEXICO] OF THE ABOVE
> MOST SECRETLY AT THE MOMENT WAR BREAKS OUT WITH THE
> UNITED STATES AND WILL ADD THE SUGGESTION THAT JAPAN BE
> REQUESTED TO TAKE PART AT ONCE AND THAT HE [CARRANZA]
> SIMULTANEOUSLY MEDIATE BETWEEN OURSELVES AND JAPAN.
>
> PLEASE CALL THE PRESIDENT'S ATTENTION TO THE FACT THAT
> UNRESTRICTED USE OF OUR SUBMARINES OFFERS THE PROSPECT
> OF FORCING ENGLAND TO MAKE PEACE WITHIN A FEW MONTHS.
> ACKNOWLEDGE RECEIPT.
>
> ZIMMERMANN

The German proposal was ridiculous. That Carranza, even with German help, would make war on the United States in order to gain hundreds of thousands of square miles of the "lost territories" was as fantastic as De la Rosa's mad scheme of invasion and in-surrection to gain the same ends. Zimmermann unaccountably admitted authorship of the telegram. Wilson's disillusionment with the Germans was complete.

On March 11, 1917, Carranza assumed the chair as de jure President of Mexico and was so recognized by Wilson. The world was quick to note that at Carranza's formal inauguration the German minister was received by cheers and applause, while Wilson's own emissary, Ambassador Henry P. Fletcher, was the victim of hisses and catcalls from the gallery.

When Wilson actually declared war on Imperial Germany in April, Washington was understandably keen to see if Carranza would join with Germany and try to entice Japan away from the Allies. Zimmermann wooed Carranza, with the backing of the Reichstag, and promised Carranza "vast sums of money" with which to buy arms and other hard goods, but Carranza declined to become involved and announced his intention of staying neutral. Carranza's grip on Mexico was far from secure; he could not stamp out Zapata or Villa completely, and as long as those dedicated enemies remained at large, Carranza could have no peace of mind. Serious involvement with major nations in a world war could not advance his revolution, which was far from running its course.

With Pershing's force out of the way, Villa was free to raid everywhere. In May and again in November Villa invaded Ojinaga, across the Rio Grande from Presidio, Texas, both times driving the Carrancista troops from the town to seek safety on the American side of the line. After Villa had departed, taking from the town everything of value, the Americans gave the Carranza troops back their arms and sent them home. In 1918, Villa confined his pillaging largely to the interior, looting such towns as Villa Ahumada and Cusihuiriachic, where he took $10,000 in cash from the Cusi Mining Company's strongboxes, in order to replenish his war chest.

Pershing's firm command of his troops in Mexico, his demonstrated ability to press on with the task at hand despite pressure and frustration, his coolness and stubbornness, all qualified him to lead the American Expeditionary Force to France in 1917. He emerged from the war with his reputation as a field commander of the first rank; only the French and British generals did not like him, and that was because he steadfastly refused to allow his A.E.F. to be thrown piecemeal into the grinder as replacements. Pershing wanted to fight his divisions as an integrated army, and he succeeded. As General of the Armies, Pershing died quietly at Walter Reed Hospital in Washington, D.C., at the great age of eighty-seven. He outlived every one of his major opponents in Mexico, all of whom died violently.

Emiliano Zapata was finally removed from Carranza's path on April 10, 1919, when he was shot to death in a carefully laid trap. Carranza did not outlive him long. Carranza and his followers in Mexico City had systematically looted the country's wealth, swollen by taxes and from the sale of oil to belligerents during the European war, and Álvaro Obregón left the Carranza camp and declared for himself. Carranza fled the city before the advance of Obregón's forces, taking with him state ministers and most of the contents of the national treasury, but was caught and killed while trying to make his way to Veracruz. He died on May 21, 1920, and was succeeded by interim President Adolfo de la Huerta, a mild Obregonista, who was only filling in the time before Obregón himself could be elected. As expected, Obregón won most of the votes during the election held on September 5, 1920. He served one term, then again sought and won the Presidency in the summer of 1928. On July 17 of that same year, Obregón was assassinated by a pistol bullet fired by a young radical who believed he was acting for the benefit of the Catholic Church.

Pancho Villa staged his last major raid near the United States on June 14, 1919, when he launched a night attack against Juárez. Once again the citizens of El Paso were roused from sleep by the frantic sounds of combat coming from across the river. Before dawn much of Juárez was in Villa's hands, but a late-morning Carrancista counterattack pushed Villa back. There was a lull, then the battle picked up again and raged throughout the afternoon and into the evening. Bullets flew indiscriminately, killing and wounding American soldiers and civilians in El Paso. Commanding at El Paso was General James B. Erwin, who had been a colonel with the 7th Cavalry during the Punitive Expedition, and Erwin was furious. He moved his artillery into position and had the gunners range on one of Villa's favorite Juárez strongpoints, the large race track not far from the river, and he ordered Colonel S. R. H. "Tommy" Tompkins, one of the heroes of Guerrero, to cross the Rio Grande. The cavalry moved on Villa's flank, the artillery began shelling Villa's men concentrated near the race track, and Negro infantrymen poured directly into Juárez from El Paso with fixed bayonets. Harassed on all sides, Villa began pulling his men away from Juárez. The retreat became a rout when Tommy Tompkins put in a mounted pistol charge, and the fleeing Villistas were followed as far as the Americans' horses could take them. It was Villa's last appearance on the Texas border.

Two months after Carranza's death, Francisco Villa decided to lay down his arms. He got in touch with interim President de la Huerta and told him he wished to surrender to the government, asking in return that the government grant him land, a house and total amnesty. Villa said that he wanted to live out his days as a peaceful rancher experimenting with scientific methods of cattle and crop raising. De la Huerta thought this an excellent idea, but Obregón, then on campaign tour, did not. He wired De la Huerta: "General Villa assaulted the town of Columbus where he committed misbehaviors and acts of violence. It is natural that the United States Foreign Office, on seeing him protected by the Mexican Government, should ask for extradition of the Durango warrior. And what are we going to do?"

De la Huerta nevertheless signed a pact on July 28, 1920, giving Villa title to 25,000 acres and a handsome hacienda at Canutillo, thirty-five miles south of Parral. Villa was allowed to keep fifty of his soldiers as a personal bodyguard, whose salaries were paid by the Ministry of War, and he discharged the others, six hundred and fifty men in all. The United States was not interested in extraditing Villa, and when Obregón came to power he made no effort to renege on the De la Huerta pact; instead he presented Villa with a pair of machine guns as a sentimental token of the Revolution.

But the desire for vengeance dies hard in Mexico, and Villa had earned numerous enemies during the years before he lay down his guns. Several attempts were made on his life while he lived at Canutillo, but it was not until the summer of 1923 that he was finally assassinated. When Villa moved into the hacienda he had discovered that the most valuable furnishings were already gone, sold for the previous owner by a citizen of Parral named Melitón Lozoya. Villa had lost heavily to Lozoya wagering on cockfights, but instead of paying his debts, Villa perversely turned on Lozoya and demanded that "his" furnishings be returned or else Lozoya would have to face the consequences. Lozoya was in a hopeless position; he was not wealthy and he could not retrieve the goods Villa demanded. Lozoya decided that Villa must be killed before Villa killed him. He discussed the problem with friends, mostly cowboys and farmers, one of whom, José Barraza, approached a cousin, Jesús Salas Barraza, a member of the Durango legislature. Jesús Barraza had no love for Villa and agreed to supply the conspirators with guns and ammunition to do the job. Moreover, Barraza promised the killers immunity.

Villa frequently drove into Parral in his Dodge touring car, always with a bodyguard, sometimes on business but usually to satisfy a lust for different women that had not abated with middle age. He always proceeded to the heart of town along Calle Juárez, and it was on this street that the assassins, eight in number, rented a house that offered a clear field of fire.

On July 20, with Villa at the wheel, the Dodge rounded a corner and headed up Calle Juárez. Besides Villa, there were six other men in the car, and when the fusillade of shots erupted from the assassins' house nobody had time to reach for his gun. Villa, hit several times, was killed immediately. Only one of Villa's bodyguards, Ramón Contreras, escaped with his life. Jesús Salas Barraza assumed full responsibility for the killing and was given twenty years in the penitentiary, but Obregón saw to it that he was released from jail before the year was out.

Before his death Villa had built himself a handsome stone mausoleum in Chihuahua City's main cemetery, and it was here that he instructed his only "church wife," Luz Corral, to have him buried. The Mexican government, however, not then ready to make General Villa a national hero, instructed that Villa be buried instead in the small cemetery at Parral, the grave marked only by a simple stone. He lies there to this day, headless; a year after his burial the grave was opened by persons unknown and the body decapitated, for what reason no one knows, or will reveal.

Luz Corral lives today in Chihuahua City in a large pink house located on a side street. The home is a museum filled with mementos of Francisco Villa's tempestuous life, and Luz Corral Villa is the curator and guide. The fatal Dodge, rusted and punctured, sits encased in glass at the rear of the home. Visitors who leave behind a few pesos are always welcome by Señora Villa, who is a poor woman. She denies rumors that Villa left her wealthy from buried treasure taken during his years of brigandage.

"All he left," she says, "were bills."

APPENDIX A

---

*Munitions exported to Mexico
through U. S. border ports from
February 1, 1914, to March 15, 1916*

Small Arms

rifles, .30-30	43,209
rifles, .30-40	866
rifles, 7 mm.	950
Springfield .44	3,756
Remington	500
.22 caliber	1
rifles, unclassified	23,000
carbines, assorted	1,150
revolvers, Colt .38	1,166
pistols, assorted	3
pistols, automatic	1
shotguns	11
sabers	50

Artillery

Hotchkiss	5
3-in. field guns	4
caissons, limbers	2
tool boxes	1

Small Arms Ammunition

cartridges, rifle, assorted	34,706,186
.22-caliber rifle	102,000
revolver, assorted	743,350

Miscellaneous

aeroplanes (via Laredo)	1
dynamite, cases	261
smokeless powder, pounds	6,075

This war matériel cleared through U. S. Customs at Brownsville, Laredo, Eagle Pass, Del Rio, Presidio and El Paso in Texas, and through Douglas, Naco and Nogales in Arizona. The munitions were used by the Villistas and the Constitutionalists against one another, and by both parties against Americans on either side of the border. This report, now in the Adjutant General's Office Files in the National Archives (AG File 2224757) does not, of course, include munitions smuggled across the river during this period, or during the heyday of gun running from 1910 onward. The report, dated March 22, 1916, was compiled from routine data submitted by customs authorities to Headquarters, Southern Department, Fort Sam Houston, Texas.

APPENDIX B

Pershing's First General Order

Headquarters, Punitive Expedition, U. S. Army
Columbus, N.M., March 14, 1916

General Orders ⎫
  No. I ⎬
       ⎭

1. The forces of this command are organized into a provisional division to be called Punitive Expedition, U. S. Army

2. The following staff is announced:

Chief of Staff: Lieut. Colonel DeR. C. Cabell, 10th Cavalry
Asst. to Chief of Staff: Capt. Wilson B. Burtt, 20th Infantry
Adjutant: Major John L. Hines, Adjutant General's Department
Intelligence Officer: Major James A. Ryan, 13th Cavalry
Inspector: Colonel Lucien G. Berry, 4th Field Artillery
Judge Advocate: Captain Allen J. Greer, 16th Infantry
Quartermaster: Major John F. Madden, Quartermaster Corps
Surgeon: Major Jere B. Clayton, Medical Corps
Engineer Officer: Major Lytle Brown, Corps of Engineers
Signal Officer: Captain Hanson B. Black, Signal Corps
Commander of the Base: Major William R. Sample, 20th Infantry
Aides: 1st Lieut. James L. Collins, 11th Cavalry
      2nd Lieut. Martin C. Schallenberger, 16th Infantry

3. The Provisional Division will consist of:

(a) First Provisional Cavalry Brigade, Colonel James Lockett, Commanding

Troops:

11th Cavalry   13th Cavalry
Battery "C," 6th Field Artillery (attached)

(b) Second Cavalry Brigade, Colonel George A. Dodd, Commanding

Troops:

7th Cavalry   10th Cavalry
Battery "B," 6th Field Artillery (attached)

(c) First Provisional Infantry Brigade, Colonel John H. Beacon, Commanding

Troops:

6th Infantry   16th Infantry
Cos. "E" & "H," 2nd Battalion Engineers (attached)

(d) Ambulance Company No. 7, Field Hospital No. 7

(e) Signal Corps Detachments, First Aero Squadron
Detachment, Signal Corps

(f) Wagon Companies, Numbers 1 and 2

4. Lieutenant Colonel Euclid B. Frick, Medical Corps, will report to the Commanding Officer (Major Sample) as surgeon in charge, Medical Base Group.

* * * * * *

II. (1) The following telegrams from Department Headquarters are quoted for the information of all concerned and compliance therewith is enjoined:

March 14, 1916

The Department Commander directs that you inform all subordinates in your command that they will report promptly by wire to proper authorities, who will report to these headquarters the names of all officers and enlisted men accompanying your command who are wounded or killed in action or who die of sickness while in the field. Commanding Officers of base and cantonment hospitals will be instructed to make reports.

March 14, 1916

The greatest caution will be exercised after crossing the border that fire is not opened on troops pertaining to the de facto Government of Mexico as such troops are very likely to be found in country which you will traverse. The greatest care and discretion will have to be exercised by all.

(2) It is enjoined by all members of the command to make the utmost endeavor to convince all Mexicans that the only purpose of this expedition is to assist in apprehending and capturing Villa and his bandits. Citizens as well as soldiers of the de facto Government will be treated with every consideration. They will not in any case be molested in the peaceful conduct of their affairs, and their property rights will be scrupulously respected.

By Command of Brigadier General Pershing
DeR. C. Cabell,
Lieutenant Colonel, 10th Cavalry
Chief of Staff

APPENDIX C

*Elements of the U. S. Army that served in
the interior of Mexico with the Punitive Expedition;
date entered Mexico, points of deepest penetration*

UNIT	ENTRY DATE	DEEPEST PENETRATION
6th Infantry*	March 15, 1916	San Antonio de los Arenales, 304 miles; Detachment, M Company, Satevó, 394 miles
16th Infantry	March 15, 1916	San Geronimo, 260 miles; D Company, Santa Cruz de Villegas, 484 miles
13th Cavalry	March 15, 1916	Parral, 516 miles
2nd Engineers	March 15, 1916	San Antonio, 304 miles
Detachment, Signal Corps	March 15, 1916	San Antonio, 304 miles
7th Cavalry	March 16, 1916	Miñaca, 310 miles
10th Cavalry	March 16, 1916	Santa Cruz, 484 miles
4th Field Artillery, Batteries A, B and C	March 16, 1916	Lake Itascate, 272 miles
6th Field Artillery	March 16, 1916	San Antonio, 304 miles
Wagon Companies 1 and 2	March 16, 1916	San Antonio, 304 miles
11th Cavalry	March 17, 1916	Santa Cruz, 484 miles

* Among the officers of the 6th Infantry Regiment was First Lieutenant William H. Simpson, a lieutenant general during World War II and commander of the U. S. Ninth Army in Europe.

Field Hospital 7, Ambulance Company 7	March 17, 1916	Namiquipa, 240 miles
1st Aero Squadron	March 19, 1916	Satevó, 394 miles
24th Infantry	March 22, 1916	El Valle, 140 miles
5th Cavalry	March 28, 1916	San Antonio, 304 miles
12th Cavalry	April 14, 1916	Boca Chica, 40 miles
Field Hospital 3, Ambulance Company 3	April 18, 1916	Casas Grandes, 120 miles
17th Infantry, 1st and 3rd Battalions	April 23, 1916	Las Cruces, 210 miles
6th Cavalry	April 25, 1916	Casas Grandes, 120 miles

APPENDIX D

---

*General Villa's Manifesto
to the Nation*

FELLOW CITIZENS: All peoples of the earth are capable at certain times of the greatest sacrifices when they see their national integrity threatened and when their rights as freemen are trampled under foot. We have a fine example of this in the titanic European conflict, and particularly in heroic Belgium, which, conscious of being one of the most civilized nations in Europe, went into this devastating war without the remotest hope of victory but with the consciousness of duty fulfilled, and succumbed when the greater part of its sons had disappeared among the ruins of Namur and Liège, when they fired their last cartridge in order not to have their beloved country encroached upon with impunity by the invader. Our own beloved country has also arrived at one of those solemn moments when, in order to oppose the unjustified invasion of our eternal enemies, the barbarians of the North, we ought to be united in imitation of the example of that host of valiant men who sacrificed their lives, calmly and smilingly, in behalf of the beloved country which gave us birth, of those Mexicans who astound Europe itself with their magnificent—[word cut out] and who became immortal by inscribing their glorious names in indelible characters on the pages of history. Unfortunately there can be no unification among us, for while it is true that our country has had patriotic and self-denying sons, it also has Carrancistas, who necessarily now govern the destinies of the country, which, impoverished, defenseless and manacled, was surrendered by them to the invader when there is no fortress to defend its already weakened frontiers. As an irrefutable proof of this there has been there, since March last, in the Galeana District the American army commanded by Pershing, it being engaged in constructing cement highways from beyond the Rio Grande to the Valley of San Buenaventura, which is at present the basis of operations of the abhorred Yankee, with the knowledge and tolerance of the Constitutionalist Government, which would like to establish ammunition factories in order to go on saturating the fertile fields of our country with the blood of its sons and thus facilitate the entrance of its allies and protectors into the interior of the Republic. Therefore, dear countrymen, the task which we must perform as Mexicans is very great and very arduous. I call upon you to take up arms in order to overthrow the most corrupt Government that we have had, these office holders who, through their extreme radicalism and in order to perpetuate themselves in power and enrich themselves shamelessly, have covered themselves with ignominy, going so far in their sordid conduct as to criminally disregard the plaints and cries of our troubled country, which, in these times of anxiety, demands the cooperation of its sons in order to save it.

Victory will crown our efforts, do not doubt it, for just causes always triumph; and if destiny is adverse to us, we shall fall in the arena with our faces to the sky, similarly to the ancient gladiators; we shall fall with the crash of a volcano in eruption; we shall collapse as do the masses of granite under the impulse of seismic trepidations; we shall disappear proudly and haughtily, shouting in a chorus: "Beloved Country, thy sons swear they will expire on thy altars."

And upon the traitors let fall the curse of history and the humiliating contempt of Mexicans, for on the morrow they will hurl at them the anathema of spurious sons of the race of Hidalgo and Morelos.

Intentionally and with the best of good faith did I remain inactive with my forces in the enticing and pleasant hope of seeing the activities of the so-called Constitutionalist Government in order to repel the invasion and attempt the unification of the Mexican people. Of course, the bitterest disappointment was not long in coming, for, so far from endeavoring to oust the invaders, they showed the most refined perversity in exploiting the gravity of international relations for their personal benefit and to the absolute detriment of honor; thus we have seen how forces that were armed for no other reason than to defend the territory were deceived and submitted perfidiously and maliciously; thus we have also seen how an infinite number of patriots who were eating the bitter bread of exile owing to the convulsions in their country, crossed the boundary line in order to enlist in the national defense, and thus we have seen how, without any scruple, many of them were interned in the dungeons of the penitentiary at the Capital of the State of Chihuahua, as a reward for their abnegation and patriotism.

As I do not see the slightest hope of a change of conduct on the part of the men in power in the country, I have the honor to state to the Mexican People that, from this time on, I shall push military operations as far as possible in order to overthrow the traitors and place at the head of the Government the citizen who, through his recognized honor and civic virtues, shall cause Mexico to figure in the catalogue of civilized and free peoples, which is the place legitimately belonging to her; for which purpose the following plan will be put into force from this date on, it being subject to additions and amendments and being applicable throughout the area controlled by the revolution:

I. The supreme disposition of the Revolutionary Government shall be to call the people to election for President of the Republic, making use of free suffrage without restrictions of any kind, in order that the people may conscientiously elect the Chief Magistrate of the nation, the military vote being included in the elections, as is strictly just; and those guilty of misconduct at the elections being punished by the death penalty.

II. Not one of the armed leaders or military officers shall be permitted to run for President, as the army is an institution whose rights and duties are clearly defined.

III. Elections shall also be called for Representatives to the Congress of the Union, in accordance with the instructions which will be distributed in due time in a separate pamphlet in order that the voters may be apprised of the importance of these elections if it is taken into account that these officials go to make up the legislative branch of the Government, to which is assigned the most ardent task of the Government, it being charged with restraining the acts of the President himself. In this connection it will be remarked that the public should select persons of well known culture and humble birth who will be capable of understanding the needs of society and especially of that numerous class who are suffering in penury and poverty, viz, the proletariat. Military men shall likewise be precluded from these offices.

IV. It being of vital importance that the Representatives and Senators of Congress should, as said before, be honorable persons who concern themselves for the welfare and progress of their constituents; they must not mix up in affairs beyond their sphere of jurisdiction, such as labors on behalf of concessions, etc., which may redound to their own benefit to the detriment of the public, under penalty of being shot, and when this painful example is set, the State they represent shall be notified in order that the vacancy may be filled by the substitute.

V. The defects of the laws governing the country being well known owing to the modifications or revisions which they have been undergoing in recent years, the President shall adhere to the reform laws in governing the country.

VI. The revised codes shall be annulled and the original ones put into force, we being convinced from practical experience that the changes they have undergone have merely served to satisfy the ambitions of a certain number of persons, to the detriment of the remainder of the inhabitants.

VII. From this date on the Revolutionary Army declares void the acts of the so-called Constitutionalist Government, in the way of loans, concessions, etc., with the exception of those which, on moral grounds and out of respect to society, are inviolable, such as marriages and other acts affecting civil status.

VIII. As the revolution, in order to attain the goal of its salutary aspirations, which are based on a clearly defined ideal tending toward the general improvement of the Republic, needs the resources of its own and outsiders for the national reconstruction, it will not answer for any debt, even though it be claimed by foreigners, who, being received in the country with so much hospitality, have, most of them, trebled their fortunes here; therefore it is just and logical that they should now suffer the consequences inherent to any country at war.

IX. From the date of this statement no foreigner shall be allowed to acquire real estate except such as have been naturalized 25 years ago and have resided continually in this country; however, for the time being, in order to meet the requirements of the war, all interests (property) of foreigners shall be confiscated in behalf of the nation. In future an essential prerequisite for acquiring real estate shall be to become naturalized as aforesaid, and such property may be acquired only in the interior of the Republic.

X. It being realized that the North Americans are in large part responsible for the national disaster and that, for absolutely illegitimate purposes they have stirred up and kept on stirring up fratricidal war in our country, as is amply proven by their unwarranted stay on our soil, they are hereby disqualified, the same as Chinese subjects, from acquiring for any purpose real estate as referred to in the preceding clause.

XI. The railroad lines, together with their equipment of every kind, shall be confiscated and become the absolute property of the Mexican Government, without foreign companies being taken into account as share holders.

XII. Mining property situated in this country and owned by foreigners shall likewise be confiscated and become national property.

XIII. In order to encourage the Mexican manufacturer and further the development of the industry of the country in general, all kinds of mercantile operations with the United States shall be suspended, it being hoped by this measure to awaken greater diligence in the Mexican workman as well as his ingenuity in seeking the greatest improvement in our national products.

Telegraph and railroad communications shall accordingly be cut off to within 18 leagues of the frontiers in the United States of the North.

This stretch of territory shall be garrisoned by the rural forces of the Republic.

XIV. It being an urgent and patriotic necessity that the military leaders operating in the various States of the Republic should require the Mexican people to militarize rapidly in order to be prepared as soon as possible for any emergency in the very probable and long struggle with the invader, they are urged especially to proceed with the greatest activity and energy in this direction; it being understood that every Mexican who refuses to take part in the conflict at this time of genuine trial, in which national autonomy is jeopardized, shall be declared a traitor and his property confiscated without claim for restitution.

XV. The military leaders shall act in accordance with the strictest morality in order that they may demand of their subordinates a good, beneficial military training which shall reflect brilliancy and renown upon the Revolutionary army. Any act in contravention to this provision shall be punished by the penalty of death, without distinction as to military rank.

XVI. In order to punish all those who make a bad use of power and in order to prevent future evils which might again desolate our country and carry sorrow into our homes, we shall proceed, by all means within reach, to request the extradition of Venustiano Carranza, his advisers and accomplices, in case they go abroad, and of the Government where they seek refuge we shall ask, through legal channels, that they return and give an account of their acts; and in case such Government should refuse our just demand, the subjects of the country in which they have sought refuge shall be without the guarantees which the laws grant to good citizens.

Fellow countrymen: Thus you now know my greatest desire, which I believe will be yours, for it is a question of exterminating the most odious and shameful tyranny that the land of Cuauhtemoc has had. To war against the traitors, crying: Mexico for the Mexicans.

SAN ANDRÉS, CHIH., October, 1916   FRANCISCO VILLA
                                          Commander in Chief

Selected Bibliography

UNPUBLISHED DOCUMENTS

The Papers of John J. Pershing. Library of Congress.
The Papers of Hugh L. Scott. Library of Congress.
Records of the Punitive Expedition. War Department, Adjutant General's Office Files, National Archives.
Political Affairs, Mexico. State Department File, National Archives.

PUBLISHED DOCUMENTS

Papers Relating to the Foreign Relations of the United States, 1916, 1917. Washington: Government Printing Office.

BOOKS

Andrews, Lincoln C. *Fundamentals of Military Service.* Philadelphia: J. B. Lippincott Co., 1916.
The Army Times, the Editors of. *The Yanks Are Coming: The Story of General John J. Pershing.* New York: G. P. Putnam's Sons, 1960.
Baker, Newton D. *Why We Went to War.* New York: Harper & Brothers, 1936.
Baker, Ray Stannard. *Woodrow Wilson: Life and Letters* (8 vols.). Garden City, N.Y.: Doubleday, Doran & Co., 1927–1939.
———, and William E. Dodd. *The Public Papers of Woodrow Wilson: The New Democracy* (2 vols.). New York: Harper & Brothers, 1925 and 1927.
Bemis, Samuel Flagg. *A Diplomatic History of the United States.* New York: Henry Holt & Co., 1936.
Bernstorff, Count Johann-Heinrich. *Memoirs of Count Bernstorff.* New York: Random House, 1936.

Bernstorff, Count Johannes-Heinrich. *My Three Years in America.* New York: Charles Scribner's Sons, 1920.

Braddy, Haldeen. *Pershing's Mission in Mexico.* El Paso: Texas Western College Press, 1967.

Brenner, Anita, and George Leighton. *The Wind That Swept Mexico.* New York: Harper & Brothers, 1943.

Brimlow, George F. *Cavalryman Out Of the West.* Caldwell, Idaho: The Caxton Printers, Ltd., 1944.

Bulnes, Francisco. *The Whole Truth about Mexico: President Wilson's Responsibility.* Trans. by Dora Scott. New York: M. Bulnes Book Co., 1916.

Chandler, Melbourne C. *Garryowen and Glory.* Annandale, Va.: The Turnpike Press, 1960.

Clendenen, Clarence C. *The United States and Pancho Villa: A Study in Unconventional Diplomacy.* Ithaca, N.Y.: Cornell University Press, 1961.

Cline, Howard F. *The United States and Mexico.* Cambridge, Mass.: Harvard University Press, 1953.

Cramer, C. H. *Newton D. Baker: A Biography.* Cleveland: The World Publishing Co., 1961.

Daniels, Josephus. *The Life of Woodrow Wilson.* © Will H. Johnston, 1924.

Dulles, John W. F. *Yesterday in Mexico: A Chronicle of the Revolution 1919–1936.* Austin: University of Texas Press, 1961.

Dunn, Robert. *World Alive.* New York: Crown, 1956.

Freudenthal, Elsbeth E. *The Aviation Business.* New York: Vanguard Press, 1940.

Ganoe, William Addleman. *The History of the United States Army.* New York: D. Appleton-Century Co., 1942.

Gibbon, Thomas Edward. *Mexico Under Carranza.* Garden City, N.Y.: Doubleday, Page & Co., 1919.

Guzmán, Martín Luis. *The Eagle and the Serpent.* New York: Alfred A. Knopf, 1920.

Hart, Albert Bushnell (ed.). *America at War.* Garden City, N.Y.: George H. Doran Co., 1918.

Horgan, Paul. *Great River,* Vol. II, *Mexico and the United States.* New York: Rinehart & Co., 1954.

Houston, David F. *Eight Years with Wilson's Cabinet,* Vol. I. Garden City, N.Y.: Doubleday, Page & Co., 1926.

Huidekoper, Frederic Louis. *The Military Unpreparedness of the United States.* New York: The Macmillan Co., 1915.

Johnson, William Weber. *Heroic Mexico.* Garden City, N.Y.: Doubleday & Co., 1960.

Lane, Franklin K. *The Letters of Franklin K. Lane.* Boston: Houghton Mifflin Co., 1924.

Lansing, Robert. *War Memoirs*. Indianapolis: The Bobbs-Merrill Co., 1935.

Link, Arthur S. Biography of President Woodrow Wilson (5 vols.). *Wilson: The New Freedom*, Vol. II; *Wilson: Confusions and Crises, 1915–1916*, Vol. IV; *Wilson: Campaigns for Progressivism and Peace, 1916–1917*, Vol. V. Princeton University Press, 1956, 1964 and 1965.

————. *Woodrow Wilson and the Progressive Era, 1910–1917.* New American Nation Series. New York: Harper & Brothers, 1954.

Moore, Samuel Taylor. *U. S. Airpower*. New York: Greenberg, 1958.

Morison, Samuel Eliot. *The Oxford History of the American People.* New York: Oxford University Press, 1965.

O'Connor, Richard. *Black Jack Pershing.* Garden City, N.Y.: Doubleday & Co., 1961.

Olsmith, Vernon G. *Recollections of an Old Soldier.* Privately printed, San Antonio, 1963.

O'Shaughnessy, Edith. *A Diplomat's Wife in Mexico.* New York: Harper & Brothers, 1916.

Palmer, Frederick. *Bliss, Peacemaker.* New York: Dodd, Mead & Co., 1934.

————.*Newton D. Baker*, Vols. I and II. New York: Dodd, Mead & Co., 1931.

Pershing, John J. *My Experiences in the World War* (2 vols.). New York: Frederick A. Stokes Co., 1931.

Quirk, Robert E. *The Mexican Revolution, 1914–1915.* New York: Citadel Press, 1963.

Reed, John. *Insurgent Mexico.* New York: Appleton, 1914.

Rodney, George B. *As a Cavalryman Remembers.* Caldwell, Idaho: The Caxton Printers, Ltd., 1944.

Roosevelt, Theodore. *America and the World War.* New York: Charles Scribner's Sons, 1926.

Scott, Hugh H. *Some Memories of a Soldier.* New York: Appleton-Century Co., 1928.

Semmes, Harry H. *Portrait of Patton.* New York: Appleton-Century-Crofts, 1955.

Sweetman, Jack. *The Landing at Veracruz: 1914.* Annapolis: United States Naval Institute, 1968.

Tompkins, Frank. *Chasing Villa.* Harrisburg, Pa.: Military Service Publishing Co., 1934.

Toulmin, H. A. *With Pershing in Mexico.* Harrisburg, Pa.: Military Service Publishing Co., 1935.

Tuchman, Barbara W. *The Zimmermann Telegram.* New York: Viking Press, 1958.

Tumulty, Joseph P. *Woodrow Wilson as I Knew Him.* Garden City, N.Y.: Doubleday, Page & Co., 1921.

Turner, Timothy. *Bullets, Bottles and Gardenias.* Dallas: Turner Publishing Co., 1935.

Wilson, Henry Lane. *Diplomatic Episodes in Mexico, Belgium and Chile.* Garden City, N.Y.: Doubleday, Page & Co., 1927.

Womack, John, Jr. *Zapata and the Mexican Revolution.* New York: Alfred A. Knopf, 1969.

OTHER PUBLISHED SOURCES

Bound volumes of the *Cavalry Journal,* 1916, 1917. Washington, D.C.

Sul Ross State College Bulletin, Vol. XLIII, No. 3 (1963). Alpine, Texas. (Contains eyewitness accounts of the Glenn Springs, Texas, and other border raids.)

Thomas, Robert S., and Inez V. Allen. *The Mexican Punitive Expedition.* A monograph prepared for the War Histories Division, Office of the Chief of Military History, Department of the Army, Washington, D.C., 1954.

Air Pictorial (February, 1965). London, England.

American Legion magazine (July, 1932). New York.

Infantry Journal, 1916.

Quartermaster Review (January–February, 1933). Washington, D.C.

Texas Military History, Vol. II, No. 1 (1962). Austin. (A quarterly publication of the National Guard Association of Texas.)

U.S. Air Services magazine (1932). Washington, D.C.

New York Times
Christian Science Monitor
Springfield (Mass.) *Daily Republican*
San Antonio *Express*
San Antonio *Light*
El Paso *Herald-Post*
El Paso *Times*
Houston *Post*

Notes on Sources

The foregoing bibliography lists only those sources used directly by the author. Especially invaluable were the works of Clendenen, a former member of the 10th Cavalry, and Tompkins of the 13th, who wrote from first-hand experience about the campaign and also had access to every official after-action report, and who, of course, was intimate with most of the officers and many of the noncoms of his own and other regiments. Clendenen's study is primarily political, while Tompkins' deals chiefly with tactical military events.

For a study of the Wilson mind at work, the reader can do no better than turn to any of Link's meticulously researched and well-written volumes. In the author's opinion, the finest recent studies of the Mexican Revolution are the books written by Johnson and Womack. The earlier works by Brenner, Turner, Reed and O'Shaughnessy are extremely interesting due to the authors' participation in the Revolution and their necessarily biased, but enlightening, observations on peasants and statesmen alike.

Other material was gathered by personal interviews and correspondence with survivors of the Punitive Expedition, officers and noncoms who served in the interior of Mexico and along the Texas border. Hundreds of feet of motion picture film taken in Mexico were made available to the author at the National Archives in Washington, D.C., and several hundred contemporary photographs were studied over the years in the search for significant detail.

Aerial survey of the terrain across which Pershing's command moved in the pursuit of Villa was made in the summer of 1968 when the author and Allison B. Peery, AIA, of San Antonio, flew from El Paso to Columbus and then south to Colonia Dublán and down the Santa María Valley. The aircraft in question, a Cessna Skymaster, was equipped with every modern navigation aid, but we were flying the "iron compass," as the pilots of the 1st Aero Squadron did, and managed to get lost. The railway we were following out of Dublán simply vanished into a mountain before we reached Guerrero. To make things worse, below there are towns that are not on the charts, and there are landmarks on the charts that we could not find on the ground. Although modern light planes may be equipped with sophisticated nav aids, Chihuahua is not, and there was no choice except to land and ask where we were. The valleys we searched looking for a town with a place to land were soggy with August rains, but we finally located what approximated a strip, a very short strip that ran uphill, and Peery skillfully put the Skymaster down. We were forced to land downhill because of grazing goats and burros.

As it turned out, we landed at Namiquipa, and were greeted by the entire populace who converged on the Skymaster barefoot, in trucks and on mules. Ours may well have been the first airplane to set down at Namiquipa since Foulois and his Jennies were there fifty-two years before. Namiquipa was not on our USAF chart, but fortunately was shown on a Mexican road map, so we were able to continue on our way.

Columbus looks much as it did in 1916, except for the electricity and the total removal of old Camp Furlong, scene of such heavy fighting on that night in March 1916. The adobe ruins of Lieutenant Lucas' hut still stand, and so does the yellow wooden railway station that once received passengers coming in from El Paso aboard the "Drunkard's Special." The hill where Tompkins and Slocum stood to watch the fleeing Villistas is now planted with a variety of flowers and cactus native to the region and has been named, perversely, it seems, Pancho Villa State Park. Only two hundred or so people live permanently in Columbus, about a hundred less than lived there on the night of the raid. It is a town existing on memories.

There are many legends about the Villa raid on Columbus and various reasons have been put forth over the years as to why, exactly, Villa chose to burn and pillage the town. One of the most incredible claims put forth is that the United States Government paid Villa to raid Columbus so that the U. S. Army would have some field experience when it came time to fight in France.

In May of 1964 *The Southwesterner*, a monthly tabloid once published in Columbus, carried a lengthy story written by the editor-publisher, Bill McGaw, claiming that Villa was paid $80,000 in cash by the U. S. government three or four days after the raid. The money was, so the story runs, handed to Villa in person by the telegrapher, E. A. Van Camp, the man AP correspondent George Seese hired to send out the details of the raid. Unfortunately, McGaw was "not at liberty to identify" his "eyewitness" to the transaction, an unnamed old man of eighty years. McGaw's "eyewitness" also claimed that Van Camp returned to Mexico in the 1920s and handed Villa another $50,000 at his ranch at Canutillo in order "to keep him quiet."

It is a fantastic charge; only the Germans have resorted to raiding their own installations to get a war started, and that was in 1939 when they shot up a German radio station near the Polish frontier. Does anyone believe that Pancho Villa would risk his life by attacking a garrison town, then loiter near the border for three or four days waiting for his money?

In August 1966 the author was in Villa Acuña, Mexico, and dined with one of Coahuila's most respected citizens, General Jaime Quinoñez, who was an ardent Villista and knew Francisco Villa from his early days as a revolutionist until the time of his death. General Quinoñez had only contempt for the charge that Villa was paid to raid Columbus. "The reason is very simple," Quinoñez told me. "Francisco Villa, who I thought was a great man in many ways, he was *muy hombre*, felt betrayed by the North Americans. Villa was also quite unstable. He worked himself into a great anger, and it was this anger that drove him to raid Columbus. He was really very, very mad."

Until history provides us with documentary evidence to the contrary, the explanation by Quinoñez will stand.

Following are brief notes on sources, chapter by chapter. Quotes taken from material listed in the Bibliography are indicated by the author's last name.

1. *Villa Lights the Fuse*

National Archives; Pershing Papers; *Foreign Relations;* Clendenen, Horgan, Tompkins; *Cavalry Journal; New York Times; Christian Science Monitor.*

2. *The Cauldron*

State Department File; *Foreign Relations;* Ray Stannard Baker, Brenner and Leighton, Bulnes, Clendenen, Cline, Daniels, Guzmán, Johnson, Link, O'Shaughnessy, Quirk, Reed, Sweetman, Turner, Wilson, Womack; *Infantry Journal; New York Times.*

3. *Recognition and Revenge*

State Department File; Scott Papers; *Foreign Relations;* Baker, Bemis, Brenner and Leighton, Clendenen, Cline, Horgan, Houston, Johnson, Lane, Lansing, Link, Palmer, Scott, Tumulty; *New York Times;* Springfield *Daily Republican.*

4. *Wilson Acts*

Foreign Relations; Newton D. Baker, Ray Stannard Baker, Bemis, Clendenen, Cramer, Daniels, Houston, Lansing, Link, Scott, Tompkins, Tumulty.

5. *Pershing's Swift Sword*

National Archives; *Foreign Relations;* the Eds. of Army Times, Braddy, Clendenen, Ganoe, Link, O'Connor, Scott, Tompkins; Toulmin; *Cavalry Journal.*

6. *No Eyes for the General*

Adjutant General's Office Files; interview with Admiral E. C. Parsons; account by Lieutenant Edgar S. Gorrell in *U. S. Air Services; Air Pictorial; Texas Military History; Christian Science Monitor; New York Times.*

7. *Seek the Devil*

Pershing Papers; Scott Papers; National Archives; Adjutant General's Office Files; Dunn, Rodney, Tompkins; Thomas and Allen (monograph); *American Legion; Christian Science Monitor; New York Times.*

8. *Penelope's Web*

National Archives; Adjutant General's Office Files; *Foreign Relations;* Clendenen, Lansing, Link, Scott, Tompkins.

9. *The Charge at Ojos Azules*

Adjutant General's Office Files; Tompkins, Toulmin; *Cavalry Journal; New York Times.*

10. *Cadillac Pursuit*

Foreign Relations; Clendenen, Scott, Tompkins; *Sul Ross State College Bulletin; Cavalry Journal;* San Antonio *Express.*

11. *To the Brink at Carrizal*

Adjutant General's Office Files; Pershing Papers; *Foreign Relations;* Clendenen, Link, Semmes, Tompkins; *Christian Science Monitor; New York Times;* interview with Major Mack Emerson, San Antonio; letter from Major General Ray W. Barker, former 10th Cavalry.

12. *No Bugles, No Glory*

National Archives; Adjutant General's Office Files; *Foreign Relations;* interview with Ed Hendrix, San Antonio; Clendenen, Link, Tompkins, Olsmith; *New York Times; Cavalry Journal.*

Epilogue

Foreign Relations; Baker, Bernstorff, Dulles, Link, Pershing, Tuchman, Womack; El Paso *Herald-Post*, El Paso *Times*, Houston *Post.*

Acknowledgments

For help of every kind, from locating scarce documents, photographs and earlier published sources to providing hours of time in interviews, and for clues and information concerning the period from 1910 through 1917, the author is indebted to the following individuals and organizations:

In Washington, D.C.: Mr. Charles F. Romanus, Office of the Chief of Military History; Miss Josephine E. Sullivan, Chief, Periodicals Section, Pentagon Army Library; Mr. Craddock C. Goins, Curator, Division of Military History, the Smithsonian Institution; Mr. David C. Mearns, Chief, Manuscript Division, Library of Congress; Mr. Elmer O. Parker, Acting Chief, Army and Navy Branch, National Archives; Colonel C. V. Glines, USAF, Chief, Magazine and Book Branch; and Colonel William Coleman, Chief, SAFOI, the Pentagon.

In Alexandria, Virginia: Colonel J. W. G. Stephens, USA (Ret.)

In St. Michaels, Maryland: Brigadier General Joseph Phelps, USA (Ret.); Mr. Walter Dodd Osborne.

In El Paso, Texas: Mr. Dale L. Walker, who has provided much valuable material since the inception of this project; Mrs. Virginia P. Hoke, El Paso Public Library.

In San Antonio, Texas: Lieutenant Colonel Dave Burnett, Information Officer, Fourth Army, and Mr. Bill Scholl, Fort Sam Houston; Historical Section, Fort Sam Houston Library; the San Antonio Public Library,; Mr. Maury Maverick, Jr.; Major Mack Emerson; Sergeant Eddie Hendrix; Colonel Martyn H. Shute; Miss Marjorie Dykes; Mr. Richard Santos, Bexar County Archivist; Mrs. Sherry Kafka Wagner; Mr. Cyrus Wagner; Mr. Allison B. Peery, AIA; Mr. Lonn Taylor; Mr. Joe Valdez; Mr. W. L. Moody IV; Mr. Henry Guerra, Jr.; the Higgins Book Store; Mr. Renwick Cary; Mr. Edward R. Villastrigo; Mr. Barron Dennis; and Captain Thomas Camp, USA.

In Villa Acuña, Coahuila, Mexico: General Jaime Quinoñez; Mr. Jesús Ramón, Jr.; Lieutenant Larry LoMonico.

In Cuernavaca, Morelos, Mexico: Mr. Robert Strother.

Special thanks go to the directors of the Fort Sill, Oklahoma, Library; to my editor, Bob Loomis, for intelligent criticism and unflagging patience; and to my wife, Rigmor Hansen Mason.

H. M. M.

Index